CONTEMPORARY SHAMANISMS IN NORWAY

CONTEMPORARY SHAMANISMS IN NORWAY

RELIGION, ENTREPRENEURSHIP, AND POLITICS

TRUDE FONNELAND

OXFORD
UNIVERSITY PRESS

OXFORD
UNIVERSITY PRESS

Oxford University Press is a department of the University of Oxford. It furthers
the University's objective of excellence in research, scholarship, and education
by publishing worldwide. Oxford is a registered trade mark of Oxford University
Press in the UK and certain other countries.

Published in the United States of America by Oxford University Press
198 Madison Avenue, New York, NY 10016, United States of America.

© Oxford University Press 2017

CIP data is on file at the Library of Congress
ISBN 978-0-19-067882-1

1 3 5 7 9 8 6 4 2

Printed by Sheridan Books, Inc., United States of America

CONTENTS

LIST OF ILLUSTRATIONS

(All photographs by Trude Fonneland, except where noted)

PREFACE AND ACKNOWLEDGMENTS

In 2000, I took part in my first fieldwork among shamanic practitioners in Norway, during the shaman course "A Tribute to the Great Spirit." The things I experienced at this course sparked a curiosity and spoke to my young folklorist heart. It also laid the foundation for a desire for a deeper understanding of shamanic practitioners' worldviews, their values and attitudes, their interpretations of everyday life, of activities, experiences, identities, and strategies.

My interest in these topics became the basis for my doctoral dissertation, *Samisk nysjamanisme: I dialog med (for)tid og stad* (Sami Neo-shamanism: In Dialog with the Past and Place) (2010), and the theme has further been an important and enticing part of my field research over the last decade.

Topics and cases explored in this book have been discussed using a variety of approaches in research seminars, in papers, and in some publications. This book, however, presents new perspectives and an extended focus, and it opens the field to a wider context. Drawing on ethnographic cases, I explore the dynamics of shamanic entrepreneurships in contemporary Norway, the impulses that are at play, and how they intersect and transform. I focus on how local pasts, places, and characters are woven into global discourses on shamanism and how, in this melting pot, new forms of religion are taking shape.

I am most grateful to my prior colleagues at the Department of History and Religious Studies, UiT, The Arctic University of Norway in Tromsø; at the Department of Archaeology, History, Cultural Studies and Religion, the University in Bergen; as well as the Department for Cultural Studies, Tromsø University Museum, where I am currently employed. Their wise comments, critical insight, and support have helped immensely. I beg forgiveness for any imprecisions, misperceptions, hasty judgments, or errors that have crept into my account, and I alone take responsibility for them.

Finally, my heartfelt thanks extends to all the shamanic practitioners who throughout the years have taken the time to share their stories and experiences with me, and not least to answer my sometimes pedantic questions. Without their participation, this book would have never seen the light.

CHAPTER ONE

INTRODUCTION

CONTEMPORARY SHAMANISMS IN NORWAY

They call us a new religion, but actually we are the oldest.[1]

On September 24, 2014, the Sámi poet, journalist, and first professional Sámi shaman, Ailo Gaup, died at the age of seventy.[2] During the following weeks, newspapers all across the country published tributes and words of memory from his friends and colleagues describing Ailo as an important cultural creator who dedicated his life to the continuation of Sámi cultural heritage through his work as a writer, poet, theater pioneer, cultural mediator, advisor, and, not least of all, shaman. The tributes highlight that he met and exchanged knowledge with shamans and tradition bearers from all corners of the world and presented shamanism as "the ancient culture course."[3]

Ailo played a crucial role in the design and growth of shamanism in Norway. And as a sign of the complex interactions behind shamanisms in a Norwegian local context, Ailo's story points to global influences, as well as to local matters, including crossovers between cultural and religious revival (see Fonneland, Kraft, and Lewis 2015).

Some researchers claim that shamanism is one of the fastest growing religions in contemporary Western society (Wallis 2003:140; Partridge 2004:47).[4] In Norway, this growth is reflected in, among other things, the alternative fairs that are arranged in cities across the country. At these fairs, shamans and other New Age entrepreneurs market their goods and services, and the public's interest, and thus attendance, rises annually. A Sámi shamanic milieu is constantly evolving, and a growing number of Sámi shamans offer their services online (Fonneland 2010).

Figure 1.1 shows people gathered round the "World Drum" made by Sámi shaman Birger Mikkelsen." The World Drum was consecrated in a ceremony in front of the Norwegian Parliament in October of 2006 and has since the launching been send to more than 18 countries. According to the organizer shaman Kyrre Gram Franck, "the World Drum is a wake-up call for us to reinstate our spiritual relationship to Mother Earth."[5] From August 2010 a Sámi shamanic festival, Isogaisa, has been held in Northern Norway with shamans from all over the world taking part (Fonneland 2015a). Not the least of these, the Shamanistic Association, a shamanic denomination, performs religious ceremonies like baptisms, weddings, and funerals, and it receives financial support relative to its membership (Fonneland 2015b).

FIGURE 1.1
The "World Drum" made by Sámi shaman Birger Mikkelsen.

This book discusses the emergence and development of contemporary shamanism in Norway with a main focus on the rise of Sámi shamanism, which by 2016 constitutes what is the most profiled and active part of the local shamanic milieu. It focuses on how political and cultural differences affect religious ecologies, highlighting that the shamanic culture that was established in the United States in the late 1960s is only one part of the whole picture. Taking a starting point in the late 1980s, I will show how shamanism gained a foothold and slowly developed into one of the largest and most multifaceted of the New Age spiritualities in Norway, at the same time influencing cultural life and various secular and semisecular currents.

Both the New Age movement and the neopagan movement were shaped by the cultural milieu of the 1960s and 1970s, and especially the social movements that picked up steam in those decades: feminism, environmentalism, the sexual revolution, and the pan-Indian movement. The label "New Age" (as a notion distinct from Christian meanings), however, was already being discussed in theosophical circles in the late nineteenth and early twentieth centuries. Contemporary paganism, on the other hand, is typically dated to the initial activities of Gerald Gardner in 1950s England. Thus, as the 1960s counterculture began to wane, many former counterculturists became involved in spiritual pursuits, both pagan and New Age, in the 1970s.

Contemporary shamanism has become a global religious phenomenon with shamans in many parts of the world sharing common practices, rituals, and a nature-oriented worldview and lifestyle. The highlighting of shamanism as a universal phenomenon is inspired by the English translation of Romanian historian of religion Mircea Eliade's *Shamanism: Archaic Techniques of Ecstasy* (1964). However, within this global fellowship, diversity is still the most prominent feature and shamanism is not inevitably describable as a uniform tendency on a global scale. Diversity is displayed in terms of the various traditions that the practitioners choose to follow and revive, in terms of practices, politics, values, and where it is all taking place. What this means is that studies of the dynamics of shamanic entrepreneurships in the United

Kingdom, for instance, are not necessarily directly transferable to other local contexts. Although the United States can be described as the cradle of modern shamanism, the spread of shamanic religious practices and ideas to other habitats is not a uniform process but involves adaptations to local cultural and political climates.

This book thus ventures between the worlds of the local and the global, and it analyzes the religious innovations that occur when a global culture of shamanism interacts with a specific local culture. Through ethnographic examinations of the experiences and perceptions of particular shamans in a particular cultural setting, I try to paint a picture of contemporary shamanism in Norway, relating it both to the local mainstream cultures in which it is situated and to global networks. By this, I hope to provide the basis for a study revealing the development of inventiveness, nuances, and polyphony that occur when a global religion of shamanism is merged in a Norwegian setting colored by its own political and cultural circumstances (see also Rountree 2013).

Taking local practices and communities as a starting point offers rich opportunities for getting close to individual practitioners and their beliefs, visions, and creativity. In this type of study, variations are also displayed that can contribute to questioning some of the central assumptions within shaman and pagan research. Based on my interviews with practitioners of shamanism in Norway, one may question whether these movements can be divided along a continuum, where at one end we find reconstructionist views (aimed to reconstruct the ancient religious traditions of a particular ethnic group) and at the other end eclectic views (freely mixing traditions of different areas, peoples, and time periods) (Blain 2005; Strmiska 2005). Such a distinction is not prominent when taking a local Norwegian context as a starting point (see also Fonneland, Kraft, and Lewis 2015:2–3). A focus on Sámi shamanism also reveals cracks in theories highlighting that the "noble savage" depends upon distance in geographic or temporal terms (Bowman 1995a). Neither assumptions about pagan religions as catering primarily to white, urban romantics nor ones that differ substantially from New Age spiritualities are supported by shamanic entrepreneurs like Ailo and his colleagues in the local Norwegian shamanic environment.

4

These theoretical perspectives may very well be reasonable in other places and at different times, but they are not in this particular area of the world, at least not since the turn of the century and with ongoing developments. Various practices of shamanism, as the chapters in this book will reveal, attract people in urban as well as rural areas. Based on a Norwegian context, I will also argue that the distinction between shamanism and New Age has become increasingly blurred during the last few years. In Norway, Sámi shamanism has emerged as the foremost shamanic orientation, and the "noble savage" is thus no longer limited to distant landscapes. Finally, the distinction between reconstructionism and eclecticism is difficult to maintain among shamanic entrepreneurs situated in Norway. Even though many of the practitioners of shamanism in Norway specialize in one particular tradition, they at the same time allow for combinations and mix traditional elements with new ideas and practices from other sources (Fonneland, Kraft, and Lewis 2015).

One aim of this book is to take the diversity and hybridity within shamanic practices seriously through case studies from a Norwegian setting. Another aim is to highlight the ethnic dimension of these currents, through a particular focus on Sámi versions of shamanism. The construction of a Sámi shamanistic movement, moreover, makes sense from the perspective of the broader ethnopolitical search for a Sámi identity, with respect to connections to indigenous peoples worldwide and transhistorically. It also makes sense in economic and marketing terms. Sámi versions of shamanism are presented today as more authentic than the American Indian version, partly—some practitioners claim—due to commercialization of the latter.

The Norwegian Context

Religious Communities and Governmental Regulations

The external forces of Norwegian governmental laws and regulations have direct consequences for the design and maneuverability of shamanistic groups. The law on religious freedom has been enshrined in

Norway since 1964. This has also made it possible for groups without any affiliation to the Church of Norway to be classified legally as religious communities.[6]

The idea of equal treatment based on faith and belief is rooted in the Declaration of Human Rights, which among other things highlights the equal right to freedom of religion and belief and the right to protection against all unfair discrimination on the grounds of religion and belief. The Religious Communities Act (Lov om trudomssamfunn og ymist anna) that was introduced in 1969 provides a framework for religious organizations in Norway. The Act ensures virtually equal treatment of the Church of Norway and other religious communities and denominations by facilitating that religious communities may apply for state and municipal subsidies per member. No country provides the same level of financial support for religious communities as Norway, and by this arrangement, the country represents an outer point where state and municipal grants form most of the resource base for the Norwegian Church, and where other religious communities receive similar, public subsidies per member (see Askeland 2011).

In 2013 the report "Det livssynsåpne samfunn: En helhetlig tros- og livssynspolitikk" (nou 2013:1) (The Belief Open Society: A Coherent Religion and Belief Politics) was published that, among other things, considered the funding opportunities for religious communities in Norway. It points out that the support to the Church of Norway must entail an equal support to other religious communities, in terms of financial support as well as practical arrangements concerning religious activities and rituals. To gain support, a religious community, according to the report, must "be based on common binding perceptions of existence in which man sees himself in relation to a god or one or more transcendent powers" (confession of faith) (§ 2-1, entitled to financial subsidies). The report notes that a good deal remains to be accomplished in terms of equal treatment between religious societies and that equal conditions should be facilitated.

Governmental regulations also influence the design of the various communities' ceremonies. For a wedding to be considered legally binding, for instance, certain formulations need to be included. The only approved shamanistic organization in Norway, the Shamanistic Association, can thus be seen as a construct designed to meet the requirements for the recognition of religious communities, highlighting how religious practices are adapted, transformed, and changed to fit governmental regulations.

POLITICS AND INDIGENEITY

The dichotomy between town and country in a Norwegian context is often portrayed as the most common identification basis for spatial and social cohesion (Thuen 2003). Northern Norway has in this context come to symbolize the "country" category as opposed to the "town," which refers to characteristics such as "gemeinschaft" tradition, nature, homogeneity, and provincialism. Trond Thuen writes, "It is the urban center that is given the power to define in this context, and it is also where the economic elite and the political powers has remained" (Thuen 2003:72). The construction of a dichotomy of town and city, centre and periphery have offered both positive and negative connotations. But as Gry Paulgaard notes, "the content of the dichotomies is the same, coding people in the periphery as less civilized, more out-dated and backward, more authentic, wilder and natural" (Paulgaard 2012:193). In contemporary times, the gap between north and south in terms of economic development and political power has decreased, but some fifty years ago, the region stood out in many important ways. Northerners had less education, earned less than most Norwegians, worked to a greater extent in the primary industries, and lived in rural areas. In Northern Norway, as Willy Guneriussen stresses, symbolic efforts to deal with the "country category" have been pursued by tearing down traditional notions of the region as an outdated and underdeveloped periphery. The goal has been to build up a picture of a knowledgeable, innovative, and proud region that is not dependent on subsidies and old-fashioned regional policy (2012:347).

Since the 1970s, aboriginality has been increasingly valorized as an integral part of the renovated postcolonial, multicultural national fabric, particularly for the purpose of international projection in tourism and cultural diplomacy. The Alta conflict is in this context an important political marker and a watershed in Sámi political history that caused Norway to change its official policy toward Sámi. The "Alta affair" was triggered by the Norwegian Parliament's decision in November 1978 to approve a hydroelectric project that involved the damming of the Alta-Kautokeino River, which flows through central parts of Finnmark, Norway's northernmost county, and the heartland of the Sámi settlement.[7] The Alta Affair that started as an environmental issue became an indigenous people issue, and the ensuing protests and demonstrations brought the Sámi case to the world stage. As pointed out by anthropologist Ivar Bjørklund: "The Sámi issue was no longer just a question of cultural preservation and language, henceforth the debates would revolve around the rights of the Sami population as an indigenous people" (2000:42).

Despite that the river system was eventually dammed, the Alta conflict had striking consequences. An important successor was the 1988 amendment to the Norwegian Constitution stating that "It is the responsibility of the authorities of the State to create conditions enabling the Sami people to preserve and develop its language, culture, and way of life" (§ 110A). A manifestation of this amendment was the establishment of the Sámediggi (Sámi Parliament) officially inaugurated by King Olav V on October 9, 1989. At the 1997 opening session, King Harald V held a radical political speech on Sámi rights and apologized for the past actions of the Norwegian government toward the Sámi. In 1990, Norway ratified the International Convention on Indigenous Populations (No. 169) of the International Labor Organisation (ILO). According to it, Sámi are recognized as an aboriginal people, not merely an ethnic minority, such as, for example, immigrants and refugees.[8]

Indigenous peoples increasingly exist in a global framework, both self-consciously drawing on globalized strategies of rights and identity, as well as being objectively situated through international legal frameworks. Sámi have from the very beginning been engaging in indigenous people's affairs. The impact of Sámi membership in the World Council of Indigenous People (WCIP), as well as their active participation in UN activities, has consequences for how Sámi issues are dealt with in regional and national contexts, and for the national governments' abilities to function in an international capacity (see Lehtola 2004).

In the case of indigenous people globally, spirituality has been recognized as a common marker associated not only with identity but also with an authenticity that native peoples are presumed to possess. These notions of indigenous people as one spiritual community, have, as scholar of religion Siv Ellen Kraft argues, become part of the common terminology of indigeneity, both in UN fora and international law (2010).[9]

CONTESTED TERMS

Choosing a terminology for an investigation of shamanism in contemporary Norway has been a challenge and is not entirely without problems. In contemporary society, the words *shaman* and *shamanism* have become part of everyday language and thousands of popular as well as academic texts have been written about the subject. In recent years the term *shaman* has become an umbrella term for the Sámi *noaidi* (the Sámi indigenous religious specialist), as is the case with religious specialists among people referred to as "indigenous," more or less regardless of the content of their expertise and practices. However, the *noaidi* has not always been perceived as a shaman. The word *shaman* is an example of the complexities often involved in translation processes over time and across space (see Johnson and Kraft 2017). The term is widely regarded as having entered Russian from the Tungus *samán*, transferring to German as *schamane*, and then into other European languages in the seventeenth century—added to academic vocabularies by anthropologists and historians of religion and further related to indigenous people elsewhere (see Wilson 2014:117). In the 1960s, the term spread to the neopagan milieu where the shaman is not only recognized as an indigenous religious specialist but as a potential enshrined in all humans. However, as Graham Harvey warns us, the use of the term *shaman* can generalize a number of people, as there are numerous local words for shamans (Harvey 2003:1). The term *shamanism*, in other words, can be seen as an expression of Western scholarly denial of the complexity of "primitive" religions and the reduction of their diversity to a simplistic unity. When it comes to these types of translation processes that the term *shaman* has been subjected to, it is important to have in mind what James Clifford highlights in terms of the concept of translation: "Translation is not transmission.... Cultural translation is always uneven, always betrayed. But this very interference and lack of smoothness is a source of new meanings, of historical traction" (Clifford 2013:48–49).

During the past decades, several researchers have opposed the term *shamanism* (see, among others, Stuckrad 2002; Svanberg 2003; Znamenski 2007; Rydving 2011). As Fonneland, Kraft, and Lewis argue, this is partly "due to the historical trajectories and to their results, including widespread notions of shamanism as an *ism*" (2015:2). In this book, I take account of emic categories and connections, focusing on which notions of "shamanism" are used today by shamanic entrepreneurs and others who share these types of spiritual beliefs. From this scholarly standpoint, I find it important to avoid the debate of whether shamanism is "genuine" or not. As a folklorist, I look at the invention of traditions as something ubiquitous, noting that indigenous religions also change. Tradition is not a static thing but an ongoing process. I support folklorist Sabina Magliocco who underlines, "What some scholars have called 'inventions', 'folklorism', or 'fakelore' I see as integral steps in the formation and elaboration of tradition, worthy of investigation in their own right" (2004:10).

Terminology is an equally debated issue among shamanic practitioners. The shamans I have interviewed reject the term *neoshaman* due both to its biased tone and primarily to designate their affinity with the past and eschew any distinction between their practices and those of ancient and indigenous cultures. In regard to what is highlighted earlier, the word *neoshaman* is nonsensical. What I can observe and know is that in contemporary Norwegian society there exist numerous shamans. What was found and which terms made sense in local indigenous communities several hundred years ago are much more complicated questions, and they are related to various scholars' interpretations of the past.

The terms *pagan* and *paganism*, which are often highlighted by scholars as common phrases for practitioners of shamanism, Wicca, Åsatru, and Celtic religions, are not commonly used words in Norwegian daily language, and I have not yet experienced that Norwegian practitioners of shamanism have embraced these as emblems of identity. Although the words *paganism* and *pagan* in this book are abandoned as synonyms for local shamanic practitioners, contemporary shamanism has a lot in common with neopagan groups (see York 2001). For instance, many of the shamanic entrepreneurs I have talked to at the festival Isogaisa and in the alternative fairs include symbols, chants, and trance rituals from Wiccan, Celtic, and Northern European traditions in their workshops and courses, as a spiritual background of their shamanic practices. It is also difficult, in the landscapes explored in this case, to distinguish clearly between "New Age" and "neopaganism," and it is not necessarily fruitful to do so. Practitioners of both traditions operate on the same market and draw upon similar ideas of self-development and self-realization. Many of them also combine techniques and therapies connected to both New Age and paganism.

A last important terminological issue has to do with the term *religion*. This is important because until recently, many Sámi shamans, such as, for example, Ailo Gaup, were adamant in rejecting the term *religion* in connection with their practices. In keeping with his teacher Michael Harner, Ailo regarded core shamanism as a "technique" (Eliade's term) and not as a religion. When shamanism was approved as an individual religion by the Norwegian government in 2012, the attitudes gradually changed. In contemporary times it is more common to see the word *shamanism* used synonymously with the word *religion* in the alternative fairs, during festivals, and in workshops. This shift from "technique" to "religion" is also transparent in Harner's latest work. His new book *Cave and Cosmos* (2013) comes much closer to accepting the idea of the supernatural as integral to shamanic practices and seems more comfortable with the idea of core shamanism being seen as a religious tradition. Scholars of religion have long debated whether shamanism can be actually called a religion, and most often shamanism does not meet the definitional threshold of "religion" due to a seeming lack of a body of dogmas and policies, a professional priesthood, and an institutional identity (see DuBois 2009:3–11). Building on Timothy Fitzgerald (2000) and Hans Kippenberg (2002), Thomas DuBois notes: "such views have in practice more to do with the history and development of the academic study of 'religion' than with the phenomena at the centre of the (individual's) supernatural experiences" (2009:5).

INTO THE FIELD—PRESENTATION OF INTERVIEWEES

The concept of culture, as ethnologist Jonas Frykman and philosopher Nils Gilje note, is not a package, system, or accumulation of texts. "There is nothing finished about it. Instead of being the final point, the concept is the starting point for a voyage of discovery" (2003:29). As a folklorist and culture researcher, I aim at understanding how people create culture and form systems of meaning that organize everyday life. I seek to track changes, boundary markers, and the complex, procedural, and polysemic.

I have chosen to examine the field of shamanism in Norway ethnographically by focusing particularly on some specific contexts and personalities using interviews, observation, and document analysis as my main research tools. Even though these tools all represent different approaches to the field, I experienced that the combination of them opened for more depth as well as understanding. Cultural analysis forms a central basis for my academic understanding. The cultural analysis has its roots in the 1980s and was developed within Swedish ethnology with Orvar Löfgren, Billy Ehn, and Jonas Frykman as key contributors (see Frykman and Löfgren 1979; Ehn and Löfgren 1982). The cultural analytical perspective is included in a postmodern science–theoretical paradigm, and it is characterized by scientific scepticism and an antipositivistic understanding of science. Cultural analysis must not be understood as an overarching cultural theory or explanation model, but rather as a model characterized by theoretical pluralism and where a diversity of sources are taken into use.

The goal of a cultural analyst is to turn to many different approaches that all might help to increase the understanding of the object of study as a cultural phenomenon. Allowing for the use of different approaches, such as combining the qualitative research interview with observation and document analysis, helps the researcher to get on the trail of her informant's assessments and notions and to investigate, ask questions, and throw light on a cultural phenomenon.

A culture analytical approach is about understanding and interpreting what is meaningful for members of a culture. It is about seeing how meaning is created and re-created. The focus is directed toward everyday reality, to the participants' lives, their experiences, and their meetings and negotiations in relation to dominant discourses. For me, cultural analysis constitutes a tool to highlight perspectives that say something about contemporary shamans' values and attitudes, their interpretations of everyday life, of activities, experiences, identities, and strategies.

The book draws on interviews with a variety of practitioners of shamanism in Norway, both Sámi and non-Sámi, as well as on participant observation at ceremonies, rituals, fairs, and festivals. The fieldwork has been conducted over a period of eleven years from 2005 to 2016. During these years, I have had the opportunity and great pleasure to talk with and get to know many people involved in shamanic practices. These conversations both informal and formal have all provided me with a broader contextualization of the environment.

The interview is a social meeting and represents a situation in which two or more persons interact and where experiences are interpreted and meaning is created (Järvinen 2005). The stories that come into sight during the interview serve as door openers for knowledge about the narrator and her or his lifeworld, and the researcher is an active cocreator in this process. Embodied in my portrayal of my fieldwork as a social meeting thus lies an understanding that the knowledge that is expressed during interviews is based on interactions and relations.

Knowledge and opinions have been created intersubjectively between me as researcher and the ones that I am researching.

All of the persons whom I contacted expressed joy that I was interested in writing about shamanism. They welcomed me without apparent skepticism and critical questions, and showed that they wanted to give me the opportunity to do research *with* them.

It is almost impossible to identify accurately the number of shamanic practitioners in Norway. Shamanism is characterized by fluidity, and far from all participants make any strong commitment to a shamanic group or organization, but rather choose to drift in and out of spiritual practices. Only the Shamanistic Association and shamanic groups on Facebook operate with concrete numbers of main and/or support members, but these still say little about the overall interest in shamanism in Norway. As is apparent, my interviewees are all people with strong commitments, and my analysis will primarily shed light on shamanic practices on the basis of this stance. (For a closer presentation of each interview person, see the Presentation of Interviewees in the back of the book.)

I have chosen to anonymize two of the interviewees because these women are no longer as active in the environment as they were when the interviews were taking place. I have given them the fictional names Lisa and Anna, and they were both in their thirties at the time of the interviews. Also conversations with shamanic practitioners at the Isogaisa festival and at the annually arranged alternative fairs in Tromsø, Northern Norway, form part of my analysis, although these are not referred to in the form of direct quotes.

Shamanism in Norway is not a unified, organized movement but a patchwork of shifting and elastic networks, stretching across both regional and national borders. This complexity is also reflected in the group of informants. The interviewees do not belong to a unifying shamanic organization. Some choose not to be affiliated with any groups and practice rituals and ceremonies alone. Others are organized in various local and national networks like the Shamanic Association, Cosmological Life Faith, or the Holistic Association. There are still some events that act as focal points where shamans from all over the country meet to socialize and share their knowledge. This primarily applies to the annually arranged alternative fairs organized in cities all over the country and the Isogaisa festival held once a year from 2010. The intent of this book is thus not to provide a full picture of what contemporary shamanism is in terms of a fully fledged worldview or system, but to throw light on some active and profiled personalities, organizations, and tendencies related to the practice of shamanism in Norway in the present.

Studying religious practices and expressions involves taking belief seriously both existentially and emotionally. In shamanic performances there is no room for detached observers (see also Lindquist 1997; Magliocco 2004; Roundtree 2010; Trulsson 2010). During courses, rituals, and performances I have participated on equal terms with fellow practitioners and tried to experience the world of the other, without imagining that I could ever see or feel the way the individual practitioner does. The field of modern shamanism is a venue where people meet and exchange knowledge and experience, knowing that the experience can never be completely identical but varies from individual to individual. Even though my view is not that of an insider, I study shamanism without prejudice and hope to have been able to attain a sympathetic, but critical approach. Not all participants might agree on the terms and labels I have chosen, but I hope that they will be able to recognize themselves.

Even though I committed myself to construct a mostly neutral basis for the interviews, I cannot disregard the asymmetry of power that is implicit in this type of meeting. In a research encounter, a fully symmetrical dialogue is not possible. The researcher and the informant have their respective interests, and I do not think they are often, if ever, the same (Vasenkari 1999:57). As folklorists Bente Alver and Torunn Selberg point out: "The interviewer defines the situation and the framework around what is going to happen. She is familiar with the questions and issues and knows best what it is all about" (1992:35; see also Briggs 1986:89). This imbalance in power is also reflected in the analysis. It is my task as a researcher to select which of the interviewees' quotes and portrayals should receive attention and be included in the final text and what should be omitted.

RESEARCH ON NEW RELIGIOSITY AND INDIGENOUS RELIGION (S) IN NORWAY—A VERY BRIEF OVERVIEW

Until the 1990s, research on new religiosity in Norway was rather limited. The first joint effort to study New Age/alternative spirituality was the project "Myth, Magic and Miracle meet Modernity (MMMM)," which still has importance for the study of new religiosity in Norway (see Gilhus and Mikaelsson 2015:179). The project was led by folklorist Bente Alver, Torunn Selberg, and scholars of religion Ingvild Sælid Gilhus and Lisbeth Mikaelsson and put particular focus on the commercial and fluent character of new religiosity and its links with traditional folk religiosity (see Alver et al 1999).

When it comes to the study of neopaganism, theologian Jone Salomonsen at the University in Oslo is a prominent scholar, focusing particularly on the goddess and witchcraft movement. Salomonsen has conducted ethnographic fieldwork in the United States at the Reclaiming collective in San Francisco, which has been the base for Starhawk, a leading figure in contemporary paganism. In her doctoral dissertation, *"I Am a Witch—A Healer and a Bender": An Expression of Women's Religiosity in Contemporary USA* (1996), Salomonsen focuses on the study of feminist witchcraft and interpretation of new symbols and rites (Salomonsen 1996:179–180).[10]

UiT, The Artic University of Norway, houses what is today the largest Nordic research milieu on Sámi and indigenous issues. UiT also possesses one of the leading environments in Norway for the study of indigenous religion. In 2015 the research project "Indigenous Religion (s): Local Ground Global Networks," headed by scholar of religion Siv Ellen Kraft, received funding from the Norwegian Research Council (NRC). The point of departure for this project are the dynamics with regard to indigenous religion-making on global and local levels. Researchers aim to investigate and compare indigenous religions (s) on global and local sites, as well as to explore the relationship between them, thereby providing research-based knowledge of developments that have potential global reach.

THE ROLE OF THE INTERNET

Cyberspace is currently one of the most important arenas for shamanic practitioners. With members and devotees spread across the globe, the Internet has become a key component in the organization and marketing of shamanistic courses, groups, and performances in large part because it allows widely separated individuals to communicate with each other and information to be disseminated more easily. The Internet has thus played an important role in popularizing these traditions and making them accessible to seekers everywhere (Pike 2004:18).

Every shamanic organization in Norway and each individual entrepreneur have designed their own website to guide the uninitiated who are browsing for information on shamanism and to distribute information about courses, happenings, and products. In addition, social media and Internet forums such as Facebook remain important arenas where people with an interest in shamanism keep in touch with others who share their spiritual concerns. Most of these forums are open to everyone, but some are also only available for specially invited participants. I have been lucky enough to be included in some of the Facebook groups, which have, among other things, provided me with necessary insight into the ritual production of the Shamanic Association.

As Magliocco argues, "Thanks to the Internet, the field of research is available on a daily basis and the categories of field and home are no longer clearly separated" (2004:36). Through e-mail and Internet forums, daily travels to and from the field, wherever I happen to be, are facilitated (2004:36).

THE BOOK'S FUTURE STRUCTURE

Drawing on interviews, participant observation, and document analysis, this book will focus on the development of the field of Sámi shamanism in Norway. Although obviously not exhaustive, nor even representative of the contemporary setting, the project represents a rare opportunity to study a late modern religious tradition in the process of evolution. The book highlights some of the diversity and breath in the contemporary shamanic setting, as well as important currents and currencies.

Chapter 2 highlights some of the key contexts and events that influenced the rise of a Sámi shamanistic movement in Norway. The emergence of Sámi shamanism has also shaped a new understanding of the Arctic wilderness. In Chapter 3, I explore the shamans' relationship with nature in the high North by focusing on how nature is included in their practices and how the use of nature relates to the legitimization of modern Sámi shamanism. Religion is a core unit in terms of how gender stereotypes are produced and realized. By exploring how shamans use the past to construct narratives of gender in the present, my presentation in Chapter 4 represents an attempt to localize religion and culture in social and gendered reality. In Chapter 5, I examine stories, products, and services that take shape as a Sámi shaman festival opens its doors to the public for the first time. I ask what is included in the marketing of the Isogaisa festival as an appealing happening. I further explore the role that the past and Sámi indigenous religion play in the production of experiences that take place, and I examine how what is distinctly local at Isogaisa is highlighted on the basis of global structures and organizations to create interest for a chosen product and a specific destination. On March 13, 2012, a local shamanic association concerned with preserving Sámi and Norse shamanic traditions was granted status as a distinct religious community by the County Governor of Troms, northern Norway. In Chapter 6, I am concerned with what kinds of local, national, and global trends and discussions have contributed to the formation of this particular local group. Finally, by focusing on the mechanisms of contemporary shamanism in Norway, in Chapter 7, I argue that the spiritual quest has developed some very surprising and innovative forms of spirituality that make it necessary to rethink the relationship between the religious and the secular world.

Overall, I try to paint a picture of shamanism in Norway in its cultural context and describe key contexts and events behind the rise of local shamanistic milieus. The book explores the dynamics through which abstract concepts and ideas find moorings in a local community and in participants' reality here and now, gradually generating distinct cultural fields. The history of shamanism provides insight into Western assumptions about religion and religiosity in general. It stands as an example of how religious labels are formed in ever-changing contexts—as a by-product of broader historical processes.

CHAPTER TWO

THE DEVELOPMENT OF SÁMI SHAMANISM

My starting point is Sámi; the local Sámi traditions of power animals, joik and ancestral spirits.... The understanding of the sacrifice—that we share energy. All of this I bring with me from the Sámi tradition. Later I moved from the local tradition to the spiritual world heritage. It can be found everywhere. Sámi Shamanism has local characteristics, but the adventures and experiences are similar in all traditions and belong to the spiritual world heritage. I gather strength.... I go where inspiration leads me.[1]

Prior to the late 1990s, contemporary shamanism in Norway differed little from core shamanic practices developed in the United States by Michael Harner, often referred to as the pioneer of modern shamanism. Since then, a Sámi version of shamanism has been established, along with a new focus on the uniqueness of the Arctic North, expressed through New Age courses and events, as well as through various secular or semisecular currents. Highlighted as the wisdom of indigenous people in general and the Sámi in particular, Sámi shamanism caters to spiritual needs but also to the more mundane needs of tourism, place branding, entertainment, and—last but not least—for Sámi nation building and the ethnopolitical field of indigenous revival.

The cultural creation developed by practitioners of shamanism in Norway provides insight into processes of religious creation and creativity. These developments and increasing spiritual inventiveness are the focus of this chapter. I am particularly interested in how and what happens when the global culture of shamanism interacts with a specific local culture, in this case, Norwegian

FIGURE 2.1
Shaman Ailo Gaup (photo by Linda Bournane Engelberth).

society. Drawing on developments within the field of shamanism in
Norway, the chapter ventures between the local and global, highlighting how American Indian symbolism might serve as a spark
that prompts a spiritual seeker to step onto the path of spirituality,
making what is perceived as local traditions the basis for a new
global religious movement.

Precisely when the interest in and the revitalization of symbols and
beliefs from the indigenous Sámi religion began is unclear. Political
upheaval and struggles in the Sámi community in the late 1970s, such
as the protests related to the expansion of the Alta-Kautokeino River,
can nevertheless be highlighted as a spark for some of that which is

expressed within the shamanic environment in Norway today (see also Kraft 2015 and Alver 2015).

The demonstrations, roadblocks, and hunger strikes that took place in connection with the "Alta affair" sparked a Sámi ethnic revival, and they are generally regarded as the beginning of the Sámi cultural revival movement (Hætta 2002).[2] They also served as premises for what shaman Ailo Gaup has referred to as "the 78 generation"—the Sámi version of the 1968 generation (*Klassekampen* March 11–12, 2006). The Sámi 1978 generation consisted of young people as well as scholars, musicians, and artists who had more or less been cut off from the Sámi culture and language and who wanted to improve the political situation of the Sámi people. This was a generation whose parents, due to strong assimilation processes, had shielded their children from a cultural baggage they considered shameful, in order to secure them a better life and more positive prospects (see Fonneland and Kraft 2013:133).

Shaman Eirik Myrhaug, who led one of the hunger strikes outside the Norwegian Parliament in 1981, describes the demonstrations as an awakening concerning Sámi rights, traditions, and heritage:

> The authorities claimed that the core of the Alta case was to carry out a resolution passed lawfully by parliament to dam large areas in order to build a power plant in what was then perhaps Europe's most magnificent and unspoilt wilderness. Many saw more sides of the case. The Sámi and many others viewed it as a crime against the indigenous populace perpetrated by society at large. The environmental movement saw in it a symbolic cause. However, this was also true of the protection of cultural heritage, and many thought it was a matter of prestige at the centre of the political establishment, and many people and many politicians were really opponents. It was grist to the mill for the prestige theory when [Prime minister] Gro Harlem Brundtland admitted that the development was probably not necessary. But, even if the dam was built, the publicity would make out that the Sámi had won a victory in achieving a positive outlook for Sámi autonomy. It was also a victory for the environmental movement. (Myrhaug in Brunvoll and Brynn 2011:124–125, my translation)

After a prolonged period of acts of civil disobedience, hunger strikes, and an occupation of the Prime minister's office (see Alver 2015), the decision was effectuated in January 1981, despite massive protests. But as Myrhaug points out, "Thanks to the Alta conflict the Sámi achieved a great deal both when it comes to publicity, an extended focus on Sámi rights, and it also put the question of Sámi indigenous status on the national political agenda" (see Thuen 1995:13).[3]

At the same time as these protests and demonstrations were being played out, new cross-Atlantic religious ideas and trends were introduced into Norwegian society, providing the basis for a shamanic movement with an international scope.

A Point of Departure

Scholarly research has contributed to the globalization of shamanism in substantial ways. Shamans in Norway, like their colleagues elsewhere, turn to studies by anthropologists and historians of religion in order to revive and reconstruct the religions of their ancient past (see Stuckrad 2003).

Largely there are three academics who are highlighted when the movements' intellectual background is drawn up, namely Mircea Eliade (1907–1986), Carlos Castaneda (1925–1998), and Michael Harner (1929–).[4] Their texts on the subject have been so influential that one might call them the canonical texts of Western shamanism (see Hammer 2015).

Mircea Eliade's *Shamanism: Archaic Techniques of Ecstasy* (1964), first published in French in 1951, presents shamanism as the oldest of the world's religions and provides a foundation for the interpretation of shamanism as a universal and singular phenomenon. Eliade's work has been central to both the academic world's understanding of the phenomenon and to the popular imagination.

Equally central to the popularization of shamanism was anthropologist and author Carlos Castaneda. His master thesis, which was published as a book in 1968 entitled *The Teachings of Don Juan, A Yaqui Way of Knowledge*, became a bestseller. In 1973, Castaneda was awarded a doctoral degree on the same subject, and his writings continued to influence the counterculture's interests in shamanism. In the scholarly community, the discussions about Castaneda's writings have been fiery. Among other things he is blamed for having made up his key informant, the shaman Don Juan, and that his books are works of fiction. His writings also gave rise to discussions related to methodological and ethical aspects, where the scholarly community, among other things, expressed criticism concerning Castaneda's descriptions of his use of drugs and peyote trips during fieldwork among the Yaqui people. Despite criticism, Castaneda's books have sold millions of copies and have been translated into a number of languages. As pointed out by Gerhard Mayer, "For many people the books of Castaneda presented a fascinating introduction to the subject, defining the role of the shaman in distant countries for many years" (2008:71).

The anthropologist Michael Harner took things one step further. Having earned his PhD in anthropology at the University of Berkeley, he left academia to teach shamanic techniques in workshops on what he called "core shamanism" at his Centre for Shamanic Studies in Esalen, California, from 1979. Core shamanism is presented as a practical project that can be undertaken by everyone. The most central ritual is the "drumming journey," which is described in detail in *The Way of the Shaman* (Harner 1980). The objective of the drumming journey is that the participant, to the sound of the drum, reach an alternate dimension. In 1987, Harner renamed this organization the Foundation for Shamanic Studies (FSS). Harner's school of shamanism, the FSS, as presented on his website (http://www.shamanism.org) is open to anyone who wishes to learn more about the subject. FSS even offers scholarships to natives who wish to "regain" their own shamanic heritage. As Harner underlines: "The Foundation's work to bring knowledge of shamanism and shamanic healing back to the West has been one of its major educational tasks, since shamanism essentially disappeared from Europe during the last two millennia" (2013:130). Today the FSS is present in industrialized countries around the world, but its major branches are located in North America as well as in Europe, where the Scandinavian Centre for Shamanic Studies run by Annette Høst and Jonathan Horowitz has gained particular influence.[5]

Harner's seminal text, *The Way of the Shaman*, published in 1980, holds status as one of the most prominent textbooks for contemporary shamans. According to Harner, a core content exists in the multitude of traditions that together constitute core shamanism. Part of the vision that is expressed in *The Way of the Shaman* is that people from different backgrounds and cultures could build upon this core shamanism by adding elements from their own backgrounds and religious traditions (Harner 1980). Harner's core shamanism promotes the idea that central features of shamanism from tribal people all over the world were and are the same, and they can be learned and practiced by following Harner's courses and methods.

Today, Harner's ideas are contested among practitioners, but many of the pioneers behind Nordic-style shamanism, including some who are currently critical of his ideas, received their first training at Harner's center in the United States. Ongoing debates and controversies about core shamanism and Harner's teaching also indicate his continuing relevance (see Fonneland and Kraft 2013).

During the 1980s, a growing popular literature on shamanism was emerging, drawing many concepts from romantic notions of indigenous spirituality, and written predominantly by Westerners. The Swedish shaman entrepreneur Jørgen I. Eriksson, a proponent of northern and especially Sámi shamanism, has published several books on the subject, among them *Sejd—en vägledning i nordlig shamanism* (1988) (Seid-a Guidance in Northern Shamanism), *Runmagi och* shamanism 2.0 (2006) (Rune Magic and Shamanism 2.0), *Var tids Noaidi-Samisk Shamanism* (2009) (A Noaidi of Our Times – Sami Shamanism), and *Rune Magic and Shamanism: Original Nordic Knowledge from Mother Earth* (2012).[6] As early as in 1982, Eriksson called a meeting at cafe Vega in Stockholm to coordinate the work of remaking Nordic shaman traditions. The outcome of this meeting was the formalization of the Yggdrasil network, which was the first group in Scandinavia to organize a shamanic *seid* ceremony (Lindquist 1997).[7] According to scholar of religion Fredrik Gregorius, in Sweden the practice of *seid* became synonymous with shamanism (2008:97). In *Runmagi och shamanism* (2006), Eriksson and Astrid Grimsson emphasize why a shaman living in the Nordic area should seek nourishment from "Nordic roots." They write, "the shaman is effective in a spiritual or religious dimension and undoubtedly a shaman apprentice should select the tradition that has grown out of and in his or her own landscape" (2006:10, my translation).

In 1983, Michael Harner held his first course on shamanism in Sweden, where he, among other things, presented practical exercises in shamanistic techniques, including the drum journey, which he portrays as having virtually unlimited applications. His presence also further influenced the development of Yggdrasil.

Harner also visited Finnmark to gain knowledge about Sámi culture and religion. Searching for traces of Sámi shamanism, he visited Ailo Gaup's uncle, the Sámi Mikkel Gaup, a well-known "wise-man"[8] in Norway as well as in a broader Scandinavian context, bearing the nicknames "Miracle Mikkel" and "Healing Fox." Harner describes this meeting in *Cave and Cosmos* (2013) as one of the high points in his anthropological fieldwork:

Hearing that the shaman's drum had finally disappeared among the Sámi, I wanted to see for myself. In the early 1980s, I twice went north of the Arctic Circle in Finland, Sweden, and Norway. There I learned that the past was not entirely the past.... Wishing to learn if anything remained of shamanic healing methods among the Sami, ... I was able to make an appointment with the famous Sami healer, the late Mikhail ("Miracle Fox") Gaup, at his home near Alta in northernmost Norway. When Heimo Lappalainen and I arrived at the appointed time, the house was dark and appeared empty. Heimo knocked on the door several times. No answer. We waited more than half an hour. Finally, he went back to the door and pushed on it. The heavy wooden door slowly opened, making a creaking sound like something from a horror film.... Suddenly I was shocked by someone who came from behind and threw me to the floor.... Dazed I looked up to find a huge young man towering over me who shouted loudly in a language I could not understand....

Heimo helped me off the floor and explained what the young man had shouted, more as a challenge than a question: "Do you believe in the power of the Sun?" ... Not only had I learned, dramatically, that Sun worship survived in this remote part of the European continent, but so did an ancient Sami shamanic practice of shocking the patient prior to doing the healing.... Now I had learned that some shamanism was still alive in Europe. (2013:130–131)

Harner further points out that Mikkel Gaup did not use the drum journey nor even the drum in his healing, and that most of the practices connected with the drum had disappeared among the Sámi in Finnmark. Later he refers to a turning point with regard to the use of the drum in this region: "drum journeying is now slowly starting to return there, partly because of help from the FSS and my former students, one of them a Sámi" (Harner 2013:131). Harner's visit can be seen as an important catalyst that paved the way for new religious ideas to impact on prevailing local practices. Until the early 1980s, Mikkel Gaup described himself, as did those around him, as a "reader" or healer of folk traditions (Fonneland 2010:156).[9] Later, and most likely influenced by Harner, he referred to himself as a shaman. Inspired by the shamanic movement, the term *shaman* came to be used more commonly through the 1980s and beyond. Harner's focus on a core shamanism free from cultural and social contexts makes his religious practices easy to integrate into almost every sacred symbolic language (see Harner 1980). The Sámi student that Harner refers to as an important contributor who ensured that shamanism got a foothold in the Norwegian society is precisely Ailo Gaup, recognized as the founder of the Norwegian shamanic movement.

THE RISE OF SÁMI SHAMANISM

Ailo tells the story of his personal spiritual development in his semiautobiographical *The Shamanic Zone* (2005). Ailo was born at Mount Rávdooaivi/Røyehodet on the Finnmark plateau June 18, 1944, by a young Sámi woman. Shortly after the birth, he was handed over to a woman who led the same mission infirmary in Guovdageaidnu (Kautokeino). When Ailo was seven years old, The Sámi Mission gave him up for adoption, and he was sent to a foster family in southeastern Norway, far away from Sámi culture, language, and the land of his birth. Ailo describes this period in his life as a dark chapter where he both physically and mentally faced the negative impacts of the assimilation of the Sámi (2005).

As a young adult, Ailo began studying to become a journalist, but due to strong interests and curiosity, he also included studies of scholarly literature on the indigenous Sámi religion. What he found these studies lacked was the practicalities, in terms of how to initiate a trance and embark upon journeys. Searching for his Sámi roots, not least for traces of Sámi shamanism, Ailo travelled back to northern Norway in 1975, where he stayed for ten years. Among other things, he engaged in the Sámi political environment by participating in the founding of *Beaivvás Sámi Nasunálateáhter* and by fighting for Sámi rights in the demonstrations against the damming of the Alta Kautokeino River. The early phase of the ethnopolitical movement was concerned with rights and politics, as well as identity issues, but for Ailo it also served as a spark for a religious revival (see Fonneland 2010).

However, what Ailo found in Finnmark that could be related to the practice of shamanism had no apparent connection to the *noaidi* (the Sámi indigenous religious specialist) traditions for which he was searching. At the Tourist Hotel in Guovdageaidnu (Kautokeino), Ailo met the Chilean refugee Ernesto, who practiced drum journeys and was willing teach him the art. This was also how Ailo's first ritual visit to the spirit world of his ancestors came about, by way of Chilean traditions, and accompanied by an African djembe-drum (Gaup 2005:86–98). Ailo comments: "And so it happened that I, who had travelled around the Polar Circle to find a Sámi *noaidi* to learn from, wound up in an attic in Oslo with a half-breed Indian carrying a djembe drum. I thought it was a good mix of cultural elements" (ibid:95).

In 1986, Ailo decided to step onto the path of the shaman and moved to California to take part in Harner's shamanic courses at his shaman center in California. Besides Ailo, another shaman from Norway has been a student of Harner, namely Arthur Sørenssen. Both Ailo and Arthur wrote books about their experiences at Esalen. These books— *Shaman: En rituell invielse* (*Shaman: A Ritual Initiation*) (Sørenssen 1988), *Sjamansonen* (*The Shamanic Zone*) (Gaup 2005), and *Inn i naturen: Utsyn fra sjamansonen* (*Into the Nature: View from the Shamanic Zone*) (Gaup 2007)—are central in terms of the development of shamanism in Norway. Ailo is still the one who has gained most attention and publicity for his shamanic courses and writings, something that could be due to his indigenous affiliation and his promotion of Sámi shamanism.

Having been trained in the practice of core shamanism, Ailo settled in Oslo, the Norwegian capital, and established himself as a professional shaman. He developed his own shaman school based upon his newly acquired knowledge. This school is known as the *Saivo Shaman School* (Saivo being a Sámi name for the underworld). The Saivo Shaman School was organized as a series of courses consisting of six gatherings that extended over three years. Teaching was arranged throughout the country, and it is these shaman courses that have had the broadest resonance in Norway. All the established shamans whom I interviewed for my doctoral thesis in 2010 had been trained by Ailo and had participated in one or more of his shaman gatherings.

During its first decade, the Norwegian shamanic movement was more or less a copy of the system developed by Harner in the United States. Similarly, the broader New Age scenes in Norway differed little from their counterparts in the United States and elsewhere in the world (see Fonneland and Kraft 2013). Fieldwork conducted by Bengt Ove Andreassen and Trude Fonneland on the New Age milieu in the city of Tromsø, northern Norway in 2002 indicated that what was expressed in the local New Age milieu did not seem to be marked by place-specific elements, and they found few, if any, references to the pre-Christian Sámi religion (2002/2003). In his study of articles and advertisements connected with indigenous spirituality in the Norwegian New Age magazine *Alternative Network*, Cato Christensen similarly concluded that the Sámi were more or less absent from the otherwise extensive material on shamanism, paganism, and indigenous people (2005).

However, over the course of the first five years of the new millennium, the situation gradually changed. From this period forward, professional shamans were depicted as representing an ancient Sámi shamanic tradition (Christensen 2007), and the Norwegian New Age scene was increasingly filled with Sámi shamans, symbols, and traditions, along with a new focus on local- and place-specific characteristics unique to the northern region, particularly in terms of domestic geography (Fonneland 2010).

Since this period, the annual New Age fairs in Tromsø have included indigenous Sámi symbols in their advertising material. Sámi *lavvos* (traditional Sámi tents) are placed outside the market hall, indoor market stands offer traditional Sámi craft (*duodji*), and Sámi shamanic trance journeys are represented among the selection of spiritual offerings, along with seminars on *joik* (traditional Sámi folk music) and Sámi storytelling (Fonneland 2007). Indicative of the success of this new movement, the "official" support of Sámi shamanism has been rather extensive. The Sámi People's organization (Sámisk folkeforbund) and Norgga Sáráhkká (a Sámi women's organization) have since 2006 served as co-organizers of the New Age fairs in Tromsø. In 2005, the Mayor in Tromsø, in a speech at the opening of this same festival, praised it as "an alternative, alternative fair, due to its location in a northern Norwegian city and its link to Sámi traditions (see Fonneland 2007, my translation).

Professional shamans like Ailo Gaup and Eirik Myrhaug were from this period on depicted as representatives of an ancient Sámi shamanic tradition (Christensen 2007), and a new generation of professional Sámi shamans has been established. Additionally, a wide range of new products have been developed, including courses on Sámi shamanism, on the making of ritual drums (*goavddis*), guided vision quests in the northern Norwegian region, healing sessions inspired by Sámi shamanism, and—to mention one of the latest innovations—the Sámi shamanic festival Isogaisa. Finally, yet importantly, a local shamanic association concerned with the preservation of Sámi and Norse shamanic traditions was granted status as a separate religious community by the County Governor of Troms on March 13, 2012.[10]

The various products—and information about them—are available through advertisements, local media coverage, Facebook groups, websites, and through local shops. A variety of Sámi ritual drums are currently offered, for instance, in tourist shops, at the annual New Age market, and on the websites of Sámi shamans (see Fonneland 2012a). Contemporary, Sámi shamanism thus has become a core subject of Norwegian New Age.

BROAD APPEAL

As mentioned, it is difficult to determine exactly how many people practice shamanism in Norway at present. Many of the New Age traditions border each other and are typically combined by practitioners. Shamans in Norway, who have specialized in one tradition, also allow for combinations and describe their businesses as flexible enterprises that cater to clients with different needs and interests. It is also true that the word *shaman* has gained a broad appeal in contemporary society. Compared to other New Age entrepreneurs, shamans are often highlighted as identifying with collective needs, being environmentalists and heritage supporters by virtue of reviving pre-Christian traditions. People who some years ago would have been referred to as "wise," "healers," or "alternative therapists" are today thus known as shamans. This is the case with one of the most renowned New Age entrepreneurs in contemporary Norway, Gro Helen Tørum, well known from successful television productions like "Åndenes hus" (The House of the Spirits). In 2014, she published her autobiography *Sjaman på høye hæler* (Shaman in High Heels), which became the most publicly profiled book on shamanism in Norway that year (see Selberg 2015). Tørum's New Age courses and practices still have a much wider embrace than shamanism and focus on coaching, lectures on coping with stress, and communication for individuals as well as for firms. Nevertheless, Tørum prefers to refer to herself as a shaman, and this is also how she is designated in Norwegian media (see Fonneland, Kraft, and Lewis 2015:4).

Furthermore, an interesting development noted by scholar of religion Anne Kalvig is the intersection of spiritualism and shamanism, both in Nordic settings and elsewhere (see Kalvig 2015). Several New Age entrepreneurs today make use of shamanism in various ways to render their own position meaningful, and at the same time, they expand the frames of what is recognized as contemporary shamanic practices.

SÁMI INDIGENOUS RELIGION AND A THEME OF EXILE

Sámi indigenous religious ideas and practices were not static or coherent; rather, they varied within the northern Fennoscandia area. There have also been temporal changes in religious practices (Rydving 1993; Äikäs and Salmi 2013; Spangen 2016). Often highlighted as shared ideas are the central role of the landscapes and natural elements (Rydving 1993; Äikäs 2015) as well as the reciprocal relationship people had with the spirits and gods that affected their lives (Schanche 2004:5). The *goavddis* (ritual drum), with its drumhead filled with symbols, is one of the religious instruments that has received wide attention in the descriptions of Sami religion. It is often highlighted as the most important tool of the *noaidi* during divination and trance (compare with Christoffersson 2010).[11]

The state- supported programs for assimilation and missionary activities resulted in the suppression of traditional Sámi believes and practices. The most intense period of missionary activities in the Sámi areas took place between 1650 and 1750. The missionaries' accounts include the term *religion*, but largely Sámi beliefs and practices are described as idolatry, paganism, and superstition.[12] An example of such representations of the indigenous Sami religion is dean Henric Forbus's spiteful comments on the drum:

> Oh you confounded Drum, tool and instrument of Satan, cursed are your depicted Gods: cursed your ring and "baja": cursed your hammer and drumstick: cursed anyone who serves you with beating, and anyone who avails himself of it and makes [someone] beat, yes all those who consent to such a beat and divination and have their inclination for it. Each beat that is made on you, is and will be a Satan's beat in hell for

them, among the spirits of the damned who shall torment and torture them. (Forbus in Rydving 1993:81)

Nordic missionaries managed to disrupt traditional Sámi religion as a comprehensive religious system through persecution and punishment of people who used ritual drums (*goavddis*), through collection and destruction of ritual drums, destruction of sacred sites, and building of churches. One may obtain a clear sense of this destructive process from studies such as historian of religion Håkan Rydving's *The End of Drum Time* (1993) that examines some aspects of the process of religious change among the Lule Sámi, when the indigenous religion was confronted with Christianity.

As stated by Siv Ellen Kraft and Greg Johnson, processes of indigenous revitalization often include attempts to bring to new life to ancient religious traditions that have been disrupted or erased from memory (Johnson and Kraft 2017). Among Sámi people in Norway, the indigenous Sámi religion (sometimes referred to as *noaidevuohta*) "has become increasingly important as a source of national identity symbols and tourism, as well as for the indigenisation of Christianity and of New Age and neo-shamanic milieus" (Johnson and Kraft 2017:27).[13] However, the indigenous Sámi religion has remained controversial, particularly among conservative Christians. As stated by Thomas A Dubois: "The old religion continues to be viewed as illicit among many Nordic Sámi Christians, who belong to either the Lutheran church or the Læstadian sects within it and who often view pre-Christian traditions as irreligious and idolatrous" (2000:268).[14] As more and more people began to identify themselves as Sámi shamans and as self-identified followers of traditional Sámi spirituality grew into a popular movement, observers naturally also questioned the movement's authenticity.

This problem was partly solved through a "theme of exile," which gradually came forth as a strategy among shamans in order to retrieve parts of Sámi indigenous religion. The old Sámi religion, according to this theme, lived on under the garbs of Læstadianism— a Christian conservative movement that spread among the Sámi

during the nineteenth century. Læstadianism is in this context portrayed as a preserver rather than as a destroyer of the traditional
Sámi way of life, a notion that historian Henry Minde has designated
as "the cultural preservation thesis" (2008:8). What Minde argues
is crucial to this thesis is the claim that "Læstadianism provided a
sanctuary for the minority populations, at a time—from 1870 down
to the World War II—when the authorities were tightening the screw
of Norwegianisation in the name of Social Darwinism and nation-
alism" (2008:9; see also Paine 1965). Indicative of this process the
old religion never fully disappeared, and thus the role and practices
of the *noaidi* lived on, only under new designations. Sámi historian Aage Solbakk in his writings clearly enkindles this perspective.
In the book entitled *Hva vi tror på* (What We Believe In) (2008),
he describes Sami indigenous religion in a northern Sámi context
and argues that there still are several *noaidi* in the Sámi community today. For instance, Esther Usti is presented as a *noaideáhkku*
(a female *noaidi*). Solbakk writes:

> In connection with the Christian mission, the term *noaidi* became an
> epithet and the *noaidi*'s work was reviled as devil worship. Nevertheless,
> the *noaidis*' business continued, but in other and more hidden forms and
> with different names being used, including *guvhllár* (healer), *buoridead-
> dji* (healer), *diehtti* (a person with knowledge in folk medicine) … These
> individuals carry out the tradition known today as Sámi folk medicine.
> (2008:20, my translation)

The *noaidi*, according to this perspective, lived on and found shelter in
folk religious as well as folk medical practices. The career of Ailo Gaup
was clearly influenced by this theme, and at the same time it contributed
to the further spread and institutionalization of it. An example of what
Olav Hammer has referred to as "the appeal to tradition" (Hammer
2001:85–200), the theme of exile provides a historical base to the idea
of an essential "Sámi-ness" across time and place, while at the same
time adding authenticity to the current generation of Sámi shamans.

INDIGENOUS SPIRITUALITY

In addition to the "appeal to tradition"—to a Sámi pre-Christian past—developments within the global indigenous movement and transnational indigenous coalitions have also influenced and helped to legitimize the practice of Sámi shamanism. Several scholars have referred to notions of a religious dimension of indigenism. According to James Clifford, "Indigènitude is sustained through media-disseminated images, including a shared symbolic repertoire ('the sacred,' 'Mother Earth,' 'shamanism,' 'sovereignty' the wisdom of 'elders,' stewardship over 'the land'" (Clifford 2013:16). In addition, popular culture, like music and film, has been important for the wider spread of such images (see Christensen 2013; Kraft 2015). Siv Ellen Kraft has in several articles referred to this type of shared symbolic repertoire as *indigenous spirituality* (Kraft 2008, 2009, 2010).

"Indigenous spirituality" is a late-modern term in international discourse that constructs the world's indigenous peoples as people with a common colonial past, common religious heritage, and a spiritual relationship with nature and their surroundings (Christensen and Kraft 2010:1). This representation of indigenous people as a community with shared religious values relating to nature, to the past, and to traditions can be traced back to 1960s counterculture, and in particular to the interplay between the environmental movement and the New Age movement. These movements emerged within the same period, and they have been exchanging ideas ever since, especially in terms of consciousness about ecology and fascination with the world's indigenous peoples. As several researchers have pointed out, these values are also often expressed by indigenous people themselves, in their identity constructions, in the struggle for political rights, and in cultural revitalization processes (see Beyer 1998; Kalland 2003; Kraft 2009; Niezen 2012; Clifford 2013). As Fonneland and Kraft argue:

> This new global spiritual-identity is partly a result of UN meetings and regulations, including laws that have helped standardise certain qualities by translating them into rights. In contrast to the "freedom of beliefs"

promoted by human rights discourse, the beliefs of indigenous people tend, for instance, to be explicitly connected to particular landscapes. To cite one example: ILO Convention 169, ratified by Norway in 1990, claims that governments must "respect the special importance for the cultures and spiritual values of the peoples concerning their relationship with the lands or territories." (Article 13, 1) (Fonneland and Kraft 2013:140)

Regular references to indigenous people as children of Mother Earth are similarly common in UN-fora, along with references to a holistic worldview. After a resolution in 2009, Mother Earth has even been granted a particular day, April 22, referred to as International Mother Earth Day (Fonneland and Kraft 2013:140). As Dorothy L. Hodgson notes, the UN presentations of indigenous people "draw on and reproduce familiar tropes and images of Indigenous people as colourful, spiritual 'authentic' and artistic" (2014:62). Indigenous spirituality is thus a global discourse that attributes a particular kind of spirituality to indigenous peoples, while indigenous people are also able to contribute to the shaping of this discourse and to utilize it for their own strategic purposes.

To some extent a reversal of the primitivism of the past, the discourse on indigenous spirituality qualifies for Michael Shermer's notion of "the myth of the beautiful people" (1997). Characteristics that once placed indigenous people on a lower level of the evolutionary scale today account for their position as peaceful, wise, and noble caretakers of environmental wisdom. As anthropologist Jonathan Friedman has put it:

[The] indigenous is now part of a larger inversion of Western cosmology in which the traditional other, a modern category, is no longer the starting point of a long and positive evolution of civilisation, but a voice of Wisdom, a way of life in tune with nature, a culture in harmony, a *gemeinschaft*, that we have all but lost. (Freidman 1999:391)

The creation of identity typically relies on the creation of opposites. Identity processes are framed by dichotomies and borderlines, and they are always relational. The term "indigenous spirituality" is in many ways a cultural marker defined by a contrast to Western society, religions, and worldviews (Christensen and Kraft 2010:2). Thus, when the Sámi people were incorporated into the international indigenous movement and into global discourses concerning indigenous spirituality, a political, cultural, and religious contrast was constructed between Sámi and Norwegians. While the Sámi are portrayed as a primitive people living in harmony with themselves and their surroundings, Norwegians are viewed as participating in the opposite— a hectic modern Western society associated with mobility and capitalism—with claims to ownership of the Earth, and with exploiting its resources. Values relating to nature and to the landscape mark a distinction between a place-oriented, peaceful, holistic, traditional, and eco-friendly indigenous culture and a modern Western capitalist society (see Kraft 2009:188).

EMBRACING CORE AND SEARCHING FOR LOCAL ROOTS

The interest in seeking local roots can be seen in the context of a growing reaction against Harner's core shamanism. As early as the 1980s, the Swedish shaman Jørgen I. Eriksson was already writing extensively in the Swedish shamanistic magazine *Gimle*, pointing out that Harner's core shamanism stripped shamanic traditions of their cultural uniqueness (see Svanberg 1994:30). Eriksson comments:

> After Michael Harner has peeled off the cultural differences that exist between the types of shamanism in different cultures, and developed the core that is common to all, it is up to ourselves to ... reconnect the [foreign] teachings to our own ancient shamanic traditions, as one grafts new healthy twigs onto an old apple-tree. Hopefully, this will result in a shamanism that will be well grounded in our own landscape, light, climate and culture. (Eriksson 1988:8–9)

Eriksson considers Harner's core shamanism insufficient in terms of the richness and variety of indigenous traditions. He also finds that core shamanism lacks reverence for Mother Earth and all living creatures. According to Eriksson, a return to the local is the solution to resolving this discrepancy. This type of "re-ethnicized" shamanism as a reaction against Harner's core shamanism also has international parallels in, for instance, Tom Cowan's Celtic *Fire in the Head: Shamanism an the Celtic Spirit* (1993) and Gershon Winkler's *Magic of the Ordinary: Recovering the Shamanic in Judaism* (2003). Like Eriksson, who searches for a shamanism grounded in local landscapes, Cowan and Gershon aim to trace and recover the long-lost shamanic wisdom and the shamanic roots of the "Celtic Spirit" and of "aboriginal Judaism."

Ailo, however, does not express this type of explicit criticism toward Harner's shamanic enterprises in interviews or in his books. On the other hand, he describes Harner as an important catalyst for the emergence of Sámi shamanism. As we will see in Chapter 4 on the shamanic festival Isogaisa, the criticism of core shamanism is still present among practitioners of Sámi shamanism in Norway.

A concern for many of the shamans I have interviewed is that influences from other cultures can, to some extent, help develop Nordic shamanistic practices. This is in line with one of the core pillars of contemporary shamanism, namely perennialism. In the *Shamanic Zone* (2005), Ailo emphasizes this further:

> Shamanism did not arise in the same way as Christianity, Islam or Buddhism, each of them being created by a separate religious founder. The old art has been here all the time as a possibility or an original heritage innate in human beings. Since ancient times, a "shamanic belt" has extended from Sámiland through the whole of Siberia. The migrants from Asia brought shamanism with them to North and South America. The phenomena has existed since time immemorial in Australia and within the big island cultures of the Pacific and certainly in Africa, the cradle of humankind. From a historical perspective, shamanism is the first spiritual practice and the first great cultural science. (Gaup 2005:9–10)

Shamanism is presented here as a foundation in all the world's cultures and as a spiritual heritage innate in human beings. Folklorist Torunn

Selberg notes, "as with heritage, shamanism—in its present form—is a new cultural production with recourse to the past, a past that is creating identity, authenticity, and meaning" (2015:100). Ideas of unbroken traditions and continuity with the past are fundamental premises for the emergence of this field. To bridge the traditions of the past with the present in an attempt to reconstruct the Sámi shamanic heritage, Ailo and other shamanic practitioners seek inspiration not only from local resources.

The influence from other traditions and cultures is, for instance, expressed on the skin of the drums that the shamans use in ceremonies and in rituals. In addition to the Sámi gods and goddesses—Beaivi (goddess of the sun), Lieaibolmmai (god of the hunt), Máttaráhkká (the primal godmother and the deity of motherhood), Sáráhkká (the goddess of women and all living beings), Oksáhkká (the goddess who watches the entrance and exit to the living world and cares for mothers and children after a birth), and Juksáhkká ("the bow mother," who is the goddess of boys and has the ability to transform an unborn girl into a boy)[15]—Eirik Myrhaug has also added space for both Jesus and Buddha on his drum. On Ronald Kvernmo's drum (see Figure 2.2), a symbol for Internet Explorer has been given a central position along with a symbol for Highway E6 that runs through Norway from the south to the north.[16] According to the perennial discourse, the seed of shamanism can be sought and found in every quarter of the world, and in a multitude of symbolic expressions. What has been lost in Sámi areas can thus be retrieved elsewhere, and it can be merged with contemporary values and resources. On his website, Ailo writes about some of the things that inspired and shaped him as a Sámi shaman:

I have found inspiration and knowledge from many quarters. My first experience with shamanism I received from a Sámi noaidi. Later I learned healing techniques that came from the Mapuche Indians of Chile. The first systematic training over time I got through Harner's courses on "Core Shamanism" in California. Later, I studied with Native Americans from North and South America and the Huna shamans from Hawaii. I know shamans from all continents.[17]

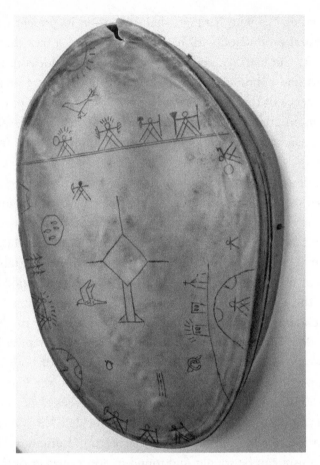

FIGURE 2.2
Shaman drum (photo by Ronald Kvernmo).

Ailo's identity as a Sámi shaman has developed through the exchange of knowledge derived from different cultures and traditions. It is also these different sources Ailo drew on when teaching his own courses. Still Ailo chose to profile his shamanic practices in relation to Sámi culture and traditions. This was achieved by naming his shaman school Saivo, offering guided vision quests to the landscape of his birth, highlighting terms and symbols from the indigenous Sámi religion, and by referring to great Sámi shamans of the past—both male and female—along with stories of their suppression, of forced assimilation, and of current revival in his books and on his website.

SAME CONTENT—NEW WRAPPING

In terms of this juggling of different sources and the openness toward traditions from various cultures, how then does Sámi shamanism differ from its US origins? In the article "Sámi Neo Shamanism and Indigenous Spirituality" (2013), Fonneland and Kraft claim that Ailo, as well as his colleagues in the Norwegian shamanic milieu, has followed a route pointed out in Harner's teachings. Having identified what he considered to be central ingredients of indigenous people's religious notions and practices, Harner urged indigenous people to trace their roots, and thereby contribute to the reservoir of shamanic resources. At the Foundation's homepage, Harner underlines:

> Core shamanism consists of the universal, near-universal, and common features of shamanism, together with journeys to other worlds, a distinguishing feature of shamanism. As originated, researched, and developed by Michael Harner, the principles of core shamanism are not bound to any specific cultural group or perspective. Since the West overwhelmingly lost its shamanic knowledge centuries ago due to religious oppression, the Foundation's programs in core shamanism are particularly intended for Westerners to reacquire access to their rightful spiritual heritage through quality workshops and training courses. Training in core shamanism includes teaching students to alter their consciousness through classic shamanic non-drug techniques such as sonic driving, especially in the form of repetitive drumming, so that they can discover their own hidden spiritual resources, transform their lives, and learn how to help others.[18]

This, one might claim, is precisely what Ailo and his colleagues have set out to achieve (Fonneland and Kraft 2013:136). We have, as Stephen Prothero in a different empirical context has argued, a change of vocabulary, but continuity in terms of basic ideas, a Nordic lexicon built upon a core-shamanic grammar (1996, see also Fonneland and Kraft 2013).

This construct, moreover, makes sense from the perspective of the broader ethnopolitical search for a Sámi identity and in regard to connections to indigenous peoples worldwide and transhistorically. It also makes sense in economic and marketing terms. Sámi versions of shamanism are presented by practitioners as more authentic than the American Indian version. In the practice of shamanism, various religious entrepreneurs obtain legitimacy through adaptation to "here." Following scholar of religion Ingvild S. Gilhus's extensions of Jonathan Z. Smith's spatial model for adaptation to postsecular conditions, the locus of here, in addition to a religion related to the family and the home, can be understood as religion connected to local geography and local history (Gilhus 2012). Featured cultural expressions are enrolled in discourses connected to tradition and continuity that legitimate the entrepreneurs' products and services, and reaffirm a certain quality and authenticity.

AUTHENTICITY FALLACY

The development of local variants of shamanic practices can also be seen as a response to the criticisms leveled by Native American leaders against "plastic shamans" as appropriators of cultural traditions that do not belong to them. Both inside as well as outside of academic circles, shamanism has been highly contested during the past several decades. One can find deep and open scholarly disapproval of contemporary shamanic practices in works like Henri-Paul Francfort and Roberte Hamayon's edited volume from 2001, *The Concept of Shamanism: Uses and Abuses*, as well as Merete Jakobsen's *Shamanism: Traditional and Contemporary Approaches* (1999). Another type of critical statement comes from both native and nonnative spokespeople who take offense whenever nonnative peoples adopt and practice select parts of indigenous spiritual systems.[19]

As anthropologist Michael F. Brown stresses: "Indigenous peoples now perceive themselves as more threatened by outsiders who claim to love their religion than by missionaries dedicated to its overthrow" (2003:23). In the article "Spiritual Hucksterism: The Rise of the Plastic Medicine Men" (2003), Ward Churchill describes how an activist in the Nisqually Nation reacts toward what she experiences as a theft of religious ideas and practices:

> First they came to take our land and water, then our fish and game. Then they wanted our mineral resource and, to get them, they tried to take our governments. Now they want our religion as well. All of a sudden, we have a lot of unscrupulous idiots running around saying they're medicine men. And they'll sell you a sweat lodge ceremony for fifty bucks. It's not only wrong it is obscene. Indians don't sell their spirituality to anybody, for any price. This is just another in a very long series of thefts from Indian people and, in some ways, this is the worst one yet. (2003:325)

Sámi scholars and activists have also expressed criticism against the reconstruction of Sámi indigenous traditions by contemporary shamans in Norway. In *I Modergudinnens fotspor* (1997) (In the Mother Goddess' Footsteps), anthropologist Marit Myrhaug asserts that:

> in its worst form of expression this romanticising has resulted in something I would describe as "reverse cultural imperialism." Earlier one was concerned with destroying Sámi religion based on an understanding that it was a bad thing. [Currently,] one is again in danger of abusing religion, but now based on a "positive" understanding of it. (1997:10, my translation)

Znamenski refers to these types of debates as "postmodern tensions." These are conflicts that a hundred years ago would have been inconceivable, because indigenous people's faith and practices at the time were portrayed as primitive superstition in the West (2007:287). The tension between some indigenous activists and shamanic practitioners represents a conflict between two different views on identity and spirituality (see among others Dubois 2009:277). For many contemporary shamans spirituality is an individual quest, related to one's individual needs and preferences. Among indigenous representatives, however, spirituality is often highlighted as a collective resource, useful in the creation of community and identity.

43

"Wannabe shamans" (Green 1988), "white shamans"(Rose 1984), and "plastic medicine men/shamans" (Churchill 1992/2003) are epithets that are used worldwide to describe modern self-proclaimed, nonindigenous shamans' practices. The problem with "plastic shamans" that often is highlighted in these types of debates is that they are corrupted by modern civilization and lack an authentic link to a true religious tradition. Equally important are the issues related to cultural appropriation and recolonization.

Both Sámi and non-Sámi practitioners of shamanism in Norway embrace and identify with the Sámi tradition. Still, to avoid accusations of cultural appropriation and colonization, there is a reluctance to don Sámi clothing and to use *joik* among shamans who cannot display Sámi descent. In our conversations, Anna relates the sharp critique from one of her course participants when she during a meditation put on a music recorder with a song that resembled *joik*. The course participant clearly stated that Anna had no right to use *joik*. The incidence raised Anna's awareness about the fragile limits of appropriation. To avoid such accusations, nonnative shamans thus bring other strategies into play to assert affiliation to native religious traditions.

Genealogical survey has long been a well-known initiative among shamans who wish to take part in an indigenous community. This is the case with several of the shamanic practitioners I have interviewed. Kyrre Gram Franck, for instance, did not claim Sámi ancestry when we first spoke in 2004; today, however, he has found Sámi ancestors on the maternal side of his family and now uses *gákti* (Sámi traditional clothing) in shamanic performances. Another practitioner whom I interviewed in 2005 asserts, due to genealogical surveys, to be one-eighteenth Sámi (see Fonneland 2010). These examples generate a feeling that in the reclamation of religious traditions, blood does indeed matter, as Pike underlines (2001:121). To be able to detect kinship and a bloodline gives the practitioner a feeling of belonging and a legitimacy to practice traditions that are perceived as immortal—endured through time and space.

Bloodlines are far from the only option for fostering belonging. Notions of blood right are also mixed with the concept of reincarnation to justify the use of a tradition. The attraction that people of different ethnic origins feel toward a particular ethnically based tradition may be the result of having been a Sámi or Norse person in a past life (see also Strmiska 2005). Some also claim to have gained access to indigenous shamanic traditions through a spiritual mentor either in this or in the spiritual world, pointing out that spirituality cannot be owned in the same way as an object, and that it knows no cultural or genealogical boundaries. In other words, they claim a spiritual inheritance and find that a sharing of ritual practices and worldviews is sufficient to take part in and market Sámi shamanism.

Also, contact with nature, and in particular the nature where the Sámi indigenous religion was practiced, offers nonindigenous shamans a strategy for conferring authenticity. As I argue in Chapter 3, shamans' narratives about their contact with northern Norwegian nature and the landscape of the indigenous Sámi religion can be seen as an act of self-positioning and as a strategy for building credibility as a shaman.

Scholar of religion James R. Lewis refers to an interesting distinction in terms of the kind of criticism self-proclaimed Sámi shamans and self-proclaimed Native American shamans have been subjected to. Lewis notes that even the most critical observations by Sámi scholars and activists, such as the Myrhaug citation earlier, are mild when compared with the harsh critiques leveled by scholars of Native American traditions. He writes:

> At the most general level, the point of the present juxtaposition of American neoshamanism with Sámi neoshamanism is clear enough: the same reconstructed neoshamanism that receives such extreme criticism in the North American context has been popularly accepted as an authentic expression of indigenous spirituality in northern Europe. (2015:136)

Nonindigenous shamans in Norway, according to Lewis, have managed to avoid the sort of intense criticism that nonindigenous shamans in the United States were met with from the very start. Although the mainstream media in Norway have been extremely critical of New

Age movements in general (Kraft 2011), anything with an "indigenous Sámi" aura, regardless of whether those responsible have a Sámi origin or not, is given a free pass (Lewis 2015).

That internal tradition-keepers react with criticism is fully understandable, whether it is among Sámi or North American "First Nations." However, it becomes strange when a third party adopts this type of statement. As scholar of religion Egil Asprem points out, we cannot escape the fact that this rhetoric is based on (Western) primitivistic perceptions of what constitutes the noble and authentic. He writes,

> The myth of an authentic religion that has long been lost to modern man, can lead the nostalgic to seek Eliade's "lost time" in exotic primitives. But it can also lead the cynic to a common fallacy: that modern applicants are (inauthentic) copies of authentic originals. This is a variant of what the logics call argumentum ad antiquitatem—a variant that we can call "authenticity fallacy." The pitfall of authenticity is based on the invalid premise that there are "pure" and "authentic" types of religion and religious practice. Outside the world of theology, this notion is pure fantasy.[20]

As noted by Fonneland and Kraft, there is no shortage of convincing examples to support charges of cultural theft and demeaning practices. However, this is not the whole story. Current conditions are, at least in the case of the Norwegian Sámi, far more complex than those depicted in the established scenario of indigenous victims of New Age abuse. Such a scenario fails to account for the presence of indigenous people on these same scenes, including Sámi shamans and the voices of indigenous spirituality (2013:144). The agency of all parties needs to be acknowledged in these types of meetings, which hence does not yield to simple theories of objectivation and appropriation. As Sámi shaman Eirik Myrhaug emphasizes in an interview with historian of religion Brita Pollan; "Without the neo-shamanistic movement, I would be in a vacuum" (Myrhaug in Pollan 2002:261). An example of what Harald Prins has called "the paradox of primitivism," the reproduction of primitivist themes is no longer limited to

"Western" circles. Primitive themes are also explored by indigenous practitioners, some of whom recognize the primitivist formula—and some of whom actively draw on it as a cross cultural "structure of comprehension and imperatives for action" (Prins 2002:56). Their motives may be economic, spiritual, connected to the search for a meaningful ethnic identity—or all of the above. Indicative of the messy character of New Age spiritualities, they belong to primitivist traditions as well as to recent processes of cultural revitalization, to global trends and local meaning-making (Fonneland and Kraft 2013:144).

As H. Glenn Penny with reference to Jolene Rickard (1998) notes in the chapter "Surrogate Indigeneity and the German Hobbyist Scene" (2014), why do we assume that to play and dress Indian is "humorous and problematic rather than understandable and perhaps even instructive?" (2014:197). According to Penny, these types of assumption prevent us from acknowledging alternative forms of knowledge production as well as cause us to overlook the interconnection between Europeans and indigenous peoples (2014:197). Rather than giving in to the temptation of constructing new elusive authenticities, our task as scholars of religion is to tell the story of why contemporary shamans, natives as well as nonnatives, search for authenticity. Living on a planet "characterised by inescapable transculturation," we need to acknowledge the constructed and deceptive nature of authenticity (Bendix 1997:228).

CONCLUSION

People engaging in Sámi shamanism generally describe themselves as part of a community dedicated to highlighting Sámi indigenous traditions as a spiritual heritage. Rather than an organized movement with identifiable doctrines, practices, and leaders, Sámi shamanism in Norway is complex, multifaceted, and loosely organized. It shows how local pasts, places, and characters are woven into global discourses on shamanism, and in this melting pot new forms of religion are taking shape.

Sámi shamanism was born as an offspring of Michael Harner's core shamanism during the late 1980s, some three hundred years after the Christianization of the Sámi. Part of Harner's vision was that people from different backgrounds could build upon core shamanism by adding elements from their own local religious and cultural traditions (Harner 1980). This, one might say, is precisely what spiritual entrepreneurs like Ailo Gaup set out to achieve when developing Sámi shamanism. In this process of adaption and indigenization, new meanings, products, and ideas occur. Sámi shamanism as a new shamanistic blend also influences the international scene, evolving constantly and providing impacts.

CHAPTER THREE

THE POWER OF NATURE
IN THE HIGH NORTH

> The land
> is different
> when you have lived there,
> wandered
> sweated,
> frozen,
> seen the sun
> set rise
> disappear, return
> the land is different
> when you know
> here are
> roots,
> ancestors
>
> —*Nils-Aslak Valkeapää, The Sun,*
> *My Father (1997)*

Sociologists Phil Macnaghten and John Urry (1998:14) argue that during the nineteenth century, the division between nature and society increasingly came to be conceived in spatial terms, with society at the center and nature as the "other," pushed out to the margins. A century later, this division has been recast as an opportunity for uniqueness and authenticity. Throughout history, humankind's association with nature has changed due to cultural, economic, and political factors. Nature is connected with strong values and moods. It has been praised and disowned, and it continues to be part of a dynamic process in which it is altered and recast in changing discourses and contexts.

In the shamanic environment in Norway, the concept of nature has come to represent opposition to globalization, technology, and modernization. Similarly, nature has been highlighted as a symbol of truth and personal growth. In this chapter, I explore Norwegian shamans' relationships with nature in the High North. How is nature included in their practices and how does the use of nature relate to the legitimizing of modern Sámi shamanism? I base the discussion on the view that landscapes are constituted as meaningful entities through events. However, different experiences, interests, and agendas make the same landscape evolve with different meanings. To shed light on these issues, I start by putting in context some of the background for the interest in nature and landscape that is expressed by the shamans I have interviewed and that can be related to the interest in nature among modern pagans as well as within the New Age spiritualites.

"THE GREEN WAVE"

The early 1970s saw a revival of the romantic view of nature, and in the Western world the yearning for a closer relationship with nature became increasingly widespread. In the Romantic period (late 1700–1830),[1] nature was depicted as having qualities that were contrasted with what was viewed as unnatural. Nature encompassed authenticity, the real thing, and the unspoiled—in contrast with the polluted, artificial, and commercial climate of the cities. Ethnologists Jonas Frykman and Orvar Löfgren express this in their book *Det kultiverte menneske* (*The Cultivated Man*) (1994): "At the same time as nature is cowed and domesticated into a consumer landscape of towers and tourists, it is also made wilder, equipped with qualities which enhance its naturalness and primitiveness—its purity" (Frykman and Löfgren 1994:54, my translation).

With the emergence of romanticism, an exotic image of the rural life and wild nature also gradually emerged. The romantic depiction of nature focuses on the aesthetic and recreational aspects, and overlooks the destructive forces of nature. Folklorists Olav Christensen and Anne Eriksen point out that "Aesthetically based frameworks were projected onto nature through artistic modes of expression such as texts and images. Nature was visited as a place for recreation and adventure" (Christensen and Eriksen 1993:27, my translation). At the same time as scientific and technical progress demystified nature, there emerged a new nature-based mysticism, which was not rooted in the cultivated landscape, but in the new landscape of leisure (Frykman and Löfgren 1994:50–51).

There were nonetheless parts of the country where nature was perceived as too wild, and the nature of the High North holds a unique position. This part of the country was pictured as barren, tough, and brutal, with a long, pitch-black dark season and a midnight sun that was mostly a nuisance. On par with the midnight sun, the tundra, the dark season, mountains, and reindeer, the Sámi people were considered an exotic element that formed part of the image of northern Norway as a natural-mythical wilderness (Conrad 2004:166–167). The master poet Bjørnstjerne Bjørnson made an honest attempt at changing the negative image of the region. His travelogues from ventures in northern Norway in 1869, published for the first time in 1872, praise the area with enthusiasm, although not everything was to his taste at first:

> One may find places which seem repugnant at first; but if one goes to a higher point to gain a more remote view, giving heed to the shapes and placement of the rocks, the deep colour of the sea, and the crispness of the air; then the notion of eternity soars across the vast, wild land, and it is wonderful. (1907:209)

Bjørnson's portrayals of the north Norwegian landscape may have been shaped by the writings of English gentleman fishermen who had already traveled to the north of Norway in the 1830s. Their writings and visits helped to create a tourist industry in the region and contributed directly to the development of "Den Norske Turistforening" (the Norwegian Tourist Association) in 1866, an organization devoted to helping Norwegians hike and enjoy the national landscape. In this sense, notions of a majestic North Norwegian nature are imports that little by little have been adopted by Norwegians.

One of the most prominent philosophers of the Romantic era, Friedrich Wilhelm Joseph von Schelling (1775–1854), claimed—in contrast with the dominant Kantian philosophy of the time—that nature is a living interaction of spiritual forces. According to Schelling, existence is an unbroken totality in which each part reflects the whole. In this context, understanding nature would be a matter of being able to interpret the secret connections that bind together each separate part of the overarching macrocosm. Similarly, one of the main proponents of transcendentalism, the author Ralph Waldo Emerson (1803–1882), viewed nature as a symbol and manifestation of the "good" in existence. According to Emerson, there is a divine power in nature that permeates everything; and all imbalance, fear, and difficulty could thus be healed simply by being in touch with the forces of nature. Emerson's depictions of nature and life have also been portrayed as a precursor to New Age philosophy (see Hammer 2004:40).

The resurgence of the romantic view of nature in the 1970s is, among other things, connected with the emergence of the modern environmentalist movement and the growing interest in New Age spirituality. This period is often labeled as "the green wave."[2] The social anthropologist Gaile McGregor points out how this period sees a shift from technophilia to technophobia (1988:1). Humankind feared the consequences of nuclear destruction and the alienating rationality which technology was believed to represent.

Modern environmentalism began as a decentralized movement in the late 1960s. The movement regarded the increasing gap between humanity and nature as an alienating process creating global imbalance. It was concerned with taking care of, showing respect for, and living in harmony with nature. The emergence of the modern environmentalist movement and other alternative movements in the years around 1970 also generated a new interest in ecological farming. The fight against nuclear power and chemical companies was an important international issue. Gradually the movement gained greater political acceptance and was able to place environmental issues on the political agenda.

In Norway, the interest in nature and the environment manifested itself in the fight against the establishment of hydroelectric power plants in Mardøla in 1971 and the Alta-Kautokeino River in 1979. The public movement against developing the Alta-Kautokeino waterway was founded in Alta on July 12, 1978, and 10,000 people took part in the protests. Both the shamans Ailo Gaup and Eirik Myrhaug (see Figure 3.1) describe their fight for the river as a turning point for their current spiritual practice. Despite the fact that the river was eventually lost, the demonstrations did contribute to raising awareness around the destruction of nature in Finnmark, and it promoted the idea that the Sámi people were the true proprietors of the nature and environment.

FIGURE 3.1
Shaman Eirik Myrhaug at Lortvannet (photo by Bente Brunvoll).

Social anthropologist Galina Lindquist, who researched urban Swedish shamans connected with the Yggdrasil organization in her thesis *Shamanic Performances on the Urban Scene* (1997), showed that many of the members have a background in the hippie movement and radical left-wing organizations. She also points out that many of these young radical left-wingers became interested in different types of alternative spirituality during the 1980s as a reaction against what they considered to be an authoritarian structure and agenda in the political movements they had been part of in the past (Lindquist 1997:269). This is the case for Eirik and Ailo as well. What began as a political engagement gradually became the basis of a form of religious practice.

NATURE AS A KEY SYMBOL

Nature has become a key symbol in Western culture. As a symbol, nature can be said to be multivocal. It points to different meanings, and it is expressed in different contexts (see Rønnow 1998:82). The yearning to return to nature is no longer reserved for protest movements. It represents an overall symbol of all that is good, original, and stimulating. However, contact with nature is not only a matter of being in contact with actual, physical nature, with its grand pristine landscapes. The orientation toward nature can be connected to primitivism in a wider sense, to an idealization of nature and the natural, in contrast with civilization and the anthropogenic. Nature represents a value bank, which is in everyone's interest to preserve and watch over. It has become a symbol of wholeness and belonging. This strong focus on nature has made several recent researchers point out that the way nature is understood in today's society has religious aspects, and nature and the landscape are often seen in connection with the sacred and transcendental (see inter alia Rønnow 2000:27–28; Szerszynski 2005:8–9).

The sociologist Alberto Melucci claims that in line with this turn toward the peripheral, many new social movements in their early stages place emphasis on values and expressions that they believe have been lost in modern society. The languages, ideologies, symbols, myths, rituals, and traditions of earlier cultures are picked up and given new meaning in light of the present context (1992:145). Melucci's hypothesis corresponds with the rhetoric expressed by the shamanic practitioners I have interviewed. Nature, the past, and the world's indigenous peoples are used as factors to justify the ideologies promoted by practitioners. They represent values that create a common ground within the group, and they serve to provide roots for the individual's personal identity and faith.

The New Age movement carries on one of the primary characteristics of the revitalizing movements that emerged around 1970; namely, the depiction of the peripheral as authentic (Hetherington 1998). In the words of Kraft: "What is true and authentic is localised to all that stands outside the established norm; all that has been rejected, repressed or suppressed by mainstream culture" (2005:32, my translation). Due to their scepticism toward modern progress, New Age communities aim to reconstruct a lifestyle that has been disrupted and threatened by the civilizing process. Thus, in these communities, nature represents a source of power, a door opener for establishing contact with the magical and spiritual world, and the goal for the individual is to move forward in his or her own spiritual development by being in close contact with the landscape. This notion that nature possesses a force that can be used for the cultivation of self is particularly prevalent in New Age circles.

The focus on the peripheral—on nature and the natural—can also be seen in connection with the struggle for a natural and balanced society that we find in many protest movements. New Age springs from the progress of modern society; yet at the same time, this movement also represents a protest against the modern, and it has been considered a countercultural wave from its beginning.[3] Scholar of religion Mikael Rothstein points out that the movement is a reaction, and an alternative, to the ideas and values that have dominated Western culture for the past two thousand years. He also emphasizes how the movement finds that the contemporary represents a type of "anti-nature" (1993:121).

Within New Age, it is claimed that this "anti-nature" is culturally rooted in dualistic thought; in reductionism; in the emphasis on the masculine; and in the focus on material values. It represents something detrimental and is regarded as a threat. New Age writers have authored a number of studies dealing mainly with these issues, such as Theodore Roszak's *The Making of a Counter Culture* (1969), Fritjof Capra's *The Turning Point* (1982), and William Irwin Thompson's *Pacific Shift* (1986). The primary target of attack in these texts is the metropolitan life. It is in the big cities that the alienation process peaks due to excessive consumption, materialism, and the pursuit of luxury. Their books anticipate a revolution of values and worldviews, and predict the emergence of a new era, of a new holistic, ecological, and integrating culture, where the old Western cultures—with their mechanistic, linear models—will collapse.

The shamans I have interviewed also reflect this strong imaginative bond with nature. Several researchers, such as Catherine Albanese, claim that this connection with nature is so strong that one may consider neopagan movements a form of *nature religions* (1990). Embedded in this is an acknowledgment of how the natural landscape is bonded with the spiritual world, and that the primary way one can get in touch with the spiritual world is by being in nature. Historian of religion Peter Beyer writes,

> Today's expressions of nature religion can be seen as an analogous counter structural reflection, critique and confirmation of contemporary social normality, namely global society with its dominant instrumental systems. To begin, nature is itself a counter-structural symbol: inasmuch as the more dominant global modernities are characterised by a priority of technical, humanly controlled and artificial constructs, so nature is all that which is not technical artifice, but also that which is deemed the condition for the possibility of this globalised world. Indeed, the nature/technique polarity is a defining feature of this arising religiosity. (1998:18)[4]

The core of the critique is related to key ideas and values in contemporary society: consumption, materialism, and dualisms such as nature/culture, mind/body, and natural/supernatural, as well as the exploitation of the environment for human gain and pleasure (see Rountree 2012). In their emphasis on nature, these communities criticize modern life-styles, saying among other things that society is afflicted by material and spiritual contamination. This contamination is interpreted as act-ing as a barrier to the spiritual flow of the body, which results in inner blockages. In this way, the imbalance of the Earth is reflected in the body. The critique of civilization among shamans may thus be said to be doubly rooted. First, one emphasizes that our way of life has inflicted an ecological crisis on the planet; but this crisis is also reflected back onto humankind, which has had its self-development hampered by the progress of postmodern society.

A clear example of how this kind of criticism is expressed is the involvement of shamans in Norway in the demonstrations at Standing Rock and the fight against the "black snake"—the 190-mile-long pipeline that is intended to transport crude oil from the border with Montana to Patoka in Illinois. Large parts of this trajectory run through indigenous sacred sites and burial grounds. An explosively growing rainbow alliance of indigenous peoples, environmental movements, peace organizations, large and small alternative groups—including shamanic practitioners and organizations in Norway—support Sitting Bull's tribe. The commitment is visible on the shamans' private Facebook profiles, but it is also expressed in more organized forms. On September 18, 2016, the Shamanistic Association led a ceremony out-side of the Norwegian *Storting* (the Norwegian Parliament building) to demonstrate their support with the Sioux tribe and with Standing Rock. The day before the Shamanistic Association's branch in Tromsø invited people to take part in a water ceremony to show that they are "standing with Standing Rock." To the news agency NRK Sápmi, the leader of the Shamanistic Association, Kyrre Gram Franck, underlines,

[The] Shamanistic Association focuses on taking care of Mother Earth and all her children. Therefore, we are now actively supporting the opponents of the Dakota Access Pipeline.... I cannot sit and watch that human rights are violated and that sacred places are destroyed. However, most important is the access to clean water.... Water is the origin to all

57

life, without water there is no life. Therefore we focus on the water, and hold a ceremony where people can go into the water and honour the water with a blessing.[5]

Norwegian shamans' struggles against the "black snake" demonstrate how shamanic ceremonies also serve as political means and resources for the fight for indigenous rights and not least for the environment.[6]

HOLISTIC PERSPECTIVES

One of the core perspectives within the New Age movement as well as within shamanism is holism (Hanegraaff 1996). Holism refers to the belief that there is an underlying connection in the world between god and nature, between nature and humanity, and between body and soul. Nature and humankind are one and the same organism, changing and alive, and the objective of each practitioner is to become one with the heartbeat of the universe. Thus, the holistic perspective gains power only when one restores one's bond with nature: with the mountains, seas, animals, and plants. This holistic perspective is also at the core of the New Age criticism of Western society and Western culture. In the words of Hanegraaff, "Holism may thus be regarded as the central core of New Age religion ... in the sense that it is an appropriate label for a generally shared pattern of cultural criticism (1996:516).

Through the focus on holism, the New Age movement seeks to distance itself from a worldview dominated by dualism and reductionism. There is a general attitude within New Age communities that dualism is rooted in the Jewish-Christian tradition. Christianity is regarded as "non-nature-friendly" in this context, as the destroyer of peoples, cultures, and spiritual traditions; and as a promoter of intolerance and persecution, including witch burning in Europe and North America; and is considered to be serving the purpose of colonialism (see Strmiska 2003:59–72; Svanberg 2003:215). Reductionism, then, developed along with the scientific revolution, and together they represent a separation of creator and creation, of spirit and matter, and of humanity and nature. "Nonholistic" worldviews, according to these communities, have been one of the main causes of our modern-day alienation from nature (see inter alia White 1967).

It is in this context that we can understand how, to shamans, nature symbolizes a state of harmony or order. Scholar of religion Tarjei Rønnow writes, "This is regarded as the normal state—a cosmic 'status quo' that is only interrupted and disturbed by the interference and contamination of modern man" (2000:32, my translation). Shamans emphasize how nature contains values and qualities that have been lost and discarded by modern times, and this is due to the "fall" of humankind. Nature may be described as the state that humanity was in prior to the "fall," a "Garden of Eden" from which we have been banished for violating the rules. Science, technology, money, and pollution are regarded as symbolic tokens of the immorality people brought upon themselves, and which has made them unclean and alienated them from the system where they originally belonged (2000:32–33, see also Rønnow 1998:165–167). Establishing contact with nature thus becomes a crucial mission and experience for all shamans. By being in nature, and by living in a "natural" way, shamans put their ideal of a holistic existence into practice.

Graham Harvey suggests that such practices make paganism a form of animism, in terms of relating to a community of persons where only some are human (2005:42). This type of animism has little to do with the original meaning put in place by Edward Tyler. Rather animism here makes reference to a relational epistemology where personhood includes not only humans or beings with human-like behavior, but also animals, plants, and natural phenomena.

URBAN SHAMANISM

Despite the fact that shamanic practices in the past few decades have been located in a modern urban environment, the city and urban life are nonetheless held as among the biggest challenges for shamans of our day (see inter alia Høst 2001 and Gaup 2005). Shamanism and the urban lifestyle can in principle be regarded as two contrasting categories. Whereas the city represents all things civilized and modern, shamanism, on the other hand, is associated with nature, spirituality, and bygone times. In contemporary Norway, shamanism is nonetheless practiced primarily in urban areas. The city serves as a backdrop to both drumming journeys and healing sessions. However, the city, unlike nature, is described within the community as something that weakens shamanic power and impedes the process of self-development. Thus, the yearning to return to nature was a recurring topic in all my interviews, and one of the main themes of the shamans' stories. The shamans described their relationship with nature's powers in different ways, and they related how they compensate for the lack of air from the sea, tundra, and mountains in the urban environment.

Being practicing shamans in Norwegian urban environments, they all expressed a sense of having lost a part of the context and closeness with nature upon which the *noaidi*s (the Sámi indigenous religious specialists) of earlier times based their practice. Both Sámi and non-Sámi shamans play on this absence of closeness with nature when naming their own practices. Urban shaman, city shaman, and asphalt shaman were some of the nicknames offered when we talked about the topic.

Having an office and a shaman center located in the center of Oslo, the self-declared "city shaman" Eirik Myrhaug emphasizes that nature is no longer a natural part of the day-to-day life of a shaman. Eirik also notes that though nature is not as close as before, he nonetheless tries to maintain contact with nature by performing some of the rituals during his outdoor shaman classes. He has established a power site close to the shaman center, where those who attend his workshops and educational seminars get to feel the soil under their feet.

According to Eirik, the "natural" contact with nature has largely been lost in modern Western society. Being in contact with forces of nature is no longer a central part of daily life, and in contemporary shamanism, experiencing nature is thus something that must be organized and facilitated. The idea is that the shamanic work loses its power if the balance between city and nature is skewed in favor of cities. Annette

Høst, one of the leaders of the Scandinavian Centre for Shamanic Studies, writes,

> If shamanic practice is "urban" in the literal sense; that is, removed from the land, the raw soil and nature; then it will have lost its potency. This is a painful fact for all of those who live in the city and try to practice shamanic art. It is one of the conditions for much of modern shamanic practice, which we need to face and be aware of. We can try to improve matters and make compensations, but we cannot mask it.[7]

The danger of being a shaman in a big city, according to Høst, is that one is at risk of losing contact with the forces of nature, and hence, also some of one's own shamanic power. Thus, maintaining contact with nature is a crucial task and experience for all urban shamans. Shamans practice the ideal of a holistic lifestyle by being with nature. Lisa goes so far as to say that if you are to call yourself a shaman at all, you must have the strength to be one with nature and be able to suffer the elements of nature on your own body:

> LISA: *Really, a proper shaman swims in icy water; indeed, you swim in rivers, you should be able to stay outside, to suffer the weather and the winds. That's something which is easy to forget when you're in the city. Yeah, I've met shamans who don't take long to freeze when they're out in nature; who only want to go home; and so they've gone soft. Sure, you can live in the city, but you have to spend a lot of time being out in nature.*

She stressed a similar point earlier in the interview:

> LISA: *And then you have what I call "shaman light"; those are the ones who are never outdoors in nature, because if you're a real shaman you can sleep outside, you become one with nature. Nature talks to you. You can talk to nature. You find a great deal of answers out in nature, and you can see things in nature, which are very hard to explain.*

So on the one hand you have the "light" variety, and then on the other hand, you have those who are a part of nature.

According to Lisa, shamans get their answers above all from nature through having animals, plants, and rocks talk to them and show them signs. The challenge for an urban shaman is thus to maintain close contact with nature and not be ensnared by the impulses of the city. In this way, Lisa establishes a hierarchy of different shaman types, where those who only rarely visit nature and are hardly able to endure the elements are at a lower tier. A proper shaman should be able to suffer exposure to the cold, wind, and weather; he or she should be able to swim in icy water and sleep outside. Those who are sensitive to the cold and long to go back to the comforts of home, on the other hand, are "shaman light"—domesticated shamans whose powers have weakened due to not being properly tempered by nature.

THE POWER OF THE HIGH NORTH

The shamans I have interviewed place emphasis on how they use nature as a power source, and they describe powerful experiences when performing rituals in nature. The personal stories of how they have used nature are rooted in specific landscapes, in specific places. Their yearning for nature is also a matter of yearning to return home, to "their own place"—to the mountains they walked in when they were children, to the rivers and rocks where they used to play. They long for the wind that blew in their hair, the familiar flavors and fragrances. In the interviews, one clearly observes a ranking of different landscapes, and the north Norwegian landscape holds a particularly prominent status. North Norway is presented as harboring mythical nature, and it represents, above all, a constructed image of an exotic homeland.

Based upon the views of geographer David Harvey, one might say that, in the eyes of the shamans, North Norway appears to be a utopian place—a constructed and ideal landscape—not a specific place, yet at the same time a place of happiness (2000:173; see also Hauan

2003:187). Nature in North Norway is generally viewed as wilder and more powerful. The steep mountains, the tundra, the sea, the proximity to Sámi sacrificial sites, the midnight sun, the dark season, and the Northern Lights are qualities that are highlighted as unique to this area. In their stories, shamans give northern Norwegian nature a direct connection to shamanic practices because of the Sámi people, who have historically lived and still live in this landscape. This is where the *noaidi*, the Sámi indigenous religious specialist, had his home and practice; and, according to the shamans, the landscape bears traces and imprints of the past.

Phenomenologically inspired local community research has emphasized how one's notions, actions, ideas, and interpretations are localized; they are rooted in a specific landscape. Humanity and place are thus mutually related. Human beings make an imprint on the place, and yet the place also makes an imprint on human beings (see Jackson 1996; Bachelard 2000; Casey 2001; Massey 2005). The philosopher Edward S. Casey writes,

> Places require human agents to become "primary places."... Personal identity is no longer a matter of sheer self-consciousness but now involves intrinsically an awareness of one's place—a specifically geographical awareness. Any effort to assess the relationship between self and place should point not just to reciprocal influence (that much any ecologically sensitive account would maintain) but, more radically, to constitutive co-ingredient: each is essential to the being of the other. In effect, there is *no place without self, and no self without place.* (2001:406)

The shamans' narratives highlight this dynamic. Their yearning for and use of nature is, both on a mental and physical level, localized in northern Norway. This yearning is connected to a collective memory of the place, but also with the individual—with his or her personal identity and development. At the same time, we see how the place interferes with and shapes the people who interact with it.

The indigenous Sámi religion was a local religion deeply connected to the local landscapes. The ancestors' spirits were thought to be found in rocks, mountains, and lakes; and as people moved through the land-scape, they also interacted with the spirits (Rydving 2003:10–15). The spirits and gods were, among other things, approached by giving offerings. The offering ritual varied both temporally and spatially, but often offerings were made at certain sacred places, for instance at sacred stones called *sieidi*. As archaeologist Tiina Äikäs notes, *sieidis* are usually rocks or rock formations unshaped by humans and their recognizing demands cultural knowledge, written sources, place name evidence, or archaeological finds (2011). Primarily the offerings consisted of animals and animal body parts, metal objects, alcohol, and tobacco (Manker 1957:40–52; Äikäs 2015).[8]

The tales of ancestors and other spiritual powers are thus rooted in specific places, in a particular landscape; and the tales take on a life of their own when one is familiar with the landscape. Places and stories mutually nourish each other and fill each other with meaning. Anthropologist Kathryn Rountree in the article "Neo-Paganism, Animism, and Kinship with Nature" (2012) argues that even though kinship with nature "is meaningful for most neopagans largely within the domains of religious belief, ritual, and recreational activity; it does not usefully determine the rules of everyday life in the ways it does or traditionally did, for indigenous animist peoples" (2012:313).

The shamans' descriptions of the north Norwegian landscape still form part of their identity. The northern Norwegian landscape reverberates in them, mirroring their origins and their own life-world. To wander in the landscape of their forefathers and to seek out sacrificial rocks, lakes, and mountains gives each of them a feeling of belonging and taking part in the history of the landscape; it further yields a religious identity that is thought to grant power and wisdom to the shaman. To "belong" in a landscape thus generates an emotional and religious ripple effect (see Christensen and Eriksen 1993; Alver 2006). In her preface to *Cultural Landscapes: Place, Narratives and Material Culture* (*Kulturelle landskap. Sted, fortelling og materiell kultur*) (2007b), Selberg points out:

> Some aspects are highlighted, others are downplayed; and a certain type of place is established; such as industrial towns, tourist towns, idylls,

mythical homelands, sacred sites, medieval sites, or alternative sites.... In the dialogue with greater narratives, cultural assessments are created which construct hierarchies of places and landscapes. (2007b:19, my translation)

In 1944, Ailo was born into the landscape, of a young Sámi mother, on the *sieidi* Mount Rávdooaivi (a Sámi sacrificial site). The narrative of being born in this type of landscape has followed Ailo all of his life; and to him it represents a symbol of belonging, identity, and strength:

> TRUDE: *But do you feel that your shamanic powers are stronger, seeing as they're in your blood?*
>
> AILO: *Yes, yes. To me there is something definite about that, absolutely, no doubt. There is something definite about that. I believe I've had many visions about that, and known that there have been shamans in my past, and I've had visions about many of them. And also a lot of mythologies related to the place where I was born, which is an ancient shamanic mountain, and I've had many queer coincidental experiences. I've had visions about how there are ancient graves located here and there, and then I've gone up there to look, and there were indeed ancient graves there; and many things like that which have happened over the years. I used that place as a learning place. I went there every year for many years on* vision quests, *and have been there many times to gather power from the landscape.*
>
> TRUDE: *So the landscape talks to you?*
>
> AILO: *Yes, definitely. And particularly seeing as it's so directly connected with being born.*

Ailo's story provides a clear image of how he as a shaman connects his life to a particular landscape, to a part of nature where he finds spirituality and the magic to be strong and present. Ailo also highlights the landscape in his story by presenting it as a vessel of tradition and knowledge about an indigenous Sámi religion, which he regards as an inspiration for the shamanic practice he is conducting today. In his book *The Shamanic Zone* (2005), he emphasizes this relationship.

> If one is a "native," that is, born into a tribe or a family that is connected with nature, one gains an intimacy with the landscape when growing up. Ever since you're a small child you get to hear tales about extraordinary things that have happened in different places. Later on, you carry this with you as the kind of faith you have as a child, even though you may have left the place where you grew up, as I have done. When you eventually reach the age of reflection, all of this comes back to you. Then the landscape returns as if it was animated, perhaps having the sacred stone at the core. (2005:200, my translation)

This story of his connection with a particular landscape signifies a kinship to a particular land and a particular people and notions that the practice of shamanism is in his blood, so to speak. This insight is expressed in dreams and visions, and Ailo claims this connects him with a shamanic community that goes back generations. To maintain this contact with his ancestors and local traditions, Ailo has, over the course of his life, often returned to Mount Rávdooaivi in order to seek out the answers offered by nature. To Ailo, Rávdooaivi functions as a place for learning: a place to find motivation and strength to go on with his practice as a shaman. The physical landscape of Rávdooaivi is also connected to a mental landscape. As Casey points out, strong, personal experiences in a particular place often lead to having that place become a reminder of events; the place leaves an imprint and activates memory (2000:189, 215).

To Ailo, Mount Rávdooaivi is such a reminder; a place where past memory and certain personal experiences become actualized. Here, the past is revived through memories of childhood and early adolescence. In this way, Rávdooaivi serves to consolidate his identity and create a sense of belonging. These are also memories that Ailo carries with him when interacting with other people and places, and thus they become further developed and strengthened.

The collective memory of the place, which is expressed through narratives, also contributes to promoting local distinctiveness. According to Ailo, the landscapes where indigenous Sámi religion originated bear traces of past events and are therefore the best carriers of shamanic knowledge. Ailo emphasizes that it is through contact with nature in this area that he, being a shaman in modern times, has gained the inspiration to continue some of the indigenous religious Sámi traditions.

In the article "'Ikke det bare vand!' Et kulturanalytisk perspektiv på vandets magiske dimension" (2006) (A cultural-analytical perspective on the magical dimension of water), Alver points out how a landscape is brought to life through tales of "sprites" ("beings of nature") which go back for generations:

> Nature has been given life and form through generations' worth of tales of sprites, through human experiences of and interaction with them. The tales create an arena for faith and action, which again serve to confirm the ideas contained in the tales, and the assessments and morality which are expressed in them. (2006:25, my translation)

The northern Norwegian landscape has traces of ancestral spirits and beings of nature, not only in tales and myths but also in actual marks on the landscape in the form of *sieidi* stones, sacred lakes, and mountains. By being aware of ancestral spirits and beings of nature, and by showing respect for the places they inhabited, it was believed that one could take part in the powers these spirits possessed. This was a type of force that could benefit or harm, and it was thus never completely without risk. If one neglected to uphold the rituals and precautions linked to parts of the landscape, it was tantamount to exposing oneself to danger. The spirits possessed the power not only to heal but also to destroy. They could cause illness, suffering, and death (see Solheim 1952; Alver and Selberg 1992:159–169; Alver 2008:69–83).

The fact that north Norwegian nature is special because of its connection with Sámi cultures is also a point stressed by shaman Esther Utsi. In an interview with the newspaper *VG* on February 15, 2009, she says:

> In Finnmark, we live in close contact with nature. The further you get away from North Norway, the stronger the hunger for something authentic becomes. We who live up here live in the centre of Sámi culture. We don't need to attend all kinds of expensive classes.[9]

In the interview, Esther placed weightage on the notion that being at a distance from North Norway involves a loss of power and authenticity. Knowledges and techniques that others need to pay for out of their pockets are in the mother's milk of northern Norwegians. To modern Sámi shamans, leaving the landscape of the ancestors is like leaving the shamanic source of knowledge. The need to keep returning to the northern Norwegian landscape and the ancient sacrificial sites was also expressed by all of them:

> TRUDE: *But one of the shamans says that although they live in Oslo, they occasionally need to go north in order to fill up their power reserves and spend time in nature. Do you feel the same way?*
> ANITA: *Yes, yes, yes. It's been like that for many years. I go there once per year; and when my parents were still alive, I was there a couple of times per year.*
> TRUDE: *But do you feel that nature up there has a stronger power?*
> ANITA: *Yes, I do. It's so ... It's so powerful to be up there, like you have no idea. You should go there. You ought to go to Finnmark. Tromsø is nothing. You need to go all the way out into the tundra and the sea there; it's amazing. There are such power sites up there that you wouldn't believe it.*

Eirik, too, says the same thing:

> TRUDE: *I have taken a look at your website, and it says that you occasionally arrange courses where you go back to Gratangen and hold*

> *courses there. Is it different to hold courses in North Norway than to*
> *have them here in Oslo?*
> EIRIK: *Yes, in a way it is stronger there. It's because up there we visit the*
> *sacrificial stone, Rikkagallo ... and can connect with the power there.*

Later I ask:

> TRUDE: *But will the forces in the nature up north have a stronger effect?*
> EIRIK: *Yes, actually, they will. They do.*

Anita, Eirik, and Ailo express the notion that in having left the landscape of their ancestors, they have also renounced the religious traditions which were anchored in the local natural surroundings. Returning to the landscape of the ancestors is thus connected with maintaining some form of contact with natural forces. It is about gaining credibility as a shaman. It is about feeling genuine and authentic; and similarly, about being able to use their Sámi identity in a marketing context.

The shamans I have interviewed as practicing city shamans represent a generation of displacement and modernity. The shamans are bearers of local traditions in a global environment. They bridge nature and culture, new generations and old, the spiritual world and the human world, the Sámi and the Norwegian, and the local and the global (see Alver 1999:151). Additionally, they all consider Sámi indigenous religion to be a direct source of inspiration and renewal. Beyer, too, emphasizes that forming a bond with local traditions and culture is one of the trademarks of "nature religions."

> Each of these religions really only gains its concrete specificity in terms
> of a particular local manifestation, a particular local tradition. The dif-
> ference between nations and religions, however, is that the latter are not
> as territorially located as are the former, although they are also that to
> some degree. This structural similarity and partial overlap with ethnic
> territory results in attempts, using Prudence Jones (1996) expression,
> to "see traditions" rooted in particular territories and then give them a

"name" through which they can join, not the family of nations, but the "family of religions." (1998:16)

The shamans highlight that they are part of a tradition, which, although having been adapted to the modern environment, remains rooted in a local landscape that is regarded as unique and authentic. The mountain Rávdooaivi was used by Ailo as a place for learning; as a place where he gathered power for his personal self-development. Similarly, Eirik talks about the sacrificial stone, Rikkagallo/Storsteinen, back home in in the county of Lavangen as a source of power and as a place where he feels that he is in touch with ancestral spirits. Eirik and Ailo place emphasis on stability and life in contrast to change. They present themselves as carriers of ancient Sámi shamanic traditions that are rooted in a local landscape. By frequently returning to the north Norwegian landscape and the ancient sacrificial places in order to replenish their powers, these shamans bring their local knowledge into a global urban environment. In line with what Rountree argues: "Spending time in natural places or visiting ancient sites is one way in which neo-pagans address the dislocation or alienation from nature and ancestral kin they experience as members of contemporary Western societies (2012:315). However, as we shall see, the connection with the local place does not affect how traditions can also be changed and adapted.

SACRED SITES

Historian of religion Louise Bäckman points out how particularly prominent natural formations in indigenous society were often regarded as power sites, described as being inhabited by spirits such as ancestors and other deities (Bäckman 1975). Such natural formations were scattered around the cultivated landscape where people were hunting, fishing, and herding reindeer. These places were special areas in nature where one believed the spirits to be present, and where one had to perform certain rituals in order to reside and travel safely. By performing sacrificial rituals, one could also establish contact with the spirits. Sources reveal that some sacred sites were used by large

groups of people, whereas others were associated with individual families (Rydving 2003:14; see also Mebius 2000:138).

The interaction that shamans and other pagan and New Age groups
have with sacred sites has received a significant amount of attention, rel-
atively speaking. Archaeologist Robert J. Wallis, in his book *Shamans/
Shamans. Ecstasy, Alternative Archaeologies and Contemporary
Pagans* (2003), discusses how shamans make use of the sacred sites of
Stonehenge, Avebury, and Seahenge. Wallis writes:

> Pagans, shamans, druids and others approach these "sacred sites" as
> places which are "alive" today, perhaps where ancestors, goddesses and
> gods, nature spirits, and persons other than humans can be felt, engaged
> with or contacted, and where the "spirit" or "energy" of the land can be
> felt most strongly. (2003:144–145)

The sacred sites referred to by Wallis (2003) are primarily used for
rituals that mark the changing of the seasons. Contemporary paganism
operates with eight such seasonal feasts. In 2015, more than 23,000
people attended the Neolithic site Stonehenge in Wiltshire to watch
the sun rise and to celebrate the summer solstice.[10] The sacred sites
are regarded as being "alive." They are places that, according to participants, hold spiritual meaning even today; and they contain forces
that have been generated throughout history. The fact that practitioners of paganism increasingly visit these sacred sites has been criticized
by nonparticipants as well as by local governments who believe that
their presence is disruptive. A number of pagan practitioners have also
expressed criticism on the "overuse" of sacred sites and propose that
rituals be performed in other places. They feel that the "original sacred
sites" primarily function as a backdrop and atmosphere for the rituals,
but that the actual rituals will be just as powerful if they are performed
in other landscapes (see Wallis 2003:178).

When the shamans I have interviewed visit ancient Sámi sacred sites,
it may be comparable with the use other pagan practitioners making
use of places such as Stonehenge, Avebury, and Seahenge. However, the
way shamans describe their practices at ancient Sámi sacrificial sites

is not limited to feasts celebrating the seasonal changes, in contrast to what Wallis describes as being the case for Stonehenge, Avebury, and Seahenge. Instead, they utilize the ancient Sámi sacrificial sites according to their own needs and desires. They visit them alone or hold classes there.

Like Eirik, when he describes the *sieidi* (Sámi sacrificial site) Rikkagallo (shown in Figure 3.2), he stresses that the ancient Sámi sites have been continuously in use throughout the ages. Although the context and meaning that people have bestowed upon their activities at the sites have varied throughout history, the shamans point out that the continuity of use boosts the energy and

FIGURE 3.2
The Sámi *sieidi* (sacrificial site) Rikkagallo in Lavangen municipality.

power of the site. During religious rituals and festivals, pagans, as Harvey, argues: "regularly renew their relationships and deepen their intimacy with their environment" (2009:8). In the interview, Eirik explained in detail what his relationship with Rikkagallo in Gratangen is like:

EIRIK: *I have a stone in Gratangen which is called Rikkagallo, Storsteinen in Norwegian, and it is a sieidi.*

TRUDE: *Yes, a sieidi stone?*

EIRIK: *Yes, or it's really a sacrificial site. It's a really big rock and very singular.*

TRUDE: *And it has been used through the ages?*

EIRIK: *It has been used through the ages, yes, since long, long ago.*

TRUDE: *So in what way is this place believed to yield power or energy?*

EIRIK: *It does, you know, because there is a tradition which has been in place throughout history. And it is the case that the more it's being used, the more it will leave traces. After all, it's an ancient sacrificial site where they've been sacrificing, and the force is still there. And there are several who have experienced, let's say, supernatural phenomena by that stone.*

TRUDE: *Yes, can you tell me about any of them?*

EIRIK: *Well, they've been hearing voices, and they have felt a special energy there. I mean, I personally haven't experienced anything which could be regarded as supernatural there, but there is an immense power, and I can feel that in the energy.*

TRUDE: *But is the site used in the same way today as in the older days, or has the way the site is being used, changed?*

EIRIK: *Well, the kinds of sacrifices that were done in the past, sacrificing animal blood and such, that's a tradition which is gone now. But then again, we do leave things there. I have used both bones and coins, but then again there aren't a lot of people herding reindeer in our area, so that's not such a natural thing to do, really. But we use stones; if you find some nice rocks and gather them in nature, then you can ask for a wish to be fulfilled via that stone. And there is a huge chasm into which we throw the stones, so that no human being will ever come*

near them. And that's how these places are often used; the things one
sacrifices should remain untouched.

TRUDE: *So is it believed that it's the ancestral spirits who are at play in*
this landscape?

EIRIK: *Yes, that's what it is. That, after all, is the kind of power they*
possess.

TRUDE: *But can these powers be dangerous if one doesn't respect them?*

EIRIK: *They sure can, so one should show respect when visiting such*
a place; and one should consider carefully what one asks for, too. It
must be ethical, and for a good purpose.

Eirik says Rikkagallo is a *sieidi* that has been used as a sacrificial site
throughout history. By continuing the use of this place, Eirik writes
himself into a past and history where the Sámi ancestral spirits play
a central part. Although the use of Rikkagallo has continued into the
modern era, Eirik still finds it to be an ancestral place where one can
connect with earlier users of the site. As in the past, Eirik indicates, the
ancestors grant power to the individual practitioner. At the same time,
they have the ability to influence the future though granting wishes,
laid down by the stone in the shape of coins, bones, or small stones.
The sacred sites are thus something the practitioners themselves must
"make happen." They require action in order to yield power. These
actions also serve to consolidate the practitioners' sense of identity and
belonging to the shamanic community.[11]

When shamans such as Eirik visit and conduct rituals at ancient
sacred sites, it can also be seen in the light of one of the key categories of religious studies: the pilgrimage or religious journey (Gilhus
and Kraft 2007:13). One characteristic of contemporary pilgrimages
is that the road is made as you walk. At the core are individual experiences, religious cultivation, freedom, and a break from day-to-day
tedium but also more commonplace objectives such as enjoying nature
and meeting people (Gilhus and Kraft 2007:15–17, Kraft 2007a:47).
The walk to the *sieidi* takes several hours and Eirik encourages participants to spend some time on mediation while walking. When shamans
and other participants visit ancient sacred sites, they are travelers on a

religious journey through history and across the landscape. They cross the boundary between past and present and between city and countryside. The pilgrimage to the sacred site is also a journey that encompasses both the inner and outer world, and it is meant to contribute to religious insight.

Linking the ancient Sámi power sites to the term "pilgrimage" also shows that the way the sites are being used has changed and evolved. To the shamans, sacred sites are power centers which are visited in order to gain energy; to get in touch with the spirit; for personal development and growth—and after that, one leaves the site. These are places where one should show respect regarding both the journey and the site itself; but it is not necessary to concern oneself with it in one's daily work and life.

Adventure and experience are two of the key terms within the contemporary tourist and pilgrim sector (see inter alia Gilhus and Kraft 2007:13; Selberg 2007a:66). In walking to Rikkagallo, the religious and the magical become tangible; something you feel in your body, something personal and concrete. In a realm of sound, scents, movements, and touch, a presence of magic and mystery is generated, bringing the ancestors back from oblivion and triggering a sense of power. The material place, Rikkagallo, makes the magical tangible, and it shows how magic is located in a certain place—in a certain landscape. The chasm shows the way down into the world of the ancestors, and one personally joins in on the magic by taking part in the ritual. Here, the magical is something the individual participant can experience by touching the stone, making a wish for the future, and tossing a coin or something of personal value to fall deep, deep down into the chasm—where it merges, like an echo of the past, with a thousand other wishes in the shape of coins, stones, and bones. The ritual act re-creates the past, and the past becomes part of the shaping of the present. Figure 3.3 shows Eirik offering at Rikkagallo summer 2014.

In Eirik's stories, Rikkagallo is described as being a liminal place, a place where only a thin veil separates the different worlds. This also enables the traveler to cross the threshold between this world and the world of the ancestors. In the words of historian of religion Phillip

75

FIGURE 3.3
Shaman Eirik Myrhaug at the *sieidi* Rikkagallo.

Jenkins, "These are places were the veils are thin between planes and forces, where the three dimensional and the more dimensional sometimes meet and merge" (2004:201). In this way, sacred sites become part of a mythical landscape.

Adventures and experiences always take place. They are being shaped by the contact between human beings and the landscape. As folklorist Anne Eriksen points out, the role of monuments, such as Rikkagallo and Mount Rávdooaivi, is to contribute to a dialogue between memory and history. At the same time, these monuments have a double function in the context of memory, in reminding us of bygone history as well as reminding participants of the value the place possessed in the past and still possesses. "Through their materiality and accessibility, they also serve as *connection hubs*. This is where history and the individual meet, and something happens: A personal experience; fertile ground for one's own memories" (Eriksen 1999:95, my translation).

In this context, Rikkagallo and other sacred sites can be interpreted as belonging to the category that the French historian Pierre Nora terms *Lieu the Memoire*, or memory sites. Places of memory are defined by Nora as: "any significant entity, whether material or non-material in nature, which by dint of human will or the work of time has become a symbolic element of the memorial heritage of any community" (1996:xvii).[12] These sites have in common the fact that they have been equipped with symbolic intent and given meaning beyond the original context of the place. Rikkagallo and other sacred sites are charged with strong symbols, which not only bring us back in time and present us with narratives of the past, but they also yield an insight into the values we regard as meaningful in the present day (see also Eriksen 1999:87ff).

Stories of sacred sites thus also contain tales, thoughts, ideas, and discourses that go beyond the boundaries of the place itself (Selberg 2007a:69; see also Selberg 2005; Massey 1997). In Eirik's descriptions of how he uses Rikkagallo, we see clear traces of the global New Age worldview that emphasizes how the will must be used for good purposes in order not to spread negative energies. Shamans stress that those who use the sacred sites must control their thoughts and only wish for what is good, because nature can also be used for causing harm. The magical dimension of nature is thus not scrubbed clean of reference to the hazardous and uncontrollable, in contrast to what has been suggested by several researchers (see, for example, Jakobsen 1999).

The marginalisation of all things Sámi has generated a need for new contexts where Sámi aspects of places can be displayed in new ways which go beyond the past marginalisation of and discrimination against Sámi culture. (Mathisen 2002:88–89)

When shamans make use of ancient Sámi sacred sites, it is in many ways representative of such new ways of narrating Sámi culture, as folklorist Stein R. Mathisen notes in the quote. By making Rikkagallo and other sacred sites serve as religious destinations, shamans open up these places for new and varied—but also controversial—interpretations and narratives of what is considered Sámi. When the contemporary shamans use ancient Sámi sacred sites, these places are "updated" and provided with a new existence as authentic, powerful, and magical places. The fact that sacred sites in North Norway have largely been left unheeded by tourists, and are not found beside busy, well-known tourist trails, amplifies the authentic and magical aspects of the site. These are not places for the masses; they are for the select few.

The sacred sites are not only a basis for physical journeys and rituals; the mental image of the site is also used in drum journeys. In *The Shamanic Zone* (2005), Ailo describes his first drum journey, in which a sacred site played a prominent part:

> When I lay down on the grey carpet, Ernesto began drumming. My free soul flew on the wings of sound into an opening under an offering stone on Finnmarksvidda. The journey went on through the inner spiral, or the previously mentioned tunnel through time…. The next trip went to the Upper World. It started at Røyehodet (Rávdooaivi), the famous mountain on Finnmarksvidda. I was elevated through sound and into light, traveling on the inside of a sunbeam through the air and up to the sun … A teacher awaited me there. He presented himself as a Sámi noaidi that belonged to my ancestors. He sat by a fire and filled me with mythology. (2005:95)

The sacred sites are regarded as being gateways to the world of the ancestors; and as such, they function as catalysts in the practice of drum journeys. They are gates to the underworld and to the over world where the spirits are present. Conjuring a mental image of the sacred site may, as pointed out by Ailo, serve as a starting point for venturing into the spirit world on a drum journey.

New Sacred Sites

The shamans I interviewed have also constructed new sacrificial sites and power sites in the elements of nature they are able to access in their daily lives. These new constructs compensate in many ways for their lack of access to ancient sacrificial sites. They also open up the possibility of having more people participate in the powers believed to be present in such places. In the biography *Eirik Myrhaug: Shaman for Life* (*Eirik Myrhaug: sjaman for livet*) (Brynn and Brunvoll 2011), we find the following passage:

> The idea behind a power site is partly that it is a place where we may easily connect with Mother Earth and the spiritual powers. Additionally, new power sites can also channel the power harboured in the ancient Sámi sacrificial sites when rituals at the new sites are carried out in the present.... A new power site compensates for the lack of access to the ancient sacrificial sites, and can also serve as a place to visit in order to "sacrifice" aspects of oneself one no longer wishes to bear in life—such as a bad habit, or other things. (2011:208–211, my translation)

In the interview, Eirik elaborates on how he established the new sacred sites he founded in connection with workshops he held in both southern and northern Norway, which he set up with a specific purpose in mind.

> EIRIK: *And I've laid out many sites; the kind of power sites we've visited, that are modern places to which one may go.*
>
> TRUDE: *But what does that mean; you've laid them out?*
>
> EIRIK: *We've created new power sites; brand-new sites where we generate energy. We use shamanic rituals and summon the various power animals from the four corners of the world, and this generates power. We pray for the forces to be present; we've chosen the places; they're there. And then energy is accumulated. That was how the old cult sites were constructed, the old sieidis, because people found power there. And then they prayed and sacrificed there. That's the historical foundation.*

When Eirik re-creates the landscape to turn it into a sacred landscape, something also happens to the people participating in this landscape: In making a landscape sacred, the landscape becomes something more than just stones, trees, grass, and mountains. It provides access to something beyond nature itself; a sacred landscape places the participants in a special mood connected with the outer, aesthetic surface as well as the inner mental processes. Eirik emphasizes how these places, like the ancient Sámi sacred sites, stand out because of special formations in the landscape. The sites are located at an elevation in the landscape, or they stand out because of a special tree or a special stone. The mood is created through rituals for establishing the sites and summoning the spirits.

> TRUDE: *The last time we talked you said something about how you, now that you live in Oslo, create new sacred sites.*
> EIRIK: *Yes I do; and then I use elements from shamanism; the medicine wheel, and summoning the powers from the south and west, and the north and east, and Mother Earth and the universe. I perform that ritual and summons, and I am sensitive when I choose such a site.*
> TRUDE: *What do you look for then?*
> EIRIK: *I take heed of the energy and how the site is located in the landscape. It must be a quiet place where not a lot of people pass by, and there should be a small hill or rock there, or a tree. Then you have to feel for the energy when you walk, feel if the place has the right vibrations. And you ask nature for permission to use it. Then you lay down an intention in the power sites. I have laid out such sites. In one such place I have laid down good intentions for the capital of Norway; that a sense of consciousness should be roused.*

Due to the particular layout of the landscape and by performing a ritual of summoning powers from the north, east, south, and west, an atmosphere is generated which distinguishes the chosen spot from other places (see Klein 1995:10–11). The site is thus not inherently sacred; it is given sacredness and power as a result of the ritual (see Smith 1998). Ailo, too, creates new sacred sites during his outdoor workshops. He points out that the act of making a place sacred is a matter of recalibrating one's own mind and the minds of other participants:

> AILO: *And you know what, I actually go around creating sacred sites here and there.... In all the sessions we have in nature, we make sacred mountains and sacred trees, or we recalibrate our minds, and that's probably what it's all about, the fact that it's just as possible to get in touch with the sacred here as in any other place; maybe even more so.*

To Ailo, what is sacred is not limited to special places in the landscape; it can be shaped and created wherever he or those participating in his classes wish. The purpose of such new constructions, according to Eirik, is to channel some of the powers he believes are present in the old Sámi sacrificial sites. The rituals performed at the new sacred sites are carried out in the present time, and they have been adapted to a contemporary shamanic universe. But to Ailo and Eirik, they also represent continuity with the past and with local traditions (compare with Gilhus and Mikaelsson 2001:140).

The construction of new sacred sites is also about facilitating nature and making it accessible to urban shamans. By arranging workshops, Ailo and Eirik aim to train participants to be outdoors and gradually become familiar with the landscape and the forces of nature. To them, the point is not that the place must be generally recognized as a sacred site, but rather that the site gives power and energy to the group, which is necessary for them to carry out their rituals and ceremonies. However, what, then, distinguishes the old from the new? Are the old and the new sites sacred in the same way? Elaborating on how these two relate, Eirik replies:

> TRUDE: *However, these sites—will they, then, become as powerful as the ancient Sámi sacred sites?*
> EIRIK: *Yes. After a while, I would say that yes, they will. They are after all being used by groups of people, and they may accumulate such*

power in the long term. They are connected to the modern society,
so, in the long run, the more people that use them, the power may
become quite strong.
TRUDE: *So it depends on use?*
EIRIK: *Yes, it does.*
TRUDE: *If so, do the Sámi sacred sites hold a different power since they*
have been used for generations?
EIRIK: *Yes, they do. They have been used for millennia.*

Eirik uses the ancient and the newly constructed sacred sites for the
same purpose, to gain power and knowledge. However, as the ancient
sites have been used for a much longer period of time, they have—
according to Eirik—accumulated more energy and power. Eirik also
points out that the energy in the new sacred sites is not connected with
the ancestral spirits. Instead, a new, more universal energy is being generated by using the site.

The insights that Eirik and Ailo convey to their students at the
newly constructed sacred sites do not primarily concern ancestral
spirits, but rather are based upon more universal and open categories such as spirituality, power, and energy. To construct new sacred
sites is thus about sorting out the elements of the past, which one
believes can be used in modern times, by a modern audience and for
a modern religious market. In accordance with New Age currents,
these elements and this information should be easily accessible. In
this way, we see that religious expressions change in contact with
new landscapes. At the same time, the connection with the ancient
Sámi sacrificial sites contributes to bestow an aura of authenticity
upon Eirik and Ailo. It generates credibility and gives them access
to the New Age market. Seen from the outside, the emphasis the
shamans place on their close ties with northern Norwegian nature
and sacred places can also be interpreted as a way of marketing their
products and services.

However, the newly constructed sacred sites nonetheless do not
replace the old ones. Although they have created new sites, Eirik and

Ailo keep returning north; and there they also arrange classes for aspiring shamans. They continually stress that the power manifested there is stronger than anything they have felt elsewhere.

VISION QUESTS

Vision quests, also known as "vision seeking" and "vision wakes," are described by the shamans themselves as being one of the most demanding of shamanic ceremonies (see Sørenssen 1988:84). In Norway, where Sámi and Old Norse traditions have been held up as inspirational sources for shamanic practices, it has been pointed out that "vision wakes" are mentioned in the Norwegian *seid* tradition (see inter alia Solli 2002:137).[13] One stanza from the epic *Voluspå* says, "Ein sat hón uti," depicting the *volve* who predicted the future during a vision wake. Vision wakes were strongly condemned in Christian medieval laws. In *Frostatingslova* part V, one may read the following:

> *Those who lose their lives due to theft or burglary, whether they be*
> *robbers at sea or land, and similarly those who lose their lives due*
> *to murder and wizardry, fortune telling and nightly vision waking*
> *in order to conjure trolls and hence promote pagan sin , , , and the*
> *same goes for sorcerers ... all such men are unrepentant criminals*
> *who have wasted their possessions and the protection of the law. (my*
> *translation)*[14]

Even in Magnus Håkonson's more recent Gulatingskristenrett of 1267, the prohibition against vision waking in order to seek counsel or conjure the *draug* or *haugbu* was emphasized. Such "pagan acts" were regarded as being in the same vein as major crimes that could not simply be remedied by paying a fine.

Eirik emphasizes how vision waking is an act that modern shamans perform in order to come closer to nature and nature's forces. The shamans of the past, however, lived in and with nature every day, and so

they did not need to set up such a ritual framework for their own practice, according to Eirik.

> TRUDE: *And vision quest, that's an ancient ritual which was also used
> in the Sámi tradition?*
>
> EIRIK: *I'm not so sure they really did that, because one was living in
> nature as it was; one was there. Today we need to create this artifi-
> cially; well, not artificially, but we have to go sit in nature. We must
> arrange it in the form of workshops. I guess that goes for the work-
> shops, too; in the past, people living in a rural town would gather in
> the evening on their own accord. The shaman would be there, and
> they would be present if anyone wanted to be healed. But today we
> need to arrange these things. Today we call them workshops; but in
> the old days they had a meeting place where they convened.*

Vision quest is a ritual that gives the practitioner experiences of nature
and the forces that are at play, and thus grants the practitioner a certain
status within the community. The idea is that nature, through the ritual,
can function as a mirror, which enables reflection and yields answers
to the individual participant. According to the shamans, a vision quest
allows one contact with the spiritual world, in the same way that rituals performed at the sacred sites do. In this setting, to "sit out" in
nature with all that it entails functions as a means for transgressing
the boundaries between our world and the spiritual world. Several of
the shamans arrange classes where vision quests and vision seeking
constitute the central part. The length of the ritual varies from class to
class, but what they all have in common is that participants spend one
or more nights alone with nature. On her web page, Anna presents the
vision wake as being a meditative journey, which opens one up for self-
development through being in close contact with nature:

Vision quest—to sit outside for wisdom
A meditative journey
August 20–22, 2010
A night spent alone in meditation

Practices where one gains a sense of presence, focus and relaxation

Nature creates a sense of calm

Nature can be a mirror

A course for cultivating the self in close contact with nature

Vision quests are ancient rituals—"to sit outside for wisdom." In the middle of big and small processes of change in one's life, it might be useful to withdraw from "the ordinary life" to a place which brings us closer to OURSELVES. To many of us, nature is such a place. During the vision quest we spend a weekend in the mountains; nature—and to some extent, a *lavvu*—is our classroom. One night is spent in solitude—awake—in meditation. The rest of the time is spent in preparation and debriefing.[15]

By attending the workshop Anna believes the closeness with nature will help participants get started on their own inner self-development. Ailo expresses a similar sentiment. In August 3–11, 2007, he went on one more journey to the Rávdooaivi Mountain with a group of followers for a vision quest. He wrote on his website:

For those who have not been out in the tundra before, this might be a chance to experience first-hand an area where few travel, except reindeer, reindeer herders, and the occasional shaman.... The vision wake involves going into nature as a meek hero or a spiritual adventurer to hunt down a vision.... Indeed, one is to be alone in Røyehodet, 2–3 days alone with the tundra, with winds and weather, with the dusk of the night; for the night is not entirely dark so early in the fall in the north; alone with your thoughts, in the quietude with your mind, your dreams. One's personal background, and the question one asks, may yield the vision one is after. As we know, outer nature can serve as a mirror for meditating on the inner landscape.[16]

When shamans step out of the city in order to "sit down" in nature, it can be arranged in the form of classes where several people go out together to be in nature, but part of it is nonetheless that the participants are to be alone with nature over a shorter or longer period of time.

As Ailo stresses, it is only when you meet nature and nature's powers face to face that visions take shape. In the article "Myths, Shamanism and Epistemologies from an Indigenous Vantage Point" (2004), social scientist Elina Helander makes this point:

> Many shamanic insights come into being in solitude. For instance, Sioux Indians search for a vision in a private ceremony in the solitude of the bushes. Sámi Shamans also search for quiet places. Mikkel Gaup, a Sámi shaman and healer, told me in an interview in 1993 that he regularly walks alone in the wilds. An Ingulik shaman, Angakkuq, receives his ability to see while in solitude. An indigenous scientist, Pamela Colorado, claims that Native Spirituality and knowledge is connected to quiet places. This allows the unknown to be present. (2004:556, my translation)

Helander establishes the notion of a common discourse on silence and nature in indigenous people's religious practices worldwide. According to Helander, it is only when one is in solitude with nature that the individual enters the gateway to the transcendental. The shamans I have interviewed have adopted this discourse. Shamans stress that gaining power and knowledge as a shaman requires that one has the strength to face the trials which nature and its powers subject one to. This is something the individual has to deal with on his or her own, and may involve both fear and solitude (see Alver 1999:150). To be alone in nature represents a contrast to the urban lives of the shamans, and going through with the vision quest, with the quiet of nature as part of the ritual, is often described as being a necessary break from city life. Anna describes in detail what it is like to do a vision quest. In the following, she recounts one of many of Ailo's workshops in which she has participated:

> ANNA: *So I've taken part in Ailo Gaup's workshops; I started with going on a vision wake with Ailo, went out in the wilds for like seven, eight, nine days, living in a lavvu and being in a group who at first work with various shamanic techniques, talking and cooking together, and going for walks and such things. And then you have three days where you*

sit outside in solitude. You often bring along a special theme to focus on, and you're asked to remain awake at night and sit outside. ... there we may experience many of those shamanic things that we work with, with regards to nature. Feeling that nature has something more and something deeper to tell you than what you see at the first glance, and then you need time, alone, outside.

When modern shamans highlight vision quests as being a core part of their practice, it is because they believe nature and nature's forces can literally help one find answers to difficult questions, and make one move onward, little by little, in his or her own self-development process. It is a matter of having the time to sit and reflect, and to personally feel the elements and human instincts. During the vision wake, one is to stay awake and continue fasting, which can make the séance physically challenging:

TRUDE: *How does it feel?*

ANNA: *To me, it's a great way to work, and an experience which I have used a great deal later on. But it can also be bloody cold; it can be boring (laughter).... I feel it to be very clarifying on my part to have such a lot of time. And simply experiencing that process in which there's a great deal of inner protest; it's uncomfortable, you want to lie down and sleep; and that's part of the package, after all, and it helps you to highlight things. Then there's the fact that the world becomes quite magical when you sit outside on your own at night; that's exciting.*

Being cold, fasting, and being bored are part of the whole, and they contribute to providing the vision quest with an air of something other than everyday routines. Vision quests break away from postmodern lifestyle, which is filled with entertainment, information, and stimuli though TV, Internet, newspapers, radio, and cell phones. Here, on the other hand, the objective is to learn to shut out this type of stimuli and to make being bored become a useful and constructive ability. By distancing oneself from busy day-to-day life and bodily needs, nature and its powers are said to come into view for the individual. When leaving life in the big city behind and going out into nature, in order to go through with a vision wake, the body is faced with new physical and mental challenges wherein one's personal situation is also challenged. Going through with a vision wake can thus be said to contribute to having the individual participant strengthen his or her position within the community. Overcoming the physical and psychological challenges embedded in the act of vision waking yields enhanced status and separates the amateurs from the more advanced.

Several researchers have been aware of how one's body and mind are changed in the face of difficulties and challenges. The sociologist John Urry emphasizes how the body "comes to life" when exposed to places which are geographically remote or which are different from the places where people spend their daily lives:

> Putting one's body through its paces demands that people physically travel from time to time to that place of difficulty and subject the body to a direct encounter of "facing-the-place" (as opposed to face-to-face). Those places where the body comes to life will typically be geographically distant—indeed "other"—to sites of work and domestic routine. These are places of "adventure," islands of life involving bodily arousal, from bodies that are in motion, natural and rejuvenated as people corporeally experience environments of adventure. (2002:4)[17]

To stand face to face with an unfamiliar and different place, according to Urry, facilitates personal change and development. In the interviews, it becomes very clear that the shape of the landscape affects the result of the vision wakes. The more dramatic and unspoiled the natural environment, the stronger the experiences and visions of participants. The Finnmark plateau and the northern Norwegian landscape clearly stand out in this regard. The nature of these places is described as being wild and magnificent. At the same time, they carry visible traces of the past. In addition to the northern Norwegian landscape, shamans also highlight national parks as being very suitable areas for vision quests. Ailo, among others, arranged workshops in national parks around the country throughout the year. Anna, too, has located several of her vision quest workshops in national parks, and like Ailo, she points to the Dividalen national park in the county of Troms as being a place where the primeval landscape yields powerful experiences:

ANNA: *Dividalen is one of the most magnificent places I know. In that landscape you have dry pine forests, you have a stream which alternates between being dramatic, wild, and canyon-like, and then open and slow-running. You have the lush birch tree forests with plenty of herbs, and then you have the mountain nearby; there are several clefts, many different things. So that is why I find it nice. There is also the fact that you can get away from the city relatively easily. There's the old-growth forest, I mean, Dividalen is a national park. The pine forest is an old-growth forest, with old trees. You have trees which fall down and are left to rot, and you have a great fauna, several big carnivores. It's exciting that bears may be lurking in the bushes (laughter). That's quite rare, though; but there are bears there, and there are lynxes, lots of them, and wolves have been visiting, and then you have snow foxes. So you can really get far away from all the cultivated stuff, if that's what you want to do.*

Dividalen, which gained the status of a national park in 1971, influenced our perception of nature in the area. From being northern Norwegian nature, Dividalen has become a primeval landscape, where modern culture does not exist. In this context, Dividalen appears as an "ancient landscape." Harboring ancient Sámi cultural sites in the shape of indigenous Sámi sacrificial sites, meat storages and *goahtis* (Sami huts), and the four big carnivores—bears, wolves, lynx, and wolverines—shamans interpret the national park as being an authentic and powerful landscape. The power in the landscape is expressed through its connection with ancient times, to the authentic and uncultivated, but it is also connected with being far from the city and the city's influences.

Through their practices the shamans construct their own folkloric narratives about sacred sites and the landscape. These narratives are shared both orally and in writing through blogs and on homepages on the Internet, and thus become part on an emergent folklore about new and old sacred sites in Norway.

Nature—A Place for Learning

According to the shamans I have interviewed, moving from the rural areas to the city can affect the depth of religious practice—from being deep to superficial. In their eyes, there is an increasing demand for even spiritual development to be achieved at a certain pace and with a certain intensity. However, this call for a faster pace in the processes is, according to shamans, not in line with how shamanic work should be practiced and can, in some cases, even be dangerous. Lisa says:

> LISA: *And maybe that's what's happening with that city shamanism; that it's kind of.... It's supposed to happen so quickly (laughter).*
> TRUDE: *We sure are pressed for time in today's society (laughter).*
> LISA: *But things take time, you know. And then, a lot of people get unsettled. They have problems, they have.... Well, I have seen many who have attended classes in order to learn shamanism. I have gone ... maybe one meter in; I mean, I've been participating a little bit in such workshops. And then I broke off; I went in my own direction. But I have seen people get psychotic. They face so many things within themselves. They could wind up in institutions. They're taking medicines. Some use drugs in order to enhance and hasten the process. So there's a lot of weird stuff going on in that community and that culture; a great many weird things. I accept that that's how it is, but I am against it. They are in such a hurry to move on; to them, it becomes like a game for entertainment purposes; but shamanism is about, say, getting to know oneself better, getting to know nature and the primeval forces; the primeval man or woman within yourself; this requires you to have both feet on the ground, and it requires you to have the right pace relative to the surroundings and to society. We do live in a ... I mean, we must be able to use this in our daily lives. There doesn't*

need to be so much secrecy about it. We should be able to use it in
our daily lives.

Later she says:

> *Well, it could be that there's too little respect for the past. Because when*
> *you enter it, you also enter history. You don't get to just go with the*
> *happy days, you have to take it all. And I don't think they have, like,*
> *hatred or vengeance in their minds when they go there, but maybe it's*
> *partly that one should also bring along the things that didn't work out*
> *in order to take some of the responsibility; to learn to enter the pain.*
> *And I think very few people do that. It's kind of like, this is going to*
> *be fun. It's regarded as a party game.*

During our conversation, Lisa presents a critical view of contemporary shamanic practitioners, which is quite common. One of the most radical critics of the shamanic movement, the social anthropologist Ward Churchill, in his article "Spiritual Hucksterism: The Rise of the Plastic Medicine Men" (2003), precisely depicts shamans as being alienated from their own lives and constantly hungering for new and ready-made spiritual experiences:

> White people in this country are so alienated from their own lives and
> so hungry for some sort of real life that they'll grasp at any straw to save
> themselves. But high tech society has given them a taste for the "quick
> fix." They want their spirituality pre-packaged in such a way as to pro-
> vide *instant* insight, the more sensational and preposterous the better.
> (2003:325)

Churchill claims that shamans are part of an increasing demand for information and knowledge, and a weekend course in shamanism can be seen as a ready-made beginner's kit for people trapped in the hustle and bustle of their daily lives. Churchill points out that shamanism seems to be shallow in the way it follows the currents of central cultural tendencies in the present; satisfying our hunger for information and knowledge by being easy and accessible. This critique is, to a large part, consistent with the image of shamans and other alternative movements featured in the media.

It is this "shallow variety" that shamans want to distance themselves from and take a stand against when they express how they have not attended all that many classes. To repeat what Lisa said earlier: "I have gone ... maybe one meter in; I mean, I've been participating a little bit in such workshops. And then I broke off; I went in my own direction." Shamans emphasize how shamanic practice is not something you can easily absorb during a weekend seminar or buy for money on the New Age market. To distance themselves from "white shamanism" (Rose 1984), "wannabe shamans" (Green 1988), and "plastic medicine men" (Churchill 1992/2003), shamans emphasize spending an extended period of time in nature. Although they have all been apprenticed through reading books and attending courses, nature itself is, in their opinion, the greatest teacher of the subject of shamanism. However, spending time in nature and getting in touch with nature's powers take time and can also be tedious and frustrating. It is not done in a jiffy over the course of a weekend seminar. It is a lifestyle, and it is a matter of using shamanic techniques and modes of thought in daily life. Northern Norwegian nature in this context is highlighted as a place for learning, a space where the power of nature and the traces left by the ancestral spirits and sprites in the shape of *sieidi* stones, sacred lakes, and mountains yield experience and strength to inexperienced, budding shamans.

LOCAL NATURE IN A GLOBAL CONTEXT

Being one of the overarching themes of shamanism, contact with nature is about building credibility as a shaman. It is a matter of authenticity, about being genuine. The shamans express this theme in narratives about their contact with northern Norwegian nature and the landscape of Sámi ancestors. Locating tales about nature in North Norway can be interpreted as a strategy for responding to the global shamanic community. This is an act of self-positioning that goes beyond the borders of locality and that serves to demonstrate how shamans try to stand out in a global shamanic context. When contemporary shamans in Norway highlight the northern Norwegian landscape as being more powerful and magical than any other landscape, it is an act of positioning, which demonstrates individuality, power, and strength. It is in *this* nature, and in *these* places, that the source of energy is the strongest; it is *here* that vision quests, rituals, and ceremonies yield the clearest visions and the strongest forces. By defining and constructing North Norway as a wild and magical landscape, the shamans draw lines between what they consider genuine and not; between the authentic and the commercial; between the unique and the universal.

By focusing on northern Norwegian nature and local Sámi shamanic traditions, the shamans I have interviewed present an alternative to, and in some cases a contrast with, the global New Age movement; a movement that, for the most part, has been criticized as commercialized and disingenuous. When shamans emphasize their connection with the northern Norwegian landscape and with Sámi culture and traditions, they weave themselves into a local tradition and shape the narratives of the local place in order to give it and themselves the glow of authenticity. The geographer Doreen Massey writes:

> Globalisation is not a single all-embracing movement (nor should it be imagined as some outward spread from the West and other centres of economic power across a passive surface of "space"). It is a making of space(s), an active reconfiguration and meeting-up through practices and relations of a multitude of trajectories, and it is there that lies the politics. (2005:83)

Today, the construction of local and particular identities is used to distinguish persons, products, and services as being particularly valuable and authentic. This is an act of positioning that allows, simultaneously, adaptation to a global world, while reacting to and opposing it (Robertson 1992; Featherstone 1995; Beyer 1998). Globalization obliges local communities to relate to the outside world and to form networks beyond the nation state. In this way, new narratives about the local community's culture and history are formed. These are often narratives that challenge the traditional perception of what is at the "center" and what is peripheral. Places that have been peripheral in a national context—which was indeed the case for North Norway— can be made central in a global context. It is precisely this recasting of the north Norwegian landscape that we see in the stories told by the shamans in this chapter. By applying characteristics to this part of the country that describe it as being magical, mystical, powerful, and authentic, shamans shake up previous conceptions of North Norway as representing the peripheral, a place marginalized in both an eco- nomic and an ethnic/cultural sense.

The emphasis on unique local spiritual values is at the same time a part of the natural process of any New Age community. That which is general, global, and universal is thus provided a local connection, which among other things rests on depicting the power of the north- ern Norwegian landscape to give meaning to the individual practitio- ner. It is also this link between local and global values that makes the shamanic movement interesting beyond simply being a countercultural current.

At the same time as the world grows ever more interconnected and deeply integrated through social, economic, and cultural changes, the focus on differences has also increased. When shamans highlight the local area, North Norway, as being powerful and authentic, it can be read as a dialectic of opposition. However, this dialectic is also played out in many other parts of the world. As sociologist Roland Robertson states, the focus on the local and particular is one of the consequences of globalization, and represents what he calls a "uni- versalisation of particularism" (Robertson 1995:25–44). Individuals and groups are to be free to evolve and to develop differently from each other. In using the term *glocalisation*, Robertson highlights the fact that cultures change, which must be studied among real-life peo- ple in the real world. I have demonstrated how such cultural changes are expressed in the shamans' pivot between the past and the present, between the central and the peripheral, and between big city life and the "natural life." The cultural changes take form in the gap between the local and the global, highlighting which parts of the past and of

94

the local traditions the shamans preserve and which parts are picked from global currents. In all, this mix of the past and the present, between the local and the global, creates a sphere for new cultural expressions. The uses of ancient sacred sites, and the construction of new sacred sites and rituals, are examples of such new expressions and innovations—of how humanity creates places, and thereby also memories and history.

CHAPTER FOUR

GENDER IN SÁMI SHAMANISM

THE PAST AS A PREMISE FOR NEW GENDER CONSTRUCTIONS

*We all have the primeval power within us. Regain this power
and continue your journey.*

As a key religious symbol in the Sámi shamanic environment, the indigenous goddess Sáráhkká has begun to dance. After several hundred years of sleep, she turned up in a red dress at the indigenous festival Riddu Riđđu in the summer of 2007. Under the auspices of the performance, *Mátki* (the journey), her message to the festival audience was to recall their own primeval forces and turn these into a vehicle on their continuing journey of life.

This chapter is an exploration of practices and expressions that are directly concerned with the embodiment of gender in Sámi shamanism in Norway in the present. I ask which positions men and women are enrolled in, and which role the past plays in shaman gender constructions. Shamans seem to fill women's absence in the historical sources with interpretation and explanations, and to present their role in history as natural and central. In this process, the Sámi indigenous goddesses Mátáhrákka, Sáráhkká, Ukksáhkká, and Juksáhkká have been given a special place in contemporary Sámi shamanistic practices (see Figure 4.1). With their link to indigenous people—to women and nature—they are highlighted as guarantors of authenticity.

FIGURE 4.1
Sáráhkká is dancing (photo by Ragnhild Enoksen).

The constructions of gender by the shamans I have interviewed, both Sámi as well as non-Sámi, are closely linked to their constructions of the past. They actualize the past as an anchor and as a basis for identity construction for women and men in the present. To commit to premodernity is a late modern action, emphasizes modernity theorist Thomas Ziehe (1986). With this initiative, he underlines that to relate to the past and to history is an integral part of the culture of our late modern society. The longing for the past also has a special position within a New Age universe. Here the past is often attributed to a sacred dimension through a longing toward a spiritual golden age characterized by intuitive knowledge from a number of different mystical and esoteric traditions (Bowman 1995a; Selberg 1998, 2001). My goal in this book is not to expose whether shamans' stories about the past are credible or not. I am concerned with what they use their narratives for, and what this tells us about the shamans themselves, about the present day and the present situation. I ask what values are being assigned to men and women in a shamanic environment and look at shamans' quest for a new social order where it is hoped that gender hierarchy be replaced by gender in interaction and balance. Even though gender issues concern both men and women, gender studies are still mainly focused on women. As Ursula King states in *Religion and Gender* (1995),

> because women have been voiceless for so long. Throughout most of human history, there has existed an asymmetry in the relations of power, representation, knowledge and scholarship between women's invisibility, marginalization and subordination in history and society. (1995:1)

Religion is central to how gender stereotypes are produced and realized. Gender is also an important factor for understanding people in a shamanic environment—for access to male and female shamanic practitioners' prospects and limits. An eye for gender helps identify interpersonal relationships in the environment and reveal the processes that produce inequality and the complex interplay of power and classification prevailing in every society. By exploring how shamans use the past to construct narratives of gender in the present, my presentation represents an attempt to localize religion and culture in the social and gendered reality. In these processes, certain bodily differences are made available while others are downplayed (see also Trulsson 2010:230).

Gender Discourses

In shamanic practices, worldwide indigenous cultures are presented as constituting a special spiritual relationship with inherent closeness to nature, forming a counterpart to values and attitudes prevailing in Western societies (see Rønnow 2000, 2003; Christensen and Kraft 2010). Indigenous cultures are highlighted as sources of inspiration for religious rituals and practices as well as for a healthier relationship with the earth.

Such types of perceptions of indigenous peoples and their cultures can also be seen as a central basis for the gender discourses highlighted in the Sámi shamanic environment, which may be generally described as an orientation from a patriarchal social order to a society where men and women no longer are polarized but live in harmony with nature and each other. This ideal corresponds to what feminist and social scientist Riane Eisler in *The Chalice and the Blade: Our History, Our Future* (1988) describes as a partnership model. The partnership model refers to a society where social relations are built on solidarity rather than rank and represent a contrast to cultures dominated by ruling structures (1988:46–50).

In the shamans' narratives, indigenous cultures, and traditions symbolize this partnership ideal—a condition in which men and women complement each other and in which neither is below the other. The Western world with its Judeo-Christian traditions, however, is described as the contrast—a patriarchal symbolism, a man's warped theology and life-remote rituals that have robbed women of their religious freedom and authority (see Salomonsen 1999:81). In his shamanic manifesto *Att bita af ödets trådar* (Biting the Threads of Fate), which is a collection of 122 declarations of a shamanistic philosophy, shaman Jörgen I. Eriksson highlights this ideal social order:

> 88: Indigenous Peoples' thinking regulates man's relationship to the world in a non-dominant manner. It's about the relationship between man and man, between man and animal, between man and the earth/landscape and between man and the spiritual world. (Eriksson 2005: 16, my translation)

According to Eriksson, indigenous cultures represent a holistic thinking and demonstrate an underlying coherence in the world with a balance between God and nature, between humankind and nature, between mind and body, and between men and women. It is also the idea about this partnership model and holistic perspective, which is said to be found in indigenous cultures, that is at the core of the shamanic movement's criticism of what is perceived as a traditional gender hierarchy in Western society.

Like pagan goddess worshipers, shamans distance themselves from the traditions that they believe reduce women's and men's drive for inner growth and development. In *Når gud blir kvinne. Blant hekser, villmenn og sjamaner I USA* (1991) (When God Is Female: Among Witches, Wild Men and Shamans in the United States), the Norwegian theologian Jone Salomonsen points out that the most important driving force in these types of religious milieus is women's and men's rebellion against the patriarchal heritage (Salomonsen 1991:14). This rebellion is directed against the Judeo-Christian traditions which the pagan communities claim have created an artificial distinction between the Creator and creation, spirit and matter, and between man and nature, and which has robbed men and women of their primal forces. The discourses of these movements about male and female power are part of a system critique emphasizing that man's oppression of nature and men's oppression of women have made both sexes alienated from their natural qualities and powers (see Kraft 2000:80).

PRIMEVAL WOMEN AND PRIMEVAL MEN

In shamanic environments, nature is symbolically linked to the female and to the woman as an intermediary between nature and civilization. In Euro-America such an equation between women and land and nature, has a long and familiar trajectory. In the now classical and also controversial essay "Is Female to Male as Nature Is to Culture?" Sherry B. Ortner aims to explain the universal devaluation of women. According to Ortner, women are universally assigned an intermediate position of both nature and culture:

> Women are seen "merely" as being closer to nature than men. That is, culture (still equated relatively unambiguously with men) recognises that women are active participants in its special processes, but at the same time sees them as being more rooted in, or having more direct affinity with, nature. (1974:7)

For Ortner and others in her wake, the idea of linking women with nature was detrimental to feminist goals. The shamans I have interviewed elevate women precisely by reinvoking this stereotype. They substantiate this image but highlight women's proximity to "nature," not as something inferior or less "cultured" but as a positive resource. Shamans convey a view of men and women as inherently different. Reclaiming and exploring are key issues in the interviews with both male and female shamans. A central point in our conversations was that it is not only a matter of thinking differently but actually starting to relate and experience bodies and practices in another way (see also Trulsson 2010). As scholar of religion Inga B. Tøllefsen argues, "It seems that the main role religious movements have concerning *gender* is to brand and manage gendered and sexual relations as a *religious* affair" (2016:296). The ascribed differences between the sexes also vouch for different religious experiences and ideas about men and women having different religious needs (see Sky 2007:69). On my request shaman Eirik Myrhaug tells me about his group of customers:

EIRIK: *Women are more about for these kinds of things. They are natu-rally open while men, I must say it so strongly—men actually have blunted emotions. There are very few men who have come so far that they seek opening and are able to recognize and sense spiritual energies—relatively few men. Women give birth to children, and are closer to life in that way, and have this contact which is also a contact with nature. And it is those values that the society must return to and, and that men to a greater extent must be open to.*

TRUDE: *Do you think there is some kind of development here, that men little by little have come to show a greater interest in these matters?*

EIRIK: *Yes, this is a trend. Men are on their way, but still women are leading.*

According to Myrhaug, being the one giving birth, the woman is more closely linked to the power of nature, and the woman's "natural" contact with nature also gives her an advantage when practicing shaman-ism. The contact with nature conceivably contributes to a stronger contact with spiritual powers and extends the ability to capture energy. In the shamanic environment, nature is perceived as the ultimate source of spirituality, sacred knowing, and creativity, which is also visible in the practitioners' constant return to the wild land for connection and prayer (see Chapter 3).

The idea of the woman being the more "natural" of the two sexes is also reflected in the various courses offered on the Norwegian New Age market. Here you can find women-only spaces focusing on the power of goddesses and female shamans as well as on female power connected to menstrual periods and to aspects in women's life cycle. In these types of gatherings, the understanding of menstruation, according to Barbara Tedlock, is inverted. "Menstrual blood becomes the material form of subtle energy—clean, beautiful, creative, and powerful" (2005:204).[1] Also in the shaman festival Isogaisa, gatherings are held focusing on female powers and the power of the *volve*.[2] The focus of these performances and course is not theoretical feminism in action. In May 2015, a weekend course was held in the city of Tromsø, Northern Norway, entitled "Sacred Woman." Twenty women took part in the course led by Lilli Bendriss known from the TV series "Åndenes makt" (The Spirits' Power). In an interview with a local newspaper, Bendriss precisely emphasizes that the theme of the course is not about women's rights but about women's power in a spiritual manner. These courses may be feminist in the sense that they put women at the center of attention and try to bring changes in existing language and power structures, but they are first and foremost concerned with woman's spiritual experiences and practices. This, in turn, provides the idea of men and women having different religious needs and abilities. A group called the "female shamans," consisting of three women based in Oslo, the Norwegian capital, describes the differences between male and female shamanic expressions connected to the practices of drumming and prayer:

—*Men drum in another way than us. The male form is firmer. There are many male shamanic traditions. Often they work within one tradition, and with habitual patterns. They use fixed songs, and the power animals they call upon are often the same each time. And their drumming is rhythmical....*

—*We listen inwards! Perhaps there is a greater sensitivity in our drumming; we know not what we need, but we know we need something. We see this in the female prayer worldwide. The male prayer is about the view that you believe you know what you need, "Give me my daily bread." We have experienced in co-drumming with men that it overwhelms our drumming. Females can drum violently and wildly, but also carefully and almost whispery. We are attracted to that which slowly appears in front of us. Women drum like moons; growing and shrinking. We wave and sway in our drumming.* (http://magic.no/magic-magasin/ reportasjer/sjamadamer-pa-reise, accessed September 7, 2015)

According to this group of female shamans, there is a clear distinction between how men and women exert shamanic techniques. Whereas men's shamanic performances are described as determined and focused, the women's drumming performances are portrayed as impulsive, but still calm and humble. Tedlock in her study *The Woman in the Shaman's Body* (2005) supports this emphasis on distinctiveness between feminine and masculine shamanic traditions. When it comes to shamanistic healing processes, Tedlock refers to the "feminine tradition" as interpersonally oriented, whereas in the "masculine tradition" shamans take on a heroic role and encourage patients to act as "passive spectators, at their dramatic performances" (2005:282).

This clear distinction between the sexes also creates an understanding that some shamanistic rituals and practices are more suited for one or the other gender. For example, the physical challenges associated with rituals such as vision quests seem especially to appeal to men.[3] One of the female shamans I have interviewed nevertheless questions whether women may have an advantage that can make them endure the challenges in nature more easily than men.

ANNA: *Well, that's a funny story, because the first time I was out doing this, there were three men with us, and I remember that two of them were particularly adamant that they would do it the hard way; they didn't bring sleeping bags and certainly no tent; and carried but little food and only cold water. Whereas we ladies had been thinking that ... Well, we're in the mountains; and we had brought tents and sleeping bags. And both the guys cracked after one day (laughter). Of course, it is tough in its own way,*

As Anna emphasizes, to endure the vision quest is all about maintaining a balance between comfort and discomfort, between culture and nature. For the men who wanted to meet with and conquer nature the hard way, the needs of the body were stronger. The women, with their tents and sleeping bags, went through with the wake as planned. The women in Anna's story represent *culture in nature*; and it was the women's culture that enabled survival by adapting to the premises set by nature and equipping them with the ability to face nature's trials. This story must also be seen in light of how women hold a special position in New Age communities; they represent a special bond with nature, intuition, spontaneity, and sensitivity (see inter alia Hammer 2004:294–295; Kraft 2000:78–82). These are qualities that the community claims provide women an advantage in the type of self-development processes of which vision quests are a part.

The dichotomy between the sexes is also mirrored in the terms "primeval man" and "primeval woman," which are both central in shamanic literature. These concepts point toward a gendered essence and refer to a loss of spiritual wisdom which once belonged to the primitive man, and which it is now our task and challenge to return to (Sky 2007:83). What is expressed here is an archetypal understanding of the feminine and the masculine in which primeval qualities of the two sexes have gained a central value. Gender stereotypes are thematized, cultivated, and established as a cosmological "truth" underlining that men and women are intrinsically different (Kalvig 2001:33).

These types of conceptions of men and women and their different qualities can be traced in the two-sex model developed during the 1800s. In this period the religious field became associated with a female sphere and women were seen as particularly open to emotional life and as natural intermediaries between the visible world and the world of spirits (see Sky 2007:69).

DISTRIBUTION OF GENDER ON THE NORDIC
NEW AGE MARKET

The distribution of gender on the Nordic New Age market has been debated (see Hammer 1997; Sky 2007; Kraft 2011). Several researchers emphasize that New Age enterprises have a predominance of female participants. A survey conducted in the New Age environment in Sweden in 1994 showed that women are more positive about New Age philosophies than men (Hammer 1997:27–29). Although the numbers may indicate that women dominate the field, New Age is characterized by loose organizational structures and such numbers are thus uncertain. Shamans in Norway nevertheless substantiate the results from the Swedish survey. Questioned about who participates in their courses and who seeks consultation and treatment, the shamans Anna, Eirik, and Ailo reply:

ANNA: *It's mostly women, clearly.*

EIRIK: *There is a predominance of women, so if I have a group where fourteen persons take part, so if there are four men taking part it can be considered as many, maybe three men perhaps two in a group of this size is normal. I've had a group that was mostly equally weighted, but that is very rare.*

AILO: *Well, it also depends on the context in which they come. I have a shaman school and here both men and women take part. But when it comes to my clients, there is a predominance of women. Maybe this is because the feeling of powerlessness is stronger among women. And it is often the women who drop out when the environment is tough and characterized by competition—so I must say yes, there are quite a few women.*

Even though women are in a majority, certain aspects of the practice of shamanism also appeal to men. The difference seems to be contained in the various offers men and women request. When it comes to the shamanic education seminars, which both Ailo and Eirik have organized, the distribution of men and women is steadier, while the client group is still dominated by women. Looking at the shamanic environment in Norway as a whole, one finds a preponderance of male entrepreneurs and organization builders. There are also persons who can be said to exert greater influence and power on the environment than others. Although Ailo is not the only conduit for shamanic teaching in Norway, several of the shamans I have interviewed have participated in his courses and vision quests. His presentations of Sámi indigenous mythology and religious traditions through books, courses, and lectures have provided guidelines for how Sámi shamanism is reflected in contemporary Norway and also in terms of female and male shamans' possibilities and challenges.

"It is a lie, it's a blank lie" — Visioning the Past from New Contexts

To relate to the past is a fundamental feature of New Age environments worldwide. Participants create meaning regarding their own everyday lives by legitimizing their actions and notions on the basis of what are highlighted as a valuable past (Bowman 1995b; Selberg 1998, 2001). The female and male shamans I have interviewed draw inspiration from what they perceive as practices rooted in a Sámi indigenous religion, in a North Norwegian countryside and Sámi indigenous spirituality. The past, nature, and indigenous peoples are enrolled in a spiritual context in relation to which the shamans in various ways construct identity and build on. This also applies to their communication of gender. Most of them criticize the mediation of feminine and masculine values found in contemporary society and look to the past in search of liberating alternatives. It is the shamans' narratives about what gender is in a Sámi pre-Christian context that constitute a basis for how gender is communicated within the contemporary field of Sámi shamanism.

The shamans' stories show that taking part in a shamanistic environment opens up new and ambiguous ways of being and acting male and female, and the practices of gender roles are altered. For many of the shamans I have interviewed, the entrance into a shamanic community also represents an opportunity to challenge what they perceive as established notions of Sámi cultures and traditions. By creating new criteria for what the past may contain, and by promoting new and powerful symbols that build on everything from spirituality to authenticity, nature, and power, the past becomes a source for inspiration and self-development in terms of the embodiment of gender, too. This is a past where the Sámi ancestors are seen as heroes, and where their knowledge of nature and the forces of nature is something we in the modern Western world have lost and should regain and learn from.

Through their practices, the interviewed shamans have used different types of strategies to gain an understanding of the Sámi past. They are all active but also selective users of research literature and sources related to the Sámi indigenous religion. Several of them highlight literature of historians of religion, such as Louise Bäckaman, Hans Mebius, and Håkan Rydving, as sources of inspiration. A general element of the shamans I have interviewed is their skepticism toward the role women are attributed in the research literature, related to their role in the Sámi indigenous religion. In his book *Inn i naturen: Utsyn fra Sjamansonen* (2007) (Into Nature: View from the Shamanic Zone) Ailo discusses this relationship over several pages in the chapter "Hvor var kvinnene?" ("Where were the Women?") The chapter highlights the author's approach to the past and his interpretations of selected source materials. His presentation aims to see the Sámi women of the past in a new light by telling the story of selected women, of their authority and power, of gender equality and harmony between the sexes:

> Most of the stories in which you can read about the *noaidi* (the Sámi indigenous religious specialist) the *noaidi* is a man. But was it only men who were *noaidi*? Or was the term used by both men and women alike, so that the word described the capabilities and skills, and was almost to be reckoned as a professional title ... ? It is mentioned in Sámi sources that Sámi women and men went hunting together on equal footing. That the old Sámi community had matriarchal features is also known. The women had their own reindeer and operated both material and spiritual values. When a couple was married, the man had to move to the woman's family and win their respect. If the woman's family was not

satisfied with him, he would get some hard lessons. If the woman was not happy, he could one day find his belongings outside the tent, and had to go back to where he came from....Thomas von Westen has left a 23-point set of "Finnenes villfarelser" (the Sámi's delusions). Number 16 on this list deals with women's domination and tyranny over their men. It is clear that Westen had no sense of the matriarchy which he came across. He himself was raised in a community where the church was ruled by men. For him it was a given that the *noaidi* had to be a man. It is thus hardly surprising that he and his peers have left few accounts of female spiritual leaders. As we all know, one only sees what one wants to see. (Gaup 2007:25–27, my translation)[4]

Like many other researchers, Ailo is concerned with highlighting that the sources connected to the Sámi indigenous religion are authored by male missionaries who do not describe the Sámi religion in its entirety, but who give us an insight into an aspect of the Sámi *men's religion*. In the aforementioned chapter, Ailo makes it his task to tell the women's history by picking up snippets of texts from those few sources in which women nevertheless *are* mentioned. The Sámi women, Silba Gåmmoe, Rike Maja, Kristin Klemet Daughter, Spå Ella, Lapp-Stina, and the mother of the *noaidi* Anders Paulsen, play the main role in Ailo's version of the past. These women are all described, by Ailo, as female *noaidis* with the ability to perform white as well as black magic for their own and the surrounding community's gain. According to Ailo, they were all feared, yet respected and admired for their ability to heal animals and humans and many of them used the Sámi drum (*goavddis*) in their work (Gaup 2007:27–30). Although Ailo claims that Sámi pre-Christian society had matriarchal traits, it is the equilibrium between the two sexes that is mostly focused on in the chapter. Ailo is concerned about conveying that the Sámi in the past held a social order in which women and men constituted a whole and had responsibilities and characteristics that complemented each other.

The chapter also provides stories about continuity where Ailo draws lines from the past into the present. Based on the book *Norge i Sameland* (Norway in Sámi land) (Gjessing 1973), he points out that the last person who was convicted in a trial for her *noaidi* practices in this country was a woman, and it happened, according to the author, in the area of Polmak, in the county of Finnmark, in 1948. Today, however, female shamans convey their stories and reach out to the audience through new types of media. Ailo writes:

> In a TV program recently a female *noaidi-guaps-diette-guvlar* from Kautokeino proclaimed that her abilities were recognised not only in Sápmi, but throughout Scandinavia and also by people from other countries in Europe. Then she said that one of her relatives had become an apprentice of hers and that this young woman would eventually take over her business. "There's a noaidi for all times," wasn't that what Louise Bäckman said? (2007: 26)

Ailo is concerned with continuity and with the transfer of knowledge about the Sámi indigenous religion from generation to generation up to the present—even among women. By linking the recognized researcher voice of Louise Bäckman to the story of female shamans in contemporary times, Ailo takes a grip that enhances the narrative's legitimacy. Ailo's interpretations of the sources and his portrayal of the Sámi past as a social system with equilibrium among the sexes, created ripple effects in the shamanic environment. For most shamans, Ailo's books and texts are more accessible than Thomas von Westen's texts and other authors of literary sources. Thus, Ailo can also be said to provide the framework for contemporary shamans' interpretations of the past.

Based on the position that women and men hold in the shamanic environment in Norway in the present, shamans look back on the past, interpret it, and make it operate in a late modern world. They fill women's absence in the various sources with interpretations and explanations, and they present women's role in history as natural and central. This is also evident in my conversation with shaman Anita Biong:

> TRUDE: *But how do you relate to the sources of the Sámi indigenous religion where it is emphasized that the noaidis mostly were men?*

ANITA: *It is a lie, it's a blank lie. The oldest findings underline that it was the women who were shamans. And this you can imagine. It was the women who gathered herbs and knew all about herbs.... So it was the women who were shamans, but suddenly, all traces disappeared.... And then men began to take over at a certain point, but they dressed in women's clothing. And this I told Ailo because he said it was the men who worked as shamans at first, but I said, "No, you're lying, Ailo. It's not true." So I told him about my reflections, and suddenly he realized something and he said: "Oh, yes, maybe that's why, when I got on my kofte (traditional Sámi clothing) for the first time that it felt feminine." It's a feminine garment, it is a dress.*

ANITA: *It was the women who started it. The elder shamans were women. The oldest traces of shamans in Scandinavia are found at the place where my grandfather and my grandmother came from.*

Both Ailo and Anita actualize the past as an anchor and a basis for identity construction for both women and men in the present. This implies a recovery and an active reconstruction of the sources that are available. Women's position in the Sámi indigenous religion is, according to both Ailo and Anita, a misrepresentation—a blank lie—which derives from a dominant male culture's oppression and disregard of women's active role. The interpretations of the past and the Sámi community as an environment in which women and men were equal partners has an important symbolic value and works for Anita as well as for Ailo as a legitimating factor for both male and female practitioners of shamanism in the present.

SÁRÁHKKÁ IS DANCING

This new perception of the past has also ensured for the Sámi indigenous goddesses a particular status in the shamanic environment. In the introduction, we met a dancing Sáráhkká at the indigenous festival Riddu Riđđu in the performance *Mátki* (the journey). Together with her sisters Ukksáhkká and Juksáhkká and her mother Mátáhrákka, she plays a central role as a symbol of female power and also of nature's power. As scholar of religion Åsa Trulsson argues, this type of gendering of the divine as female poses as oppositional because the main religious traditions in Euro-America conceptualize divinity as exclusively male and, at times, as a genderless spirit (Trulsson 2010:315). She writes:

> Moreover, the Goddess as a symbol is not only about anatomy, but represents a fully-fledged gendered category including values that are often excluded from conventional conceptualisations of divinity, such as radical immanence, earth-centeredness, the embracing of sexuality and the body. (315–316)

In a Norwegian context the reception of this kind of symbolism has been ambivalent and met with criticism, particularly from researchers. Historian of religion May Lisbeth Myrhaug was one of those who first responded. In her book *I Modergudinnens fotspor* (1997) (In the Mother Goddess' Footsteps), Myrhaug expresses frustration over shamanic performers' depiction of Sámi culture as exclusively positive in relation to nature and to the status of women:

> I hope that this book will contribute to that the romanticising—and partly glorification—of indigenous religions that exist among certain groups must give way to a more realistic understanding of these religions and their form, content and function. In its worst form of expression this romanticising has resulted in something I would describe as "reverse cultural imperialism." Earlier one was concerned with destroying Sámi religion based on an understanding that it was a bad thing. Now certain groups are concerned with taking out disconnected parts of the Sámi pre-Christian belief system to use these parts for their own purposes and understanding—to search for a meaning in life. Thus, one is again in danger of abusing religión, but now based on a "positive" understanding of it, including its relation to nature and its strong feminine aspects. (Myrhaug 1997:10)

By highlighting Sámi, and other indigenous peoples as role models for the right management of nature and for gender equality, the shamanic environment is said to create an image of the world's indigenous peoples that has an unambiguously harmonious touch. According to Myrhaug, these kinds of practices involve the risk of essensializing fairly diverse cultures and, furthermore, harmonizing them against contemporary spiritual needs.

In the newspaper post "Who Knows How Sáráhkká Danced?—Riddu shamanism astray" printed in the regional paper *Nordlys* on July 19, 2007, literature and culture researcher Harald Gaski expressed his opinions on the performance Mátki. Gaski notes that the performance creates jesting and a stew of shamanism and *joik* from various regions. He also stresses that this kind of "flirting" with old Sámi religion is indecent and represents an unfortunate use of Sámi religious traditions. He writes:

> This was a fusion of different indigenous traditions and is disrespectful to all the Sámi.... I am highly critical towards this kind of use of the old Sámi faith. I want people to show respect for our old beliefs, gods and goddesses.... Showing respect means that one does not create jesting of religious beliefs.... I don't think that Sáráhkká danced. Therefore, I have no need to see a visualisation of a dance that has never taken place.... The context of the old Sámi religion has gone, and therefore the search for it becomes a regressive nostalgia rather than a liberating art experience. One could easily end up trivialising that which one wishes to praise, because the time for doing it, no longer fit the faith which was once mighty.

What Gaski suggests is a freezing of Sámi indigenous religious traditions in time, leaving them unchanged, dead, and prevented from adoption by other groups. This is not how religion works, however. As folklorist Sabina Magliocco points out, "Spiritual praxis is by nature syncretic; it incorporates elements from surrounding contexts when it finds analogous meanings and power in them (2004:7). What does it then imply to misuse religious traditions, as both Myrhaug and Gaski emphasize? To romanticize a chosen people, a chosen past, or a lost paradise is not an action that is limited to the new religions of our time.

Romanticism and essentialism are found in all religions at all times (see Geertz 1991:236; Kraft 2005:104). In different ways, all religions deal with turning back to a "Garden of Eden," to restore a lost paradise or to achieve a state of pure harmony and love. Nevertheless, we see a tendency that when such utterances are expressed within a New Age frame, they are met with much resistance and harm (Kraft 2011). Right from the start, shamanic milieus have been met with skepticism and charged with being disrespectful and blasphemous in their dealings with indigenous traditions.[5]

In contemporary shamanism, different indigenous people and pre-historical cultures are used as models and inspiration for religious practices, for gender equality as well as for a healthier relationship with the earth. As Trulsson notes:

This involves a projection of desired states or abilities of various indigenous populations, which are then perceived to provide the answer to what is experienced as an alienating and oppressive culture. It involves the risk of essentialising quite diverse cultures and, furthermore, harmonising them against contemporary Euro-American spiritual needs. (2010:239)

However, the processes involved in various shamanic workshops, seminars, and ceremonies in Norway in the present are more complex than a construction of a romanticized other (2010:239). In the Sámi shamanic environment, indigenous people are able to contribute to the shaping of the discourse of indigenous spirituality and to utilize the same for their own strategic purposes.

Shamans' focus on the balance and harmony between the sexes in a pre-Christian Sámi context should be increasingly met with questions like "What is it that makes these types of interpretations of the past perceived as valuable?" and "Why create an oppositional identity by linking with the marginalised and oppressed?" On the basis of the contemporary context in which Sámi shamans operate, the alternative—that Sáráhkká did not dance and that she as a symbol of female power and wisdom was made invisible—would have been in conflict with the milieu's prevalent thought. These are not symbolic values and ideals that are unique to a Sámi shamanic milieu, but can be traced in many shamanic orientations (see Beyer 1998). But by focusing on Sámi shamans' stories, one can get an insight into how these values are expressed and are being created.[6]

As historian of religion Peter Beyer points out, marginal groups that in different ways can be connected to nature are sought after in shamanic environments and are given added value as part of the marketing of the authentic. Beyer writes:

> Indeed, nature religion currents represent themselves precisely as the forgotten or suppressed religion of the marginal, of the weak and of the oppressed. Not only does the history of the oppression of aboriginal peoples, of women, witches, of Third World peoples and traditions not negate the validity of their religious symbols, myths and rituals; rather as with the proletariat in Marxist thought, such marginalisation from the dominant power structures is interpreted precisely as a warrant of greater authenticity. (1998:18–19)

With their connection to both indigenous people and to women, the Sámi indigenous goddesses Máttaráhkká, Sáráhkká, Ukksáhkká, and Juksáhkká are highlighted as symbols of authenticity in Sámi shamanism. In the festival Isogaisa, in Sámi shamanic courses, and in the Shamanistic Association, these goddesses play a role as guarantors of uniqueness and authenticity and are present in rituals, plays, and ceremonies. This is especially true for Sáráhkká, who is emphasized as a symbol of the feminine and fertility, of indigenous power, and the forgotten, displaced, and oppressed (see Figure 4.2). This is in line with what scholar of religion Michael F. Strmiska emphasizes, namely that goddesses of fertility are arguably the most prominent female deities in pagan traditions, even though there are pagan goddesses who preside over many other functions and forces (2005:37). The Sámi goddesses and the myths connected with them are used as inspiration for religious practices, songs, and art, but they are also perceived to be real entities that can be related to.

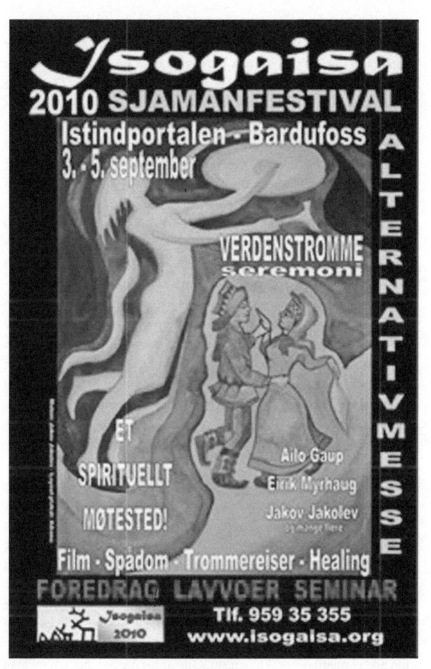

FIGURE 4.2
Isogaisa poster.

During Isogaisa the focus on the female aspect of shamanism is already visualized on the festival's poster. The eye-catcher on the poster is an outline of a woman beating on a drum; in the colors of the Northern Lights, she encapsulates a dancing Sámi couple. This image breaks away from traditional interpretations of the Sámi indigenous religion and defies the taboo of women's use of drums. According to some of the sources on the Sámi religion, sexually mature women should not touch the drum (see Olsen 1997). The festival poster, in contrast, puts the woman at the centre and presents her role as natural and central.

In "Psychiatry's conventional medicine versus Northern Norwegian folk medicine," a speech at the festival seminar in Isogaisa in 2010, Ailo emphasized that all contemporary shamans must open themselves to the earth's energy. Furthermore, he underscored that this was a challenge, especially for men, because the earth is a feminine power. Ailo conveys that the feminine houses a portal to the subconscious—to the earth, thoughts, and feelings, and that men must work hard to open up for the same type of energies. The notion of men as representing the sensible, rational, and functional sex is here replaced by new forms of manhood—by men seeking contact with the earth and nature (see also Kraft 2004:7).

Gender researcher Jørgen Lorentzen refers to such communications of the masculine as "separate masculinity" characterized by a deliberate distancing from dominant forms of masculinity (2004:50). According to Ailo, male shamans mark borders toward the "normal culture" by being open to the earth's power and the feminine. During Isogaisa's opening ceremony in 2010, when a female Sámi shaman, in a common ritual invoked the forefathers, Ailo rose quickly uttering, "But what about the foremothers, then?"

One of the exhibitors at Isogaisa 2010 was the Sámi artist Nils Anders Inga. On his stand at the festival, he presented a series of graphic works inspired by the tension between Sámi indigenous religion and contemporary shamanism. One of his images shows a woman with seven circles symbolizing the new world around her. According to

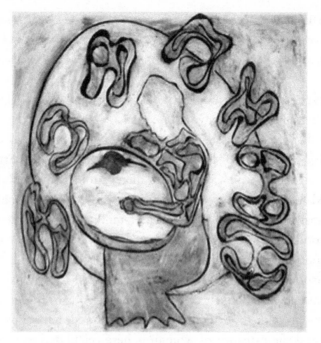

FIGURE 4.3
Woman with drum (graphic by Nils Anders Inga).

the artist, the picture illustrates women as pioneers within the spiritual world, both in the past and in the present (see Figure 4.3). With today's context as a framework, female shamans are also listed as superior to men. Eirik explains:

EIRIK: *I have an impression that there have been many female shamans in the past who used the drum in their shamanic practices. But it has also been a domination by men—that, I think, is undoubtedly correct. But again one should be a bit careful because there exist no direct transfers or sources. We have access to what the priests transferred. And perhaps it was the male shamans who stood up against the clergy, while the female shamans were left in the background and were not featured in the same way as men.... I think that historically the practice of shamanism has been strong among women, perhaps stronger than among men.*

TRUDE: *But are there any differences between male and female shamans in contemporary society? Do they have different abilities?*
EIRIK: *I think so. I think that the strongest shamans will be women.*

These types of interpretations of the past and the highlighting of a strong feminine power have consequences for male shamans in the present. In *A Community of Witches: Contemporary Neo-Paganism and Witchcraft in the United States* (1994), Helen Berger argues that there is a greater emphasis in pagan milieus for men to embrace their so-called feminine side to explore images of male energy and powers in, for instance, the pagan Gods. The feminine in this context can be understood quite loosely, argues Berger, but shows traits that are generally associated with women, such as nurturance, emotional closeness, and sensuousness (1994:41ff). This trend is also clearly expressed in the shamanic environment in Norway. Most courses that have a gender focus are aimed at highlighting womanhood, female powers and values, and the category of woman is here celebrated as specific and sacred.

THE PRESENT AS THE STARTING POINT

The longing for the past houses a creativity, where people continuously create their traditions, values, and myths, and thus the context of their own life (see Selberg 1999; Fjell 1998). With their focus on men and women's "primeval forces," shamans challenge and problematize traditional gender norms. This is also an approach to the Sámi past, which the shamans whom I have interviewed perceive as more integrating, and that opens up for both women's and men's abilities to bond with Sámi culture and traditions.

AILO: *One can cultivate whatever one wants and I have cultivated a form of unisex shamanism. But of course one can cultivate a more masculine practice and justify this mythological and shamanistic.... Or one explores things connected to the female, like birth for instance, shamanistic, and finds strength in this, that this is a female tradition and this is a male tradition. But there is something, in addition, I think. It is a historical development, where the male and female roles in society converge, and this development also influences the practice of shamanism.*

According to Ailo, the past holds premises for both unisex shamanism, where the emphasis on equality and common challenges are key entities, as well as for shamanic groups concerned with a focus on male powers or female powers. By creating new criteria for the past's contents, the past becomes a room that offers inspiration and development for men as well as for women. This is a past where foremothers and forefathers live in harmony with nature, with the spirits—and each other. According to the shamans I have interviewed, this is also a past we in our modern Western world have lost, a past that should be searched for and learned from. Questions about intact transfers and about real continuity are not relevant in these types of traditionalization processes, because tradition here can be described as a selective symbolic construction of the past in the present.

Through the shamans' stories and writings, an outline of their constructions of the past comes into view. This is a past that is located and which belongs somewhere, while at the same time is also open to interpretations and personal adjustments in terms of gender. Through a focus on female goddesses and on women as mediators between nature and civilization, between this world and a spiritual world, shamans create new stories about men's and women's abilities and powers. These stories communicate a critique of traditional interpretations of the gender's values that can be imagined to make women and men alienated from their "natural" or "primeval" qualities.

The past, which is revived during shamanic performances, stories, and literature, is not the past we know from history books and the discourses of scholars. Here it is the link between memory and the imaginary world that is being staged (see Lowenthal 1985). For shamans in contemporary Norwegian society, the past is not a closed chapter; it is a process that extends into the present and reaches into the future.

In these types of traditionalization processes that the shamans I have interviewed highlight, it is essential to distinguish between the past and the present. Shamans' relationship with the past is not about returning to the past in concrete terms; it is about making a selection from the past and adapting it to a modern world. This is a past that harmonizes with the shamanic environment's communication of gender where both men and women are equipped with primeval powers.

CHAPTER FIVE

THE FESTIVAL ISOGAISA

A CENTER FOR CONTEMPORARY SHAMANIC PRACTITIONERS

Isogaisa is a mountain, a goal in the distance. A wish to experience something beautiful, something indescribable.

The Isogaisa festival is a social meeting place, where different cultures blend.

The old Sámi spiritual way of seeing the world is combined with modern ways of thinking. Indigenous people present their own culture and then take part in the performances of other groups.

In this way shamanism is brought to a higher level and achieves broader professional content.[1]

In 2010, a new arena for practitioners of shamanism was established, namely the festival Isogaisa, held in the county of Lavangen, Northern Norway, and presented as an indigenous festival highlighting spiritual traditions of indigenous people (see Figure 5.1).[2] Here, shamans from all over the world gather annually to perform ceremonies and exchange knowledge. Isogaisa is thus a clear example of how Sámi shamanism as a new shamanistic blend influences the international scene and provides impact. Figure 5.1 shows the first Isogaisa festival poster, promoting the festival arena as a spiritual meeting place.

Isogaisa is but one of many examples of how shamanism is expressed in contemporary society; still the festival can be described as a major venue for shamanic as well as indigenous religious meaning-making. Shamanism in Norway is not a unified, organized movement, but a patchwork of shifting and elastic networks, stretching across both

FIGURE 5.1
Isogaisa poster.

regional and national borders (Fonneland 2010). There are still some events that can be said to act as focal points where shamans from all over the country meet to socialize and share their knowledge. This primarily applies to the annually arranged alternative fairs organized in cities all over the country since the early 1990s and not least to the Isogaisa festival.

At Isogaisa various indigenous cultures and traditions, symbols and narratives serve as inspirational sources for the program and for the products on offer. At the same time, festival organizers say that they want to convey these expressions in a modern language, making them inspiring and relevant for people in contemporary society. Although festivals, like Isogaisa, are important vehicles for cultural continuity and passing on of tradition, they are also important instruments employed in situations of cultural and religious renewal. By virtue of being the first Norwegian festival oriented toward New Age spirituality, Isogaisa contributes to a broadening of the religious field in Norway. The festival can be characterized as a manifestation of spiritual entrepreneurship that combines New Age core values with Sámi indigenous symbols and stories. Isogaisa is thus also a key arena for the further development of the field of Sámi shamanism and a central catalyst for shamanic meaning-making in the present.

PREFACE

Isogaisa, which is presented as being an indigenous festival focusing on the spiritual, was held for the first time on September 3–5, 2010. For the first two years, the festival was organized in Heggelia, both on the inside and outside of the military welfare arena Istindportalen in the Målselv municipality of Nord-Troms. After 2012, the festival moved to the guesthouse Fjellkysten in Lavangen municipality, where the festival is now permanently located. The establishment of a winter festival arena in Fjellkysten is also on the cards: the Isogaisa *siida* (*siida* is a traditional Sámi local community), which will consist of an octagon—an eight-sided *lavvu* and eight peat *goahtis* (traditional Sámi turf huts) for overnight stays.[3]

The shaman Ronald Kvernmo is the founder of Isogaisa, and together with the Isogaisa Association (*Foreningen Isogaisa*), he is responsible for organizing the festival.[4] The Isogaisa Association invites the audience to take part in an annual festival weekend of inner travel—to magical adventures in a Sámi landscape. According to the festival program, the motivation behind the festival is to unite an indigenous Sámi worldview with modern ways of thinking and thus create "a spiritual meeting place where different cultures are fused together."[5]

Isogaisa is an innovative festival concept. Sámi indigenous religion and New Age philosophy are used as symbols in rituals and ideas to enrich the experience of the audience. In this way, Isogaisa also exemplifies cultural production through reinterpreting and redefining the past. One of the products that takes shape in this way is Sámi spiritual cultural heritage, which can not only be seen as being part of one's personal negotiation of identity (see Lowenthal 1998) but also as part of the marketing of the local, which is conveyed as being beyond—and thus is of interest to—postmodern society (see Kirshenblatt-Gimblett 1998:149–153).

The objective of Isogaisa organizers is to reach as many interested people as possible, by tailoring a festival program that targets all age groups. When asked what type of audience Isogaisa is intended for, Ronald says:

> People of all ages, from all parts of society, from all countries! Some go there to meet like-minded people, some go there to attend seminars and workshops, and some go because they are curious. Isogaisa is suitable for families. There are arrangements for children, young people, and adults. The volume of the music will be comfortable, and there are no age restrictions.[6]

Over the past two years, we have seen that around five hundred people visit the festival each year. The majority of these are women. People working in the health sector also constitute a large portion of the attendees. This is comparable with the demographics of those who attend

Norwegian alternative fairs and New Age workshops and seminars (see Hammer 1997:27–29). However, there is one area where Isogaisa deviates from the traditional interest in New Age activities, and that is, that it attracts tourists in the form of Norwegian and international travelers in the region. To them, Isogaisa is probably not regarded primarily as a New Age gathering, but rather as an event that allows them to experience unique religious and cultural traditions.

Concerned with sense-making on emic grounds, this chapter focuses on ways in which contemporary shamans anchor their practices in ancient indigenous pasts. Focusing on the *local aspect*, namely the role that the landscape of Sámi ancestors and the Sámi indigenous religion play in the thematic production at the festival, I investigate how the local and distinctive features of Isogaisa are highlighted based upon global structures and organizations in order to generate interest. Furthermore, I explore the resistance against the Sámi shamanic practices that take place and are communicated at Isogaisa.

The chapter is based upon my own fieldwork at Isogaisa from 2010 to 2016, as well as on meetings and interviews with festival leader Ronald Kvernmo and festival participants. The information about the event as presented on Isogaisa's home page and Facebook page also forms a central part of my analysis.[7]

Isogaisa—A Focal Point for Shamanism in Norway

The Norwegian festival scene is steadily growing and evolving. According to the umbrella organization "Norwegian festivals" ("Norske Festivaler"), around eight hundred festivals are arranged in this country every year, mostly during the summer season. In the present, several indigenous festivals are annually arranged in Norway. These events range from one-day happenings with a focus on film, music, culture, history, literature, or sports, to a small number of larger arrangements with a national or international outline. As festivals, these events offer a break from daily life; they provide a sense of community and yield an abundance of stimuli for the senses. Festivals are often held up as being an expression of a changing cultural scene. Music, art, literature, and sports, as well as religious rituals and expressions, are extracted here from their traditional contexts. These types of arrangements also blur the boundaries between the hall and the stage; between the performers and the audience; between the organizers and the volunteers. They create new arenas, reach a wide audience, and represent opportunities to be seen and heard (Pedersen and Viken 2009:185). Isogaisa belongs to the category of indigenous festivals with an international profile. Here shamanic practitioners and sympathizers from all over the world gather for a whole week, to take part in workshops, rituals, markets, ceremonies, and concerts.

The alternative fairs, which are annually arranged in cities all over Norway, should not be underestimated in terms of helping to shape central networks for shamanic practitioners and participants. Still these fairs are primarily marketplaces for a plethora of New Age products and services that have a global scope. The unique aspect about a festival like Isogaisa is precisely the local connection and the emphasis on the particular and local flavor—unique local culture and local religious traditions. Like the Norwegian alternative fairs, Isogaisa is an arena for promoting New Age thoughts and trends; but the products that are on offer here have a glow of authenticity by virtue of their connection with a local place and local history.

Unlike the alternative fairs that only run for a weekend, Isogaisa is an arrangement that lasts a whole week and where people are gathered in a small, confined space. For many, Isogaisa has also become an important arena for social gathering where memories of previous years' festivals and the people met there are shared. In *Earthly Bodies, Magical Selves: Contemporary Pagans and the Search for Community* (2001), Sarah M. Pike notes that pagan identities are primarily expressed at festivals through music and dance. According to Pike, shamanic identities are performative. They seek to control the impression they make upon others in ways that vary according to the context. It is primarily at festivals and other major happenings that the performance of a shamanic identity reaches a peak point concerning both costuming and performances (Pike 2001). This is highly relevant in terms of what is expressed at Isogaisa. From start to finish Isogaisa is a festival packed with shamanistic ceremonies, rituals, and performances. Participants and performers dress up in clothing inspired by indigenous customs; indigenous religions are revitalized along with traditional handcraft, like the making of ritual drums; and people taking part in the festival week have the opportunity to explore and cultivate their shamanic identities.

"IT FEELS SO MUCH MORE NATURAL THAN THAT AMERICAN THING"

Sámi indigenous religious expressions, symbols, and narratives serve as inspirational sources for the program and for the products for sale. At the same time, festival organizers say they want to communicate these expressions in a modern language on the New Age scene. In this way, Isogaisa can be seen as a significant contributor to Sámi indigenous spirituality and to the growing and evolving Sámi shamanic scene.

Festival organizer and shaman Ronald Kvernmo has been apprenticed to Ailo Gaup, who was the first person to orient himself toward Sámi indigenous spirituality, and who looked to Sámi indigenous religion as an inspiration for modern shamans. Ronald became part of this shamanic movement in the middle of the clash between local and global currents.

The Isogaisa festival is presented as being a celebration of this new local scene—and Sámi shamanism, according to the organizer, is intended to contribute to further development in this field. The festival serves as an arena in which to educate society on the virtues of shamanic ideas and practices, to craft new visions, and to highlight shamans as important actors in contemporary cultural and political processes. To create room for growth and development, Isogaisa allows for the gathering and uniting of Sámi religious traditions from all of Sápmi, as well as searching for inspiration from artists and culture workers outside of Sápmi.

Each year, a specially selected group of international artists are invited to take part in the arrangement. In 2010, eight shamans from the Murmansk region participated: one interpreter, two shamans, two dancers, and three *duodji* (Sámi traditional handcraft) performers. In 2011, the youth organization Nurash from Lovozero in Russia was invited, in addition to some of the Sámi cultural workers and shamans that participated in the festival the year before. The purpose of these invitations is to establish a bond between Sámi shamans in Norway and Russia.[8] Figure 5.2 shows Ronald together with Sámi cultural workers at a "Mini Isogaisa" festival outside of Murmansk on May 5, 2012.

FIGURE 5.2
Shaman Ronald Kvernmo and Sámi cultural workers from Russia (photo by Ronald Kvernmo).

"Mini Isogaisa" festivals are also arranged throughout the year in both Norway and Russia, and the objective is the same—that is, to spread information about the festival and to link different Sámi cultures. The program of a "Mini Isogaisa" spans the course of one day and focuses on socializing and performing of rituals; it usually concludes with a concert featuring Sámi performers.

To create room for this type of coming together in a remote place like Lavangen, the festival is financially supported by the Barents Secretariat, the Norwegian Cultural Council, and the Sámi Parliament. The main intention behind the funding is to establish a bond between Sámi shamans in Norway and indigenous cultural workers from other countries. From the perspective of these institutions, Isogaisa is seen as a venue for intercultural negotiation, and the festival week is embraced as a potent site for cultivating understanding and dialog on indigenous histories, cultures, and religions on indigenous terms.

According to the festival leader, Isogaisa can be seen as a cradle for a Sámi spiritual cultural heritage and locally rooted Sámi identities, which are cultivated and grow stronger through the meeting of cultures during the festival week. In our conversation, Ronald stresses this point:

> ... the things that are coming from the US via Michael Harner, that's a lot of stuff; that's where the main beacon is. But we don't have to go further than just past Murmansk, to the Komi and the Nenets people—and then there are the Sámi; that's three different peoples in a small geographical area just over the border, and they ... at least the Nenets people, many of them haven't had contact with the Russians, so shamanism is a living culture among many of the people within the tribe. There's a lot of solid culture to be found there, plain and simple. So, the things that have been lost to the Sámi can be borrowed from them, because they are so close. And it feels so much more natural than that American thing. I mean, Michael Harner has done a great job.... He has, in a way, mixed together a lot of cultures, and that's when you get that kind of world shamanism. But being a good Sámi activist, I'm not sure I like it (laughter). I prefer to turn it the other way around: If we are to make a festival, we should

rather base ourselves on the Norwegian, the local, the Sámi region. And if we are to borrow from other cultures, we should go to Sámi areas in Russia or the South Sámi regions. If we have to go even further, it shouldn't be any further than to the next people who may be regarded as distant relatives. That would feel a lot more natural than taking something from the US, or South America or Peru or Africa.

In emphasizing the connection with similar religious traditions all over Sápmi, the festival sets itself apart from its American roots and supports a brand of shamanism that is becoming increasingly culturally and place rooted. The Russian delegations are assigned the role of bridging new and old shamanic traditions, and they are presented by Ronald as being important vessels of tradition and authorities on the subject. In this turn toward the local, festival organizers emphasize that the type of shamanism that is practiced at Isogaisa is not artificial or synthesized; it is founded on traditions rooted in a local and recent past.

The creation of a Sámi shamanic milieu that is being formed at Isogaisa is a matter of writing oneself into a local tradition, and creating narratives about the local place and local religious traditions to give them a sheen of authenticity. The festival takes part in the global by highlighting the local. Global New Age currents are colored by local tradition and culture, and they become transformed into something that the practitioners can present as being local and unique. In this way, the festival becomes a resource when it meets the global New Age field, by making a distinction between what is considered to be genuine and what is considered universal.

Festival Life at Isogaisa

The program of the festival changes from year to year, with different shamans taking part and different artists and musicians responsible for the entertainment. Thus, some program posts are stable. Further analysis of the festival will be based upon four different sections and events that together make up the core of Isogaisa; namely, courses and workshops, the alternative fair, socializing, and ceremonies. Although some of these overlap to a certain extent and are arranged simultaneously, I have chosen to present them separately in order to provide a comprehensive idea of the sum of the experiences that are being generated in the thematic production of the festival area.

COURSES AND WORKSHOPS

Every year the festival offers a range of courses and workshops arranged by different exhibitors. The program for Isogaisa 2015 includes twenty-five different offerings spanning from workshops in throat song, Kildin Sámi shamanic healing methods, and workshops on the making of Sámi earrings. Some of the workshops last only for a few hours whereas others span multiple days; it also varies if the courses must be paid for or are free.

For the past five years, the professional *duodji* (Sámi traditional handcraft) artist, Fredrik Prost from Viikusjärvi—a small village in the northernmost part of Sweden—has held a workshop in the making of ritual drums at Isogaisa. Prost trains participants for three days in creating their own ritual drums inspired by the traditional Sámi *goavddis*. These drums, according to festival organizer Ronald, "will be very special and exclusive drums with enormous energy."[9] The course ends with a ceremony in which the drums are inaugurated.

Another stable program post is a mountain hike to the Sámi *sieidi* Rikkagallo (Sámi indigenous sacrificial stone), where participants take part in a ritual and a sacrifice under the guidance of Sámi shaman Eirik Myrhaug (see Chapter 3). This hike lasts for a whole day, and the walk to the *sieidi* and back to Isogaisa is described as a pilgrimage (see Fonneland 2017a). Eirik emphasizes that the sacrifice at Rikkagallo helps to strengthen Isogaisa and creates good energies during the festival week. On the festival's website homepage one can read, "The sacrifice to the stone is an ancient tradition that through the Isogaisa festival has been revitalized and where we do a ceremony and sacrifice inline with our new understanding of a shamanic reality."[10] The goal for the trip to the *sieidi* is, in other words, to combine modern spiritual practices with indigenous religious traditions.

The Sámi artist Ingor Ánte Áilu Gaup has been a central contributor to the festival program for several years. On the festival homepage, Gaup is presented as "one of the foremost contemporary artists throughout Sápmi."[11] In addition to holding concerts in the main *lavvu*, Gaup also arranges courses where participants are invited to learn to *joik*. At these courses, the *joik* is made available for people without a Sámi heritage and the *joik* is presented as an instrument available for everyone searching for their inner voice and for self-development. In relation to the discussions in Chapter 2 on appropriation of indigenous traditions, Myrhaug, Gaup, and Prost, who are all of Sámi descent, have chosen to make the *joik*, drum, and *sieidi* accessible for anyone who wishes to perform, articulate, and reclaim a shamanic identity. At the festival, old and local traditions are merged with global discourses on pagan rituals, spirituality, and indigeneity, practiced by Sámi and non-Sámi alike, and incorporated in a contemporary shamanic context.

In the process of shaping and developing a cultural heritage, there is a clear focus on objects. At Isogaisa, the traditional Sámi drums (*govaddis*), the Sámi *sieidi*, and the *joik* are used as the basis for new constructs, and they become symbols of continuity with the traditions of the past. In the words of the geographer David Lowenthal, "To be certain there was a past we must see at least some of its traces" (1985:247). The Sámi drum, the *sieidi*, and the sound of the *joik* are precisely such traces. In shaping their festival drums, taking part in a sacrifice at the *sieidi*, and learning to *joik*, Isogaisa provides the festival attendants with access to a firsthand personal taste of the past. The objects, the Sámi drum, *sieidi*, and the *joik*, are in this context messengers that enable a dialogue between the past and the present. As folklorist Jonas Frykman says about the role of objects in cultural production: "Things like this—and many more—have become something more than symbols. They bear secrets and have to be induced to speak" (2002:49).

At Isogaisa, the Sámi drum, the *sieidi* Rikkagallo, and *joik* no longer have the stigma of being reminders of a pagan past; they are powerful, authentic, and magical symbols of a vital Sámi culture and available to everyone taking part in Isogaisa.

THE ALTERNATIVE FAIR

The second main part of the festival program is an alternative fair, which operates in parallel with the other festival activities right up until the festival, concludes on Sunday afternoon. Compared with alternative fairs, *which* are arranged annually in small and big Norwegian cities, this festival fair is a "mini alternative fair" with about twenty exhibitors. Whereas the traditional alternative fairs gather a wide range of exhibitors, the focus of the Isogaisa fair is on the Sámi tradition; selling Sámi drums, brass rings, *duodji*, and other products related to the practice of shamanism.

As festival organizers have chosen to have an alternative fair as one of the main parts of the festival, the obvious dialogue Isogaisa has with New Age currents is highlighted. This also shows that the distinction between shamanism and New Age has become increasingly blurred. An alternative fair is a New Age market in miniature, which, despite its wide range of topics and products, conveys a standard repertoire that provides insight into the core values of the community—the New Age lingua franca . In a study of people offering alternative treatments in Denmark, scholar of religion Lars Ahlin characterizes the New Age core in terms of four themes; namely, self-spirituality, self-authority, self-responsibility, and holism (2007). At the festival fair, just as at other alternative fairs, various healers and therapists give weightage to the *self* as a divine being within humanity, which is sovereign with regard to one's own judgment and choice. The shamans who have found their way to the festival fair venue, who receive festivalgoers for consultation and treatment, regard illness as a sign that something is wrong with the *whole* person. As therapists, they market their role as *guides*. The patients themselves are thus responsible for their own healing.

Despite the fact that Isogaisa embraces the core principles of the New Age milieu, festival organizers also want to distance themselves from traditional alternative markets. Ronald emphasizes:

> I do not know of any other events like Isogaisa. The local alternative fairs
> do try; but they lack the cultural bit. There are many good alternative events
> here in northern Norway, but you do not have any core culture; that is my

impression. My impression is, not that I want to say anything bad about how the alternative fairs are arranged, that it's a lot about business. "We sell what people want." We, on the other hand, do not do a lot of that. We try to convey a message that highlights Sámi culture and shamanism; whereas the alternative fairs are more like putting all sorts of stuff together under the same roof, and there is a lot of variety. Of course, we have to have some variety at Isogaisa, too; there will be bonfires, lavvu, and Sámi music.

Ronald has adopted the critique that many scholars and media express toward the alternative market; namely, that it is shallow and superficial, that there is too much emphasis on business and too many religious traditions mixed. In their focus on Sámi culture and tradition, the festival fair makes a move to avoid this type of criticism.

New Age spirituality and Sámi indigenous spirituality symbolize two different sets of values. Whereas the New Age movement has been criticized for lacking roots and traditions, Sámi indigenous spirituality holds a special status and is connected with values such as wisdom, the ancients, cultural heritage, environmental protection, and natural insight. By marking their distance from typical New Age markets, and by linking the religious aspects of the festival to Sámi culture rather than to the New Age, festival organizers boost the status of Isogaisa as both a festival and a business. In contrast with New Age, the links to a Sámi past and Sámi indigenous spiritual traditions become a resource that attracts attention and guarantees a unique product, service, and experience.

CEREMONIES

The third main event at Isogaisa is the many large and small ceremonies that are performed both inside and outside the festival area. The festival begins with an opening ceremony and is followed by a hunting ceremony, children's ceremony, chocolate ceremony, and various types of drumming journeys. Additionally, the announcement for the 2017 festival indicates that it will include a ceremony greeting the dawn, a tea ceremony, a pipe ceremony, and of course a closing ceremony. The various ceremonies are performed as more or less ritualized practices. This implies that Isogaisa may be regarded as a ritual field.

Every year an opening ceremony is held in the festival's main *lavvu*. Before entering the *lavvu* every participant has to go through a short act of purification where sage smoke is passed over the participants' bodies. Inside, festival attendees gather in a big circle around an unlit bonfire. The fire that is lit during the ceremony is meant to burn day and night throughout the festival weekend (see Figure 5.3). An appointed fire keeper will secure that the flames are not dying out.

The ceremony opens when all the invited indigenous representatives, together with the festival leader, enter the center of the *lavvu* in a procession, drumming and *joiking*. Then four shamans standing in opposite directions are chosen to light the festival fire while invoking

FIGURE 5.3
The festival fire.

the spirits from the different corners of the world; from north, south, east, and west. Ronald points out that the festival fire is a holy fire and people are encouraged to give an offering to it during their stay and to refrain from throwing waste and plastic in the fire. Then talks are held by some of the indigenous representatives and by Ronald, who finishes his talk by declaring that the Isogaisa festival is open. The rest of the opening ceremony is filled with various performances and with Sámi folk music performed by invited groups and established Sámi folk musicians.

Activities are a core element of all types of festivals. The audience is not a group of festival spectators; they are festival *participants*. This implies an active and tangible relationship with the products on offer, as well as with the place in which they are offered. Additionally, the series of ceremonies marketed by Isogaisa facilitate types of activities other than those we usually associate with the adventure economy of our time. Whereas theme parks, which were the subject of analysis in Joseph B. Pine and James H. Gilmore's book *The Experience Economy* (1999), allow for an immediate satisfaction of the senses, Isogaisa, on the other hand, allows for experiences of a slower kind—experiences that are supposed to affect the participants on an inner, psychological level. The various ceremonies are experiences laden with expectations of how they will, in one way or another, give the festival audience a feeling of increased energy—of inner growth and development (see O'Dell 2010:31).

Although the activities offered in food festivals, literature festivals, and music festivals may also offer experiences for the senses that will affect and change those who participate, the numerous ceremonies of Isogaisa offer an additional dimension which more "worldly festivals" do not market in the same way. The pipe ceremony, hunting ceremony, tea ceremony, and the many drumming journeys offer ritual passages in which the sensing of the landscape, the sound of the drum, and the tastes and scents represent a liminality, transformation, and inner self-development. Isogaisa is thus not a festival in which the audience is supposed to just come and be entertained; the objective is to come, experience, and *be changed*.

The ceremony and interactive theatre performance "Those Who See" was among the activities that attracted many people in 2010. It focused precisely on this change, and it took shape as a rite of passage. The performance was made by Haugen Productions, and it was also part of the program of the indigenous festival Riddu Riđđu in Mandalen in 2007, under the name Mátki (the journey). At Isogaisa, the starting point of the performance was located in the woods behind the festival venue. On Saturday and Sunday afternoons, every thirty minutes groups of eight persons stepped out into nature, meeting actors, healers, dancers, clowns, shamans, and musicians. The participants followed a forest trail that combined elements from Sámi mythology and natural medicine from various parts of the world. They took part in drumming journeys aimed at finding their power animals, in cleansing ceremonies, in *joik*, and in various creative challenges such as painting and dancing. The objective of the performance was, according to the organizers, that participants were to experience ancient indigenous traditions, and through these experiences challenge their own lives by asking questions such as, Who am I, Where do I stand today, and What is my path?

Though "Those Who See" is not an initiation rite into shamanism, it places weight on how inspiration from indigenous peoples' religious tradition can be a resource for everyone in the present. This, according to the organizers, is something we in the Western world have lost and which we should rediscover. Isogaisa presents itself as being precisely this type of learning arena, where those with inquiring minds may acquire about the values they feel we lack in Western culture. The festival offers a perceptible access to the Sámi past, and thus it forms a bond between the past and the present.

SOCIALIZING

Festivals are primarily social arenas where people come together, maintain and expand their social circles, and relax in a nice atmosphere while enjoying the entertainment. Socializing is also the final item on the festival program. As pointed out in the article "Traces of Our Ancient Religion: Meaning-Making and Shamanism at Sami Offering Sites and the Isogaisa Festival, Northern Norway" (Äikäs, Fonneland,

Kraft, Perttola, and Thomas 2017), the participants emphasize the social importance of the festival fire as a place where people gather around and share their food and stories. Festival attendees talk about the spirit in the fire, how they honor the fire by decorating it with flowers, and about the healing power of the fire. The fire is also a place for personal offerings made in solitude.

One of the highlights of the Isogaisa 2011 program was a festival dance for the general audience accompanied by *joik* developed by the Sámi artist Elin Kåven. The dance was published on YouTube and on the Isogaisa homepage prior to the festival; people were encouraged to learn the steps before the festival. The dance and the *joik* visualized the journey to the Isogaisa festival by mimicking the movements and sounds of various Arctic animals. In the festival area, the dance and the *joik* contributed to a sense of community. The simple dance steps symbolized a project of coming together, in which participants of all age groups could take part according to their abilities. The Isogaisa dance and *joik* also serve to highlight how formerly taboo cultural expressions are currently entering popular culture.

As pointed out by Äikäs, Fonneland, Kraft, Perttola, and Thomas, a central phenomenon at Isogaisa is the role given to hugging. Hugging is described as the power of the festival (2017). Several interviewees note that, in contemporary society people communicate less face to face than through social media and mobile phones. They find that there is a great need for human closeness, and this is why it is important that this perspective is emphasized at Isogaisa. Hugs are deemed so important that a festival hugger is selected every year. The task of the festival hugger is to spread joy among festival participants and to ensure that strong, social bands are tied.

"THE PEOPLE IN LAVANGEN MUST BE PROTECTED AGAINST SHAMANIC THOUGHTS AND INFLUENCES"

In the aftermath of Isogaisa 2013, a local newspaper announced that some Sámi communities were highly critical of the funding of the festival because of Isogaisa's promotions of parts of Sámi culture that, from ancient times, are not to be made public, such as the practices surrounding healing and the contact with spiritual powers.[12]

The Barents Secretariat, which is one of the institutions that provide financial support, thus ordered an independent review of the ethical aspects to support the event, and in February 2014 two researchers at the Norwegian Institute for Cultural Heritage Research (NIKU) drew up a report.

The report highlights that the festival's marketing of shamanism violates the traditional principle of secrecy of spiritual and healing powers or abilities, but it also further points out that this is how Sámi shamanism generally is practiced in contemporary society and that the festival is an important arena where the Sámi can take part in shaping a global indigenous spirituality. The researchers underline:

> The festival is based upon a global concept that has been given a local anchoring.... We [will] say that the differences between old and new practices are greater than the similarities and they should be considered as different practices. There is no evidence that Sámi neo-shamans represent a threat for practitioners of healing in today's Sámi Christian tradition.... Based on our impressions the festival reaches out to an audience that would not otherwise be affiliated with Sámi cultural offers. It supports local culture, but at the same time, it connects to a global movement where Sámi spirituality already circulates as part of the multifaceted offers. That Sámi people actively participate in this movement with their own offerings and on their own terms is a matter of strength for the Sámi community and indigenous peoples in general. The fact that Sámi people can represent themselves in the religious field can counteract the global tendency that indigenous spirituality is separated from its historical and local context and is represented by others. (Brattland and Myrvoll 2014:5–6, my translation)

A parish priest in Lavangen, John Syver Norbye, was one of those who opposed NIKU's conclusions, and in the aftermath of Isogaisa 2014 he expressed his criticism toward the festival in the Christian online forum

"For Bibel og Bekjennelse" (For Bible and Confession). On September 13, 2014, Norbye writes,

> The invocation of such spirits are in basic conflict with the Bible's first commandment and must be described as idolatry. Lavangen is an administrative district for Sami language and culture. As a priest here, I am concerned that the Sámi people must be protected against shamanic thoughts and influences. Also, people who have a Sámi identity, are at risk to be attracted to forces and experiences that bring them under influence of evil powers. (http://www.fbb.nu/artikkel/sjamanisme-og-kristentro/, my translation)

Norbye's critique was spread through local, regional, and national media, and during Isogaisa 2016 the debates reached a peak point.[13] Both Norbye and several festival participants were interviewed and conveyed opposing views and attitudes on Isogaisa. The tension surrounding the festival gives us a glimpse into the ways in which communities cope with social flux and cultivate creativity. What we have here is a tension between competing worldviews, views of nature, and relationships between nature and man and between good and evil powers. Another key issue deals with how people imagine and relate to the past, and what happens when competing stakeholders disagree on the interpretations of the past and what can be communicated as a resource for the Sámi community in the present. What some local voices see as an assault against Sámi religious traditions is by others described as an important Sámi resource and voice in the development of global indigenous identity as well as religion.

A large majority of the newspaper articles spoke in favor of the festival. The parish priest's attitudes toward Sámi shamanism are presented as a cultural assault, as colonialism, and as an unwanted interference. Parallels to the church's abuse against the Sámi people under the mission processes and under periods of assimilation are drawn. To the local newspaper *Fremover*, festival director Ronald Kvernmo emphasizes, "The church has condemned Sami understanding of nature for 500 years" (September 25, 2016). Shaman

Eirik Myrhaug highlights similar arguments to the Sámi cultural newscast *Ardna*:

> The Sámi people have suffered enough by the church's missionary work. We have lost much of our culture. I have personally lost my mother tongue. Now we return to all this through the Isogaisa festival. (https://tv.nrk.no/ serie/ardna-tv/SAPP67006215/02-11-2015#t=30s, my translation)

In light of these types of statements, Isogaisa may be described as a religious, social, and political resource to legitimize personal, social, and political conditions in the present.

Isogaisa as Venue for the Development of Indigenous Identity

In the NIKU report, Isogaisa is also welcomed as a resource for the development of local knowledge on the Sámi past as well as for a growing discourse on global indigenous spirituality. Brattland and Myrvoll point out:

> The festival's local roots and the inclusion of local Sámi culture are supportive to Sámi culture and society in southern Troms and northern Nordland and for the Sámi community beyond the region. It contributes to greater knowledge about the pre-Christian Sámi society, about ... the Sámi sacred sites (*sieidi*) that are of great importance not only for Lavangen, but also for the entire society. The fact that the festival in addition has an international flavour makes it no less important.... Isogaisa does not contribute to ethical concerns for the Barents Secretariat and similar institutions that provide support. The alternative Sámi movement should be welcomed as a resource for local Sámi communities and for the global movement on indigenous spirituality. (Brattland and Myrvoll 2014:6, my translation)

Isogaisa is presented as being a learning arena where a dynamic process of remembering brings forth elements from the past. Assumptions that religious traditions that have been lost can be retrieved and shared are here generated. And by sharing and exchanging spiritual knowledge, this type of expertise, according to Brattland and Myrvoll, will develop and grow for the benefit of the local community as well as for indigenous people globally.

That the festival may serve as a cradle for the development of indigenous identities, as pointed out in the NIKU report, is a primary concern to the festival leader. He himself grew up in an environment and a time where being Sámi felt like a stigma. When during adolescence he moved to Guovdageaidnu (Kautokeino), a county in the Sámi core area, he experienced that, neither practicing a Sámi language nor having close family in the herding culture, he did not fill the "requirements" to call himself a Sámi (see Hovland 1996; Stordahl 1996; Gaski 2008).

Selecting a Sámi identity in spite of the experienced lack of prerequisites can be demanding (see also Gaski 2008:222). It was not until adulthood and through contact with a shamanistic environment that Ronald felt he could be proud of his own background and history and choose to call himself Sámi. This personal development also triggered a desire to learn more about shamanism, and eventually to teach others about the subject.[14] As Ronald points out in our conversation, common conceptions about Sámi culture and identity are challenged in the shamanistic environment. According to him, to be Sámi deals with more than practicing a language or engaging in traditional reindeer herding. Getting to know shamanism, he found that to be Sámi also includes a spiritual and mythical dimension. In this perspective, the shamanic environment represents a context that challenges the traditional concept of identity and allows new and ambiguous ways to be Sámi.

Isogaisa offers a perceptible access to the Sámi past, and thus it forms a bond between the past and the present. The festival generates a feeling of how it all happened *here*; and that here it is all happening *now*. It is loaded with powerful symbols, which not only take us back in time, presenting tales of the past, but also conveys information about which types of values we regard as important in the present (see Eriksen 1999:87ff). The past, which is revived during the festival, is not the past we know from history books and the discourses of scholars.

At Isogaisa, it is a link between the memory and the imaginary world that is being staged (Lowenthal 1998). Here, the past is not a closed chapter; it is a process that extends into the present and reaches into the future.

In this way, Isogaisa can be said to be a monument to Sámi pre-Christian traditions as well as indigenous spiritual expressions that are being created within a certain framework every year. Being a monument, Isogaisa contributes to a "coding" of the local place, which can be deciphered by the participants at the festival. The Isogaisa monument, however, is not solely based on the local landscape but considers the festival arena to be a center and a specially selected representative for shamanism globally. The festival participants are mobile and fluid, and thus the practices and ideas cultivated in the local landscape during the week of the festival are transported to contexts far away from Lavangen.

This development, it is noted, also takes shape through contact with indigenous culture workers from other countries. It is, in particular, these types of exchanges and developments in local traditions that the Sámi Parliament, the Cultural Council, and the Barents Secretariat wish to encourage through their yearly financial support, and why Isogaisa is marketed as a resource for local Sámi communities and the global indigenous movement.

"Isogaisa, the beating heart of a counter culture"

Festivals are events which serve to profile and expand the local, as explained by ethnologist Kjell Hansen in the article "Festivals, Spatiality and the New Europe" (2002). The special aspect of festivals is the fact that they are indeed taking place (2002:20). Isogaisa, too, takes place in a specially selected landscape. During the festival weekend, the local north Norwegian landscape is transformed into a spiritual venue for Sámi culture, both nationally and internationally. When I asked Ronald about what he considers the most important aspect of Isogaisa, he replied, "The forming of bonds. We are in the center, the south Sámi area is represented, and Russia is also here." From having been peripheral, Isogaisa transforms the place where the festival is held into a creative cross-national arena for religious innovation and a focal point in Sápmi.

The prerequisite for having Isogaisa's landscape take the shape of a center is to market the place as being unique: as being different from all other places. In most cases, this type of marketing is done by creating a clear local connection, and the easiest way to do this is through its name (Hansen 2002:29). The name Isogaisa means "big peak," or "the biggest peak among many big mountains." The word is also familiar from several poems and songs. The festival organizers aim to use the festival to make "Isogaisa" a brand name, not only covering the festival itself but also the growing, evolving Sámi shamanic movement in general. Ronald says:

> Branding. The name Isogaisa…. now we are establishing the term Isogaisa, we are anchoring it in the "top of the mind" of people. So the next time people think of shamanism, the name Isogaisa should come up, and it should be a broad term. It is not only a festival; it is a shamanic centre. We may even launch a CD soon, which is going to be called the "Power of Isogaisa."

By marketing and spreading the name Isogaisa and its local connection, the objective is to expand the local by making the municipality a center for practitioners of Sámi shamanism.

Dreams of having religious experiences, often at remote centers, has been a prevalent pattern in religious history. The tales and visions of journeys to holy places such as Jerusalem, Rome, and Mecca have been many. In the postmodern religious landscape, the distance to these centers has grown shorter, and the number of centers has increased in pace with the developments within the religious sphere (see Kraft 2011). Isogaisa is a clear example of how the northern Norwegian region is marketed to be such a spiritual center.

The connection between local development and the marketing of spiritual values makes the festival an agent of change in extended cultural innovation and development processes. At Isogaisa, the identity of the region is recast in a way that replaces the traditional image of North Norway as being "peripheral," and as being a politically, economically, and culturally repressed region. For this reason, Isogaisa is not situated in a political vacuum, despite the fact that the festival is primarily intended to be an arena of activity and entertainment (see Hall 2007:306; Hansen 2002:28). This is highlighted by the statement made by festival goer and exhibitor Wilhelm Strindberg in the headline, "Isogaisa; creator of a separate identity and sense of pride; but also a spearhead of counter-culture. Isogaisa: the beating heart of the counter-culture."

CONCLUDING REMARKS

Isogaisa is an important venue for the expression of people's ideas, values, memories, traditions, and aspirations. As a festival, Isogaisa acts as a contact zone where people negotiate and reflect on their identities. Understanding the significance of festivals like Isogaisa in a globalizing sphere of indigenous cultural production thus has implications beyond the aspect of entertainment. The various cultural performances that are expressed at the festival can be simultaneously commodities, spiritual rituals, and transformative political projects; "these are not necessarily mutually exclusive, nor are they without occasional contradictions and tensions" (Phipps 2009:32–33). Like Peter Phipps, I see indigenous cultural festivals as places for political action that it is time to look more closely at "as significant, playful and urgent acts of cultural politics" (2010:237).

At Isogaisa, different indigenous cultures and prehistorical traditions are highlighted as sources of inspiration for religious practice and environmental-friendly relationships with the earth, though shamanic practices are shaped in relation to contemporary Euro-American society. This involves a projection of desired states or abilities of various indigenous populations, which are then perceived to provide the answer to what is experienced as an alienating and oppressive culture. As Åsa Trulson argues, "It involves the risk of

essentialising quite diverse cultures and, furthermore, harmonizing them against contemporary Euro-American spiritual needs"
(2010:328). However, the processes involved in various workshops,
seminars, and ceremonies at Isogaisa are more complex than a construction of a romanticized other (2010:328). At Isogaisa, indigenous
people and other attendees are able to contribute to the shaping of
the discourse of indigenous spirituality and to utilize it for their own
strategic purposes.

The study of newly emerging festivals, such as Isogaisa, provides
a window to the processes of ritual creativity. The festival is, in my
view, a clear example of how religious labels are formed in ever-
changing contexts—as a by-product of broader historical processes.
Isogaisa, with its seminars, alternative fair, and ceremonies, is like
other festivals in that it is a place for socializing, enjoyment, and
leisure—nevertheless, it is also a place where the local and global are
merged, where power relationships come into play, where political
interests are materialized, where cultural identities are tested, and
where new visions take shape.

CHAPTER SIX

THE SHAMANISTIC ASSOCIATION

THE RISE OF SHAMANISM AS AN APPROVED RELIGIOUS COMMUNITY

[The] Shamanistic Association is a religious community that aims to promote a shamanistic belief system and preserve individuals' and groups' rights to seek and exercise shamanistic practices.

Shamanism is a 30,000-year-old spiritual practice where one uses trance techniques to communicate with the forces of nature and the world of the spirits. The Shamanistic Association is a religious group that wishes to promote a positive image of shamanistic religions, and to preserve individual and group rights to seek and pursue shamanistic practices.

Holding shamanistic religious views means acknowledging that all things are animated and that they are our relatives.[1]

In Norway, a shamanic association concerned with the preservation of Sámi and Norse shamanic traditions was granted status as a religion by the Norwegian authorities on March 13, 2012. This means that, according to the laws regulating religious bodies in Norway, they may perform such religious ceremonies as baptisms, conformations, weddings, and funerals, and, additionally, gain financial support from the membership. In this chapter, I will focus on how the Shamanistic Association, which is the name of the newborn religion, came into being, as well as delineate its primary concerns (see Figure 6.1 which shows the Shamanistic Association's logo). I will show how a transnational movement has taken on local features in the framework of

SJAMANISTISK FORBUND

FIGURE 6.1
Shamanistic Association's logo.

the Shamanistic Association's establishment in the city of Tromsø. The chapter will also examine the process connected to the association's development of shamanistic ceremonies and rituals.[2]

As James Beckford notes, "Disputes about what counts as religion, and attempts to devise new ways of controlling what is permitted under the label of religion have all increased" (2003:1). The Shamanistic Association (SA) appears to have been created for the purpose of meeting the criteria required for obtaining the rights of a Norwegian religious community; the national legal framework thus inspired a diverse group of professional entrepreneurs to join forces and organize themselves into a religious association. In Norway, this was the first time a shamanic movement was able to obtain the status of an official religious community with the right to offer and perform life cycle ceremonies and gain financial support relative to its membership.[3]

Drawing on interviews with the leader and board members of SA, participant observation at seminars and in ritual performances, and document analysis, this chapter will focus on the processes that led to the rise of the Shamanistic Association in Norway, as well as on some of the association's major concerns, significant events, and developments.

As a result of the rise of the Shamanistic Association, decontextualized and transplanted ideas have been pinned down to specific ideas of time and space. In other words, shamanism has been embedded in a local northern Norwegian environment. A central theme of this chapter is thus devoted to showing how transnational religious ideas and practices take on local distinguishing features to acquire meaning and define community. At the same time, it will focus on how local constructs can be said to alter transnational movements. It describes the dynamics of a cultural creation whereby abstract concepts and ideas find moorings in a local community and in participants' reality here and now—gradually generating a distinct cultural field, the field of northern shamanism.

This can also be described as a study of cultural border zones, where the production of meaning takes shape in the encounter between religions and nations, local and global myths and stories, and laws and regulations, as well as in the encounter between the past and the present.

THE VISION

The development of new religious organizations often starts with a vision. In the case of the Shamanistic Association, this vision is linked to a single person's religious interaction with the world of his spirits and spiritual helpers—a world that generated a revelation. The person who received this revelation was Kyrre Gram Franck, also known as White Cougar, now a leader of the Shamanistic Association at the national level. Kyrre has been involved in shamanism since the early 1990s and says that he has had shamanic teachers inspired by American Indian as well as Sámi indigenous traditions. In Tromsø, Kyrre has been a well-known local shaman and healer for a long time. He is also the organizer behind "The World Drum Project," a shamanic nonprofit organization founded in Norway in October 2006, with a focus on peace and environmental issues.[4] Kyrre can be viewed as a soteriological entrepreneur.

He is a founder, organization builder, role model, and motivator. As the association's appointed leader, Kyrre's personal background, his interests, friendships, and networks, allowed him to put his imprint on the rise and development of the association (see Lindquist 1997:189). Regarding his vision, Kyrre tells me:

> *It is difficult to express these images and feelings in words, but the vision came to me in a dream. That is, not in an ordinary dream, but in a state of trance and communication with the spirits. One of my spiritual help-ers, an old man, came to me and showed me a picture of Scandinavia. He then told me that I should start up something called the Norwegian Shamanic Association. I could see that there was a slight contradiction here, but the explanation is probably that it is not me who will be start-ing up shamanic associations in the other Scandinavian countries. The vision also brought images and feelings of people sharing spiritual knowl-edge and learning, and I was told to focus on the past. Even though the Shamanistic Association embraces shamanism in its many variations, it is at the same time important for us here in the north to protect the north-ern traditions associated with shamanism. So what we hope to accom-plish in the long term is to develop the Shamanistic Association into a tradition keeper for the northern traditions.* (my translation)

As a first step toward recognition and formalization of a shamanic asso-ciation, Kyrre shared his vision with his friends in the local shamanic milieu. One of them, Ronald Kvernmo, the prior mentioned leader of the Isogaisa festival, urged Kyrre to drop the word "Norwegian" from the association's title. According to Ronald, this word could be offen-sive to shamans involved in and inspired by Sámi shamanism. After consulting the spirits about this potential amendment, the name of the association was changed to the Shamanistic Association (SA).

The vison lends legitimacy to SA's focus on northern shamanism, and it highlights SA's role as a keeper of place-specific shamanic tradi-tions. Kyrre further argues that the vision can be seen as a concretiza-tion of the mythological notion that "the light comes from the North."[5] Consequently, it is decided that SA's main seat always will have a grounding in North Norway. The vision, in other words, portrays Northern Norway as a natural and appropriate center for shamanistic practices. On SA's homepage on the Internet we can read:

> One of shamanistic Association's clearly stated goals is to create a living shamanic culture in Norway. (We aim to) give life to old traditions— to our heritage. Throughout Norway, this is happening right no, not only under the auspices of the Shamanistic Association. Also, other organisations and individuals help to revive the fire. The drums emerge along with knowledge that has been banned for long. 300 years ago, the drums were prohibited. In 2012, with the public approval of the Shamanistic Association, the drums are again accepted.[6]

According to Kyrre, the intention behind the establishment of the SA is that the association will develop into a unifying force with the ability to strengthen individuals' and groups' rights to practice shamanism. Not least, he hopes that the association will develop into a true alternative for those who adhere to shamanistic belief systems, and that the construction of life cycle ceremonies like baptisms, confirmations, weddings, and funerals will help to increase people's interest in shamanism.

Because Kyrre can be seen as the founding father of the Shamanistic Association in Norway, his vision may also be considered as SA's "myth of origin." Historian of religion Russel T. McCutcheon argues for a modern and secular category of myth that does not define myth by its sanctity and special content, but that instead redefines myth as a strategy or a storytelling technique. From this perspective, a myth can be described as a social strategy, a technique, a tool, a special kind of social reasoning that people use to legitimize themselves and their social and cultural reality (McCutcheon 2000). In this case, Kyrre's vision can be seen as a foundation that legitimized the creation of the Shamanistic Association out of self-interest, but at the same time presented as originating from the will of the spirits. It also legitimized the focus on northern shamanism and on Kyrre as the association's natural leader. It was *he* who received the spirit's revelation. It was *he* the spirits had confidence in and chose as a contact person. Kyrre's central position is also reflected in the organization of SA, where, in addition to being a leader, he also has the status of vision keeper. According to the board protocol, in cases where decisions might lead to significant changes of vision, the vision keeper retains veto power. The position of vision keeper will follow Kyrre for life.

Due to his roles both as vision receiver and vision keeper, Kyrre is a central catalyst in terms of how the Shamanistic Association is profiled, and what is to be emphasized and possibly omitted in the creation of the group's identity and community. This is also, as anthropologist Galina Lindquist argues, what is striking in the world of shamanic performances: "an important condition of its existence, its performative expressions, hinges entirely on certain individuals" (1997:189). At the same time, the leader nevertheless exerts no strict control in relation to what members want to highlight as sources of authority and authenticity. In SA, Kyrre points out, they strive for a flat organizational structure where each member has a fair chance to take part in processes connected with developing the Association. Dialogs reflecting interactions between members, leader, and board members are realized through discussions taking place on Facebook. Here members interact, question, and take part in the process of decision making.

A member of the Facebook group asks:

> those who are actively involved and dedicate their time to the associa-
> tion are also helping to shape these visions, so the role of the Vision
> Keeper must not be to engage randomly in determining all the guidelines.
> (January 16, 2012 at 12:20 pm, my translation)

Lone Ebeltoft, who is one of SA's board members, replies:

> Thanks for these fine comments :) I also imagine a Vision Keeper as a
> tradition keeper—one who only intervenes if the board considers chang-
> ing the main paragraph (section 1.1) in SA. (January 16, 2012 at 1:15
> pm, my translation)

Further, Kyrre comments:

> That's right. A Vision Keeper is not intended to cast a veto in every-
> thing.... As mentioned this is a vision that came to me about two years
> ago. Therefore it is important for me that the vision is adhered to, but
> the ability to veto takes effect only where it would lead to substantial
> changes in the main paragraph where the vision is expressed. (January
> 16, 2012 at 3:01 pm, my translation)

Nevertheless, there is great variety in terms of each member's level of
activity and involvement. On Facebook, it is clear that some voices
are expressed more frequently than others, and that some dominate
in various dialogues. SA consists of a group of people who have
highly divergent views of what creates power in terms of shamanistic
practices and rituals, and whose dedication and engagement varies.
These participants are also actors who, to varying degrees, put their
imprint on and leave traces in the development of the Shamanistic
Association.[7]

As the same time, as an interaction between the board and individual members is highlighted as central to the development of SA, the
external forces of Norwegian governmental laws and regulations are
also playing a role in shaping the Association. Two years after receiving
the initial vision, the application process for a shamanistic association
began. In this process, governmental regulations must be dealt with in
many arenas. Initially, Kyrre applied to the County Governor for per-
mission to start a shamanistic organization. However, this proved to be
difficult because of the bureaucratic system and rules regulating freedom of beliefs. If SA was going to have a chance at getting approval to
perform shamanistic life cycle ceremonies, they first needed to establish
themselves as a religious community.[8] Groups applying for official status as a religious community need to frame their application according
to The Religious Communities Act (*Lov om trudomssamfunn og ymist
anna*). By doing this they also reproduce a certain understanding of
religion derived from Christian understandings of what constitutes the
"core essence" of religion (Owen and Taira 2015:94). Governmental

regulations also influenced the design of these ceremonies. For a wedding to be considered legally binding, for instance, certain formulations needed to be included. SA, then, is a construct designed to meet the requirements for the recognition of religious communities, highlighting how religious practices are adapted, transformed, and changed to fit governmental regulations.

THE PROCESS STARTS—THE LETTER TO THE COUNTY GOVERNOR

The Religious Communities Act's (*Lov om trudomssamfunn og ymist anna*) definition of religion favors Protestant Christian religious forms that other religions need to conform to in order to gain recognition as a religion. The letter Kyrre sent to the County Governor to establish both a national board located in Tromsø and a local shamanistic association is dated January 16, 2012. It contains certain requisite information in a number of paragraphs that deal with everything from rules for membership, to objectives, to rules for leaders of the local religious communities, to matters relating to the design of the Association's life cycle ceremonies. To gain official recognition as a religious community, the community must also submit an official creed, the contents of which must not be "in conflict with public morals."[9,10] SA's creed is highlighted in the first section in the letter to the County Governor:

§1.

1.1

The power of creation expresses itself in all parts of life and human beings are interconnected with all living beings on a spiritual plane. Mother Earth is a living being and a particular responsibility rests on us for our fellow creatures and nature. All things living are an expression of the power of creation and therefore are our brothers and sisters.

A shamanistic faith means acknowledging that all things are animated and that they are our relatives. And that by using spiritual techniques, one can acquire knowledge through contacting the power of creation, natural forces and the spiritual world. A shamanistic faith involves a collective and individual responsibility for our fellow creatures, nature beings and Mother Earth. Mother Earth is regarded as a living being.

Shamanistic practice means the use of shamanistic techniques both for one's own development and for helping our fellow humans and other creatures. This means that creation is sacred and one celebrates the unfolding of the life force. (my translation)[11]

This creed articulates, according to Kyrre, the main parts of his vision. It is with respect to this section that the vision keeper retains the power of veto. The main emphases here are the struggle to protect the environment, a holistic worldview, and Mother Earth as a key symbol for shamanistic practitioners. The symbolic values and ideals emphasized in this paragraph are not unique to Nordic shamanism, but they can be found in shamanic milieus across the globe (see Beyer 1998; Stuckrad 2005). From the very beginning, Mother Earth has been a central touchstone in shamanic practices. She is an essential figure to which one attributes power as well as offers sacrifices. A broad statement like this serves to encompass the diversity of practitioners of shamanism and excludes no one on the basis of national or ethnic identity.

To have a creed that says something about the relationship with a god/gods and that does not conflict with a "public moral" is mandatory. This requirement is still inconsistent with a religion that sees itself as fundamentally nondogmatic. Public registration challenges some of the key ideals within New Age spiritualties, namely individual religious freedom, antidogmatism and anti-institutionalization (see Heelas 1996). In one of our conversations, Kyrre and Lone reflect on this issue:

LONE: *We had to work hard to find a formulation everyone could accept. Because it is important not to force anyone into anything, especially within shamanism because where the main goal is that everyone should be free. This is at the core of the critique against SA. We notice it when we are around at fairs and stuff and tell about the Shamanistic Association, then someone always says, "I'll never join anything like that, no one will force me into anything." They have simply not understood. We only wish to facilitate for shamanistic practices.*

TRUDE: *But at the same time, you face a public law, which you need to relate to?*

KYRRE: *That has been the heaviest obstacle (laughter), to understand what they were looking for. First, we got a nice disapproval, and an encouragement to resubmit. We spent a lot of time and I thought that if we do not make it this time, we need guidance. Then, we understood that is was a wording that had to be included for the document to be approved. We had to use the term "spouse," for example. It had to be literal and in the right order. This shows that there is a bureaucracy that interferes with the religious communities' design and what we can communicate that we believe in. Much of this builds on Christian principles, so I felt a bit reluctant to go into the process.*

The call for a creed is clearly contrary to a religion to which being nondogmatic is a core value, and it forces SA to conform to Christian values. Kyrre emphasizes that it felt problematic to construct a creed but also highlights that there was no way around it, if SA was to have a chance to be approved.

One of the other points highlighted in the letter is that the group will be divided into primary members and other members. Primary members are individuals who are not members of another faith, while other members are those who want to support SA but are affiliated with another denomination. These persons cannot sit on the board, but otherwise they have the same rights as primary members. The annual fee to participate in the Association was, for 2016, 150 Norwegian crowns per member (19.99 EUR). SA receives 500 Norwegian crowns (66.62 EUR) in governmental support every year for each primary member. Currently (2016) SA consists of 238 members from all over the country, 180 of whom are primary members. SA is also registered a Facebook group, with some 3,000 persons participating.

The letter to the County Governor further states that SA is to be a focal point for persons adhering to a shamanistic faith and that their goal is to designate and educate ceremonial leaders across the country.

The ceremonial leaders' tasks are to hold regular gatherings for members and others who wish to participate, and that this is especially important at the solstices, equinoxes, and full moons. Appropriate guidelines have also been created for the people who will be appointed ceremonial leaders. The candidate must be at least twenty-three years of age and have at least five years' experience with shamanistic practices. Ceremonial leaders are to be appointed by the main board.

Kyrre emphasizes that SA's most important task is to increase the knowledge of its members. He underlines that there are more and more people offering shamanic courses and making money, but most of them also lack knowledge and training and thus degrade the milieu. One of SA's tasks is to raise the standard and to ensure that courses organized by SA guarantee high quality for customers.

THE SHAMANISTIC ASSOCIATION—A TRADITION KEEPER FOR NORTHERN SHAMANISM

Even though the Shamanistic Association emphasizes shamanism as a universal phenomenon and embraces shamanism in its many variations, at the same time it promotes an agenda of emphasizing local roots and a local connection. In his vision, Kyrre was told to focus on the past. This focus is also highlighted in SA's official statement where it is emphasized that their goal is to develop the organization into a tradition keeper for northern shamanic traditions.

According to Kyrre and Lone, northern shamanism embraces Norse and Sámi pre-Christian traditions. To gather both Norse and Sámi traditions under the same roof can be seen as a strategy for reaching out to a larger number of potential members. It is a strategy of inclusion that dissolves the taxonomies of insider and outsider, and of who has access to the traditions of the past. The term "Nordic shamanism" creates a common Nordic approach and a focus on shared traditions. In our conversation, Kyrre and Lone perceive their religion as a product of particular cultures, landscapes, and historical time. They emphasize that the goal is to restore the original roots of northern shamanism, preferably back to 5,000 to 10,000 years ago when the differences between the "nature religion practices" of the various local tribes were minimal. This is clearly a strategy for identifying a common origin and common roots. As Jenny Blane argues, these types of religious traditions are "indigenous to place, but not tied to blood or race categorizations" (2005:193).

Sámi shamanism has been marketed as an alternative to Harner's core shamanism in Norway since the early 2000s. This is a topic of contention, and there has been constant discussion about who has the right to take part in and practice what is perceived as Sámi traditions (see Myrhaug 1997). The leader and board members of SA wish to avoid such tensions and to avoid being accused of stealing traditions. Drawing inspiration from a time when the boundaries between Sámi and Norse traditions were supposedly blurred can be seen as an attempt to circumvent such tensions. Kyrre and Lone point out that SA is a peacemaker and bridge builder between Norse and Sámi pre-Christian cultures and traditions.

Also, by highlighting Norse traditions eliminated by the expansion of Christianity, SA can see themselves not as oppressors but as victims of the same forces that have marginalized indigenous peoples. As Magliocco argues in *Witching Culture: Folklore and Neo-Paganism in America* (2004), this type of historical revision is a powerful metaphor, which underlies identification with oppressed or marginalized peoples.

> Oppression such as that suffered by indigenous peoples at the hands of colonisers becomes an indicator of genuine spiritual knowledge or power—the same kind of spiritual authenticity they imagine pre-Christian European peoples must have had. (2004:232)

Parallels can also be drawn here to what Fredrik Gregorius emphasizes as the basic notions of Nordic culture in Swedish Norse organizations— namely the notion of an authentic, organic Nordic culture living on under the garb of Christianity that is seen as more appropriate for people living in the northern areas (2008:132). This is precisely what Kyrre and Lone also emphasize. Authenticity is believed to be found in distant times and places, in a Nordic pre-Christian past that the detrimental influence of civilization has not touched. Embedded in this quest for a Nordic past and a lifestyle lost, we can thus also trace a critique of civilization—a form of antimodernism and antiurbanism. What the shamans seek, what is perceived as real and organic, is found in nature prior to the modern period.

This then is a past far away in the mists of time, which, as Kyrre and Lone emphasize, can be touched only indirectly, through narratives, popular culture, myths, legends, and sagas, as well as through shamans' religious experiences. According to Lindquist, these types of "invented" traditions that take form in the shamanic milieu often refer to a past so distant that there are no living memories to challenge—or support—their images (Lindquist 1997:129). This is also the case for SA's search for a common ground for their shamanistic practices in contemporary society. Their quest for a Nordic shamanic heritage involves liberation from established discourses about what the past can accommodate, and it opens the past for individual approaches and interpretations. But as Lindquist further states:

> For such a "constructed" past to be meaningful, it has to be helpful in understanding the present, and it must be anchored to people's current social concerns. Tradition becomes living only when it is projected on to, and enlivened with, the actualities of today's life. (Lindquist 1997:129)

In SA, northern shamanism is brought to life through a focus that these are traditions that correspond to our nature, our ancestors, roots, climate, and mindset. These are traditions retained in our landscape, in old burial places, and in archaeological sites and that are thus available to everyone inhabiting the northern latitudes.[12] The idea is that nature has the power to "release" ancient energy and knowledge. The Northern Lights as well as the midnight sun are highlighted as domestic spiritual qualities that connect the past to the present. Similarly, sceneries with their plains, lakes, and mountains are interpreted as doors into the world of the ancestors. By being present in, and by using, this landscape, past and present melt together and create a totality. The landscape is interpreted as having the imprints and traces of ancestors, and this crossover between time and space gives places a touch of mystery. As Eriksen points out: "The past ceases to be a bygone age; it can be perceived as a now because it is related to a here—a here that is also part of contemporary man's own direct experiences" (1999:92 my translation).

The longing for the past houses a creativity where people continually create their traditions, values, and myths, and thus a connection with their own lives (see Selberg 1999; Fjell 1998). History lies open for reinterpretation and can be adapted to the individual's desires and needs; it is optional rather than obligatory. This contributes to unsettling the overall authority that is no longer to be found in specific religious traditions but is expressed in the individual seeker. Religious actors place the different parts together according to their own accounts, interpret with their own hearts, and replace parts when they find it appropriate to do so (see Eriksen 1999:149–151).

As Anne Kalvig argues: "The 'tension' between Sámi and Viking shamanism constitutes a fertile ground for contemporary religious creativity and production" (2015:68). This creativity is expressed, for example, in the wedding ceremony that the association has developed and which has been approved by the County Governor. During the ritual the bride and groom together hold a ring made of iron and copper. Iron in this context is meant to symbolize the Norse community, while copper is linked to the Sámi past and Sámi traditions. The wedding ceremony then not only unites a couple but also brings together different cultures and traditions, to meet and blend through the ritual.

To further turn the diffused tradition of northern shamanism into a source for SA's members' shared community and identity, key figures in SA are doing research to get closer to the sources of what they experience as a shared Nordic shamanic community. This research is distributed, popularized, commented upon, and embellished on the Association's homepages on the Internet and on Facebook. In this work, the distribution of information in Sámi has become an important issue for SA. As noted by Strmiska, knowledge of the language of a particular pagan tradition is among the means of demonstrating ethnic belonging (2005:17). Developing a Sámi profile through language use contributes to enhancing SA's position as a serious religious operator in the Norwegian society. It can also be interpreted as part of the positioning of SA as an "insider" in Sámi contexts.

Lone has chosen to embark on the work of getting closer to the sources and emphasizes that she will especially focus on the traditions connected to the *Volve*, known as a sorceress in Norse traditions. Her quest for the past concretely illustrates the creativity that characterizes this type of historiography. As Lone points out, very few literary sources document these traditions. To get closer to this tradition and to learn more, she seeks inspiration from women in the larger shamanic milieu who have been focusing on and marketing these types of traditions for years, including Annette Høst in Denmark and Runa Gudrun Bergman in Iceland. She hopes they can provide her with a deeper understanding and help her anchor traditional practices in the present. Additionally, Lone seeks inspiration from what she perceives as sources in the Celtic tradition, which she sees as enigmatic and open to interpretation, as well as from popular culture. As noted by Graham Harvey, popular culture and fictional works, especially the genre of fantasy, are often highlighted as sources of inspiration for contemporary pagans. These sources are also referred to more often than other literature on the subject, like academic works, ritual manuals, and philosophical treatises on theology (1997:181–184). What these references suggest is precisely the important role of imagination, creativity, and play in these milieus (1997:181–184).

To bring Nordic shamanism into the present, the Shamanistic Association's focus on northern traditions is also portrayed in their logo (see Figure 6.1). Here Sámi and Norse symbols are entwined into a joint expression. In the logo, the Sámi sun symbol, *beaivi*, encircles Yggdrasil, known as the tree of life in Norse mythology, with a drumming shaman in the foreground. The logo expresses their desire to unite traditions, to find a model of a community in the past that all members can view as a resource for their practices in the present—a resource for identity and community. They seek to turn time back to a period when religious traditions formed the basis of community and were not (or so they imagine) identified with specific ethnic groups. The ideal is to not exclude anyone from taking part in a reconstruction of religious traditions. These different types of approaches to the past are undertaken as part of creating new practices, enacted and endowed with meaning, revealing how a distinctive cultural milieu is gradually generated.

By underscoring their connection to "local" religious traditions, the Shamanistic Association distances itself from its American origins and focuses instead on a shamanism that gets less and less "core," and more and more locally inspired. The emergence of a Nordic shamanistic milieu takes shape through the establishment of SA, reshaping stories about the local landscape and local religious traditions so that they appear in the glow of authenticity. The Association takes part in the global by promoting the local. Global new religious currents are painted here with local traditions and cultures, and transformed into something which practitioners can present as local and particular. As such, the Association constitutes a resource in the encounter with the global New Age subculture by drawing boundaries between what is perceived as real and what is perceived as illegitimate, between the authentic and commercialized, between the unique and the common.

This, on the other hand, does not mean that SA excludes all other sources as valueless in relation to the practice of Nordic shamanism. Kyrre himself has been trained in shamanism by teachers with different sources of inspiration, and so he emphasizes that to partake of influences from other cultures can, to some extent, help develop Nordic shamanistic practices. Thus in terms of basic ideas and practices, this new construct does not differ from its US origins. However, though colored by the raw material of local concerns and resources, the teachings and practices of northern shamanism do not distinguish themselves noticeably from those developed by Michael Harner.

THE DEVELOPMENT OF LIFE CYCLE CEREMONIES

Shamans are said to gain access to the past, first and foremost through ritual performances that create links between the past and the present. From the very beginning, rituals have been strongly emphasized by the

Shamanistic Association, an emphasis found in the shamanic milieu more generally. As stated by shaman Kenneth Meadows, "In shamanism you simply do it in order to know it; knowledge comes through the doing" (1991:5). In other words, you cannot be a passive shaman. It is by practice that the production of meaning begins.

On a sunny afternoon in late August 2013, I participated in a full moon ceremony arranged by SA at Prestvannet, a natural resort centrally located on the island of Tromsø. In the midst of people strolling and children playing, ten SA devotees gathered around a fire. Almost all of the participants had brought their own drums; as the ceremony started, some of the shamans began beating their instruments and gradually the others joined in. Lone talked about the August moon's importance and the focus of the drum journeys that afternoon. All in all, the gathering consisted of the three drum journeys. Kyrre led two of them, wearing a ritual mask, while Lone was in charge of the last one. After the meditation session, people were encouraged to share their experiences, and some of the participants were welcomed to lead a joint drumming. Then it was time to socialize. Some had brought food and others brought tea made of *chaga*, a mushroom found on birch trees, which is said to have healing powers and to enhance spiritual experiences during drum journeys.[13] After a few hours, the last drumbeats faded and the area was left in silence.

SA's main activities are precisely related to the construction and performance of rituals and ceremonies that aim to consolidate a community within the group of practicing shamans. The development of ceremonies connected to rites of passage such as baptism, confirmation, wedding, and funeral; social meetings in the open air with organized drum journeys at every full moon; and, not least, major celebrations at the solstices and equinoxes function as cultural clocks that provide each member with a solid basis for his or her shamanic practices and identity. As Trulson argues, rather than a full-fledged worldview distinct from individuals and groups, the sacred is continuously cultivated by a series of ritualized practices (2010). The staging and performing of rituals can have a subjective and private meaning for each participant. At the same time, the rituals and ceremonies aim to evoke a sense of

cultural continuity. If they are seen as important, the rituals and ceremonies can develop into an internal tradition, which paves the way for
a construction of shared memories, and common myths, which are elements that contribute to creating a community (Lindquist 1997:182).

According to the laws regulating religious bodies in Norway, as an
approved religious community, SA may also perform such religious
rituals as baptism, confirmations, weddings, and funerals. A group of
members are currently working on developing a ritual repertoire that
will form the basis for the association's life cycle ceremonies.[14] This
work is organized through a closed group on Facebook, with seven-
teen people taking part.[15] Drafts and ideas concerning the development of the association's main ceremonies are shared, evaluated, and
discussed.

The process of developing life cycle ceremonies with a northern slant
began at the Isogaisa shamanic festival in August 2012. Two days were
set aside for this project, and on Thursday, August 23, a group of SA
members gathered along with indigenous representatives and shamans
from Greenland, Canada, New Zealand, and Russia. The participants
were further divided into four groups, with each group being responsible for a specific rite of passage. During these meetings, the SA members
clearly recognized their position as surrogates. The intention behind
this seminar was to learn from the guest shamans, who were viewed
as representatives of the past and the past's ancient indigenous ritual
traditions. It was asserted that through their presence and involvement,
the seminar could be a catalyst for the process of retrieving lost ritual
traditions. As Kyrre argued:

> At the seminar, we want to identify the basic elements of the various
> "Ur-cultures," which we have access to, through the guest shamans. Our
> job in the Shamanistic Association is therefore to observe, learn, and
> document, so that we can use the results of the seminar as a basis for
> developing our own rituals. We believe that there exists a knowledge of
> the old rituals that we will be able to document during the seminar and
> later rework and possibly utilize as the basis for new modern rituals
> based on ancient traditions.

The Shamanistic Association emphasizes inspiration from global indigenous cultures as a resource in their efforts to develop life cycle ceremonies with a Nordic flavor. According to Kyrre, the rituals of indigenous people are something that we in the Western world have lost, and thus something we should collect and from which we should learn. As such, SA illustrates what historian of religion Catherine Bell lists as characteristics of the new ritual paradigm, in which it is emphasized that the Western world has become a spiritual vacuum, due to the decline of "traditional religions" and our lack of rituals. To prevent this absence of rituals from making people root-less and alienated, the idea is to retrieve knowledge from "ritual-ized cultures," to borrow ritual structures and ideas and gradually develop our own (1997:223–242).

The ritual seminar at the Isogaisa festival appears to be exactly such an educational arena, where a group of practicing shamans gets a chance to acquire values and wisdom they feel are missing in Western culture. Two of the participants in the group relate how traditions connected to the use of herbs and plants that are lost in a Nordic context can be retrived through the knowledge of the Russian Sámi participants at Isogaisa:

> What we think is important regarding the use of herbs and plants is to use the ones found in our own area. Certainly, it can be cool to buy plants and herbs from places like South America, but in the end that also implies that we lose the knowledge of our own plants. The Russian women on Isogaisa used the same plants that we have here at home, juniper, nettle, and rosemary. It is very important that we work with our local plants and herbs so that the knowledge do [sic] not go into oblivion.[16]

For SA, the seminar offers a perceptible access to a common Nordic history and constitutes a bond between the past and the present. The past is not viewed as a closed chapter, but as available for the individual shaman to access and regain knowledge and traditions. As Lone points out:

> *This was one of those rare times when elders from several indigenous cultures wanted to share with us Westerners. I think they wanted to do*

this first and foremost because they see that the world has lost many of the old ritual paths and that their task is to guide us to bring the paths back.

That ceremonies entail a connection between past and present is also strongly emphasized on SA's homepage on the Internet. To achieve a desired outcome of a ceremony, the practitioners, according to Kyrre, must communicate with the spirits in an ancient ritual language that the ancestors recognize as well as to show respect for the traditions of the past. In the paper "Å holde seremonier" (To hold ceremonies) that was published online in October 2016, Kyrre argues,

> Through the ceremonies, a language that the spiritual world understands is established. This is the same language that our ancestors have used since time immemorial. Therefore, it is also important that we, when performing ancient rites, perform them exactly the way they are supposed to. If one deviates from the regular pattern, the spirits might not understand the "language" and the ceremony can be perceived as an insult. I think that the spirits have great patience with modern humans and appreciate our good intentions, yet I find it extremely important to respect the old traditions.[17]

Still, these types of returns to the old paths do not involve simply picking up types of rituals that have been practiced in the past. In the shamanic milieu, creativity, as mentioned earlier, takes precedence over tradition. The group selected to take part in the "reconstruction" of northern shamanic life cycle ceremonies see themselves as creators of culture. They do not abide by any fixed tradition, but bring into being their own. One of the participants in the group underlines precisely the creative aspect of shamanistic ceremony construction:

> Of course you can make all possible variants of the various milestone ceremonies, but what I argue make the ceremonies "shamanistic" is the relationship with nature, the attitude of those present (that they are

participants not spectators), and in particular the relationship with the spirits, especially the foremothers and forefathers.[18]

The discussions in the ceremony group say something about what has authority and what one wishes to highlight as important starting points for religious practice. There is, however, no clear limitations in terms of what types of elements and traditions can be incorporated into the ritual production. In shamanic practices, the self is highlighted as a genuine source for approaching the core of past traditions as well as for communicating in a ritual language known to the spirits. As Bell emphasizes, "What is seized upon as tradition is usually a rather new synthesis of custom and tradition.... This type of 'return' to tradition, therefore, is clearly a force that opens the tradition to many changes" (1997:256). SA focus lies on reworking and developing new rituals by using the old ones as a foundation. The founders of SA draw upon a variety of traditions and sources, and synthesize the symbolism of Sámi, Norse, and Native American myths, ideas, and values.

RECEPTION—CONCLUDING REMARKS

The domestic media has covered the activities of SA from the very beginning. Both local and national media showed great interest in the rise and approval of the Shamanistic Association in Tromsø. During the course of the Association's first year, papers carried such headlines as "Nå er sjamanisme offentlig godkjent i Norge" (Now shamanism is officially approved as a religion in Norway) (*Nordlys*, March 14, 2012), "Sjamanisme finner grobunn i Norge" (Shamanism finding fertile ground in Norway" (*Dagen*, March 15, 2012), and "Sjamaner inn fra kulden" (Shamans in from the cold) (*Bergens Tidende*, October 30, 2012).[19] The association's key figures, Kyrre and Lone, have been interviewed by local and national newspapers, radio and TV. TV2, one of Norway's largest national TV channels, covered the news about the initiation of a shamanistic association in Tromsø. In the program, it was emphasized that Lone welcomed the governor's decision and expressed her ambition for preserving and continuing the shamanistic traditions and practices of the country. It was further highlighted that the Shamanistic Association's goal is about understanding and respecting nature. Nor is shamanism in any way mysterious. Shamanism is a world religion, and in the North people are committed to preserving the Sámi and Norse (Arctic) traditions (TV2, March 14, 2012).

All relevant media stories are characterized by a positive attitude toward the newborn religious association. The positive attention is in stark contrast to how the media in general has covered New Age events and entrepreneurs. According to Kraft, the New Age does not hold a high position on the media's list of real religions and acceptable religiosity (Kraft 2011:105). In the case of SA, we thus have media contributions that show a genuine interest in the phenomenon of contemporary shamanism. In the various reports, shamanism is not portrayed as a countercultural movement, characterized by oppositional attitudes and naïve as well as unreliable social actors, but rather as a positive contribution and a necessary alternative, embodying important attitudes concerning contemporary environmental issues and materialistic lifestyles.

This also blurs SA's borders with the larger society. As Paul Heelas demonstrated, the New Age is very much a phenomenon of and for modernity, informed by the values of the host society, elaborating and radicalizing some of its dominant themes (1996). The type of spirituality highlighted by the establishment of the Shamanistic Association can also be seen as a resource that provides a shine and an aura to surrounding social milieus. This is a religious community that can claim to take care of *our* traditions, *our* common Nordic religious roots. As such, the Association can be seen as a cultural force. In this case, Nordic shamanism emerges as our common cultural heritage. According to Eriksen, the concept of cultural heritage holds everything that is nice and (slightly) old and that generally has the status of being important and valuable and is not imposed from the outside (2009:478).

By their emphasis on the local and on the city of Tromsø in northern Norway as a national center for constructing a common Nordic heritage—a center where Sámi and Norse traditions can meet, merge, and form the basis for a community across ethnic and religious boundaries—the Shamanistic Association can be said to be contributing to some of the central discourses in contemporary society concerning the High North. In the tourism industry as well as in the business community in general, Northern Norway is showcased and marketed as a region of resources, with great scenery, lighting, and colors, as well as spiritual energies (see Guneriussen 2012). Nor did it take long for the establishment of the Shamanistic Association to be appropriated into a marketing campaign for the city of Tromsø. On April 1, 2012, *ABC News* published a list of good reasons for traveling to Tromsø. One of them stated: "Byen der nysjamansime ble godkjent som egen religion" (The city where neoshamanism was approved as a religion in Norway) (*ABC Nyheter*, January 4, 2012).

SA is a spiritual entrepreneur involved in highlighting the northern region as a spectacular and unique brand in the global tourism industry and in the late modern experience economy. In different ways, the Shamanic Association is engaged in a process of replacing traditional images about Northern Norway as a premodern rural community with new and powerful stories invested with spiritual undertones. Even though SA first and foremost constitutes a religious community and is a venue for people committed to shamanistic practices, the Association is not without social and economic implications, and, as such, SA is a cultural force.

CHAPTER SEVEN

SHAMANISM IN SECULAR ARENAS

THE CASE OF ESTHER UTSI, A SÁMI SPIRITUAL ENTREPRENEUR IN THE NORWEGIAN TOURISM INDUSTRY

At Polmakmoen experiences, community, culture, health, therapy and equanimity are in focus. For those interested in exciting experiences we can offer various activities such as walks in the mountains, adventures along the Tana River, open fires, hot tub under the open sky, snowmobile tours, Sami culture and a unique opportunity to observe the magical Aurora Borealis[1]

The figure of the shaman seems to fit exceptionally well into contemporary structures of needs and motivations in different cultural areas beyond the religious-spiritual field (Mayer 2008:88). As Gerhard Mayer points out: "The variety of elements contributing to the fascination makes it a suitable chipper for many different contexts; for the healer, the actor, the artist, the DJ, the rock singer" (Mayer 2008:89)— as well as the tourist host. Approximately, since the turn of the century, references to Sámi shamanism have been represented in many sectors of Norwegian society; within experience and entertainment institutions like museums, festivals, theatres, within the film and tourism industry, and in the form of products of a more tangible nature, like books, video games, and food. Fonneland and Kraft refer to these inventions as "hybrid style Sámi shamanism" offered by both Sámi shamans and secular agents and by Sámi and ethnic Norwegians alike. These products and concepts cater for broader audiences and for a variety of needs, including tourism, regional development, and entertainment. They draw on trends in the spiritual milieu as well as in the experience economy (Fonneland and Kraft 2013:132–145).

Phrases like the "magical Aurora Borealis" (as used in the description of Polmakmoen Guesthouse in the chapter ingress) and "Arctic magic," for instance, has during the last decade been established as a common ingredient in promotional material of various sorts, with the northern Norwegian region constructed as an Arctic and magic region, situated near the borders of civilization (Fonneland 2017b).

The *goavddis* (drum) is today available in tourist shops, in museums, it can be heard in the music performed by Sámi artists, and sold by professional Sami shamans. At Sápmi Park, a tourist theme park in the village of Kárášjohka (Karasjok) in Finnmark, tourists are offered virtual encounters with the *noaidi* (Mathisen 2010). At the festival Isogaisa, Sámi shamanism is listed and marketed as both entertainment and as an important tool for self-development. In the Sámi video game "Sáivu" that was launched in 2012, children are encouraged to design their own shaman drums, which upon beating, produce a magic helper. Next, after having successfully solved a task and found certain Sámi items, the tasks and items are to be handed over at a *sieidi*, a Sámi sacrificial stone. A shamanic personal beauty care salon, *Sarahkkas Beauty*, in the Norwegian capital offers cosmetic treatments combined with shaman healing.[2] In addition, in the music industry, shamanism appears in a growing number of contexts. One such artist is the Sámi musician Elin Kåven, a recording Sámi artist for ten years, who aims to bring listeners to the arctic sphere of shamanic folklore and mythology of Sámi people.[3] Through her music, she manifests the mythological creatures from the Arctic, and her concerts are described as fairy tales in notes. To make sense of such spiritual and semispiritual settings, it is crucial to take into account the interplay between secular and religious elements and include "hybrid" products—products whose New Age components are open to different interpretations—with or without spiritual references, and which are ascribed at least one function of a more prosaic or secular character (see Fonneland and Kraft 2013).

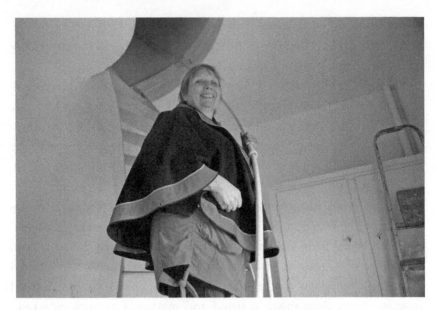

FIGURE 7.1
Spiritual entrepreneur Esther Utsi.

In this chapter, I will discuss the stories and images that are the focus of the spiritual entrepreneur Esther Utsi (see Figure 7.1). Esther, until February 2014, ran the Sámi tourist resort Polmakmoen Guesthouse and is the head organizer of a pilgrimage called "The Seven Coffee Stops," which starts at Polmakmoen and ends at Kjølnes Lighthouse in Berlevåg, which is also run by Esther and houses a restaurant and a guesthouse.[4,5] This chapter explores the role of religion, in the form of Sámi shamanism, in the construction of these tourist venues, and it focuses on the manner in which religion is part of the commodity presented—how spirituality is produced, packaged, and staged. I also discuss how one woman's religious experiences can be linked to both local and economic development, and to visions of new images of the northern region.[6]

BACKGROUND—REPRESENTATIONS
OF SÁMI PASTS AND PRESENTS

The tourism industry provides an important view into cultural heritage production as well as into place branding and marketing. It is therefore also important to look at what elements and components are selected to represent a chosen culture in the context of tourism, in which some cultural elements are put at the forefront while others are silenced. When it comes to the contemporary tourism industry in northern Scandinavia, the local tourist boards offer travels to the north to experience the Aurora Borealis in the winter and the midnight sun in the summer. Across this seasonal variation, we find the promotion of Sámi culture, often labeled as "genuine Sámi culture" as an important all-round year tourist attraction (see Mathisen 2014).

Although the prevailing narratives of Sámi people and culture in the context of tourism have changed through time, they all play on closeness to nature and landscape and can be said to be deeply embedded in old traditions of Western primitivism and imaginaries about the Noble Savage (Mathisen 2001). Representations and displays of Sámi people and culture through varying forms and with shifting purposes have taken place over a long time span. In 1822, one of the first known exhibitions of Sámi culture was arranged in the Egyptian Hall in Piccadilly, London. Together with a herd of reindeer, a Southern Sámi family bemused enthusiastic visitors. In the course of the 1800s, more such exhibitions were established and all achieved great popularity and interest (Baglo 2011). During the 1900s, Sámi culture was made available for both cruise and road travelers. Sámi camps were organized and summer homes along the road were equipped with sales sheds (Viken 2002:2).

In the marketing of Sápmi, it is primarily the nomadic herding culture, the reindeer, *lavvo*, *joik*, and *gákti* (traditional Sámi clothing) that have been highlighted as Sámi markers and become picturesque materializations of certain aspects of the Artic landscape and its inhabitants. According to folklorist Stein Mathisen, versions of Sámi reindeer-herding culture are "central symbols for a way of life that represents harmony with nature and the environment and that offers a special kind of indigenous, spiritual conscience" (2015:204).

As anthropologist Kjell Olsen notes in a study reviewing representation of Norwegian Sámi in local and regional tourism brochures, "these representations give an impression of the Sámi that perpetuates their image as radically different from Norwegians" (2006:37). Referring to the stereotypical portrayal of Sámi as "the emblematic Sámi," Olsen points out that the portrayals in contemporary tourist brochures are not significantly different from representations of the Sámi displayed during the world exhibition in London in 1822. Even though society has developed significantly in the approximately two hundred years that have passed since the world exhibition, the representations of the Sámi people has not changed appreciably (Olsen 2003, 2006).

Spiritual Entrepreneurship

The promotion of Sámi culture in the tourism industry in many ways corresponds to an increasing tendency to highlight religious symbols and conceptions in the marketing of a tourist destination. New Age spiritualities are also a part of this growing trend. As a marketing source in the context of tourism, New Age references have the ability to create an aura of magic around a given destination. By using both global New Age values in terms of words and expressions with spiritual connotations like magic, energy, and self-development, and in terms of drawing on ancient local traditions, an aura of magic is established. This connection to the New Age in the context of tourism has increased and a growing number of tour operators have discovered this market during the past twenty years (Cogswell 1996).

New Age spirituality is interpreted as part of an established reservoir of shared cultural symbols and as a tool for increased sales and productivity. This means that the tourism venues in focus are not limited to tourists in search of religious experiences. The entrepreneurships presented are flexible businesses built around a concept that can be toned down, adjusted, and extended to different groups of customers—to spiritual as well as to secular tourists.

To frame the relationship between tourism and New Age spirituality, I identify actors in the tourism sector who draw inspiration from New Age philosophy, as spiritual entrepreneurs (see Fonneland 2011, 2012a, 2012b). This concept refers to businesses in which New Age expressions, symbols, and concepts are part of the marketing strategies and the products sold. Words and intangible goods like "spirituality," "holism," "deep values," and "self-development," which are central within New Age, appear here as important concepts in the production of unique experiences for consumption in the tourist market.

The relationship between tourism and religious or spiritual experiences has been debated for a long time in anthropological, sociological, and religious historical research on tourism (see MacCannell 1976; Turner and Turner 1978; Graburn 1989; Stausberg 2011). In addition, the theories of the gurus of modern experience economy, Joseph B. Pine and James H. Gilmore, are relevant to this research. Pine and Gilmore see a significant change in contemporary consumers who are no longer only concerned with buying goods and services but who increasingly seek engaging and "transformative" adventures. In the future, Gilmore and Pine emphasize, the ability to create personal experiences will give companies and enterprises a sustainable competitive advantage, experiences being the hottest commodities the market has to offer (1999, 2007).

In "The Varieties of the Spiritual Tourist Experience" (2012), Alex Norman lists five categories which he finds are at the core of spiritual tourist experiences, namely healing, experimental, quest, retreat, and collective. Polmakmoen Guesthouse houses all of these overlapping aspects. The wording "spiritual tourism," however, does not mean that the tourist taking part in the tourism offer achieves a personal spiritual or religious experience. Rather it emphasizes the organizers' marketing strategies and their aim to create a tourist experience that breaks from everyday routines and is both in demand and unique.

The ways and the degree to which spiritual entrepreneurs connect to New Age philosophy vary. A combination of a variety of spiritual and secular offerings and services is probably more typical, because a combination makes it easier to survive financially. Many spiritual entrepreneurs work within niche markets with uncertain economic outlooks, in which the values created are of a cultural, aesthetic, or symbolic character rather than purely economic (see Hess 1993; Birch 1996; Mulcock 2001). The interaction between economic models for religious activities and religious meaning production is here central.

Several religious entrepreneurs explicitly present themselves as businesses in which you can find a combination of commercial interests with a vision of a life project that goes beyond the commercial.

POLMAKMOEN GUESTHOUSE

We are now ready for a trip to northern Norway, to Polmak in Tana municipality, where the concept of spiritual entrepreneurship will be contextualized through an encounter with the hostess of Polmakmoen Guesthouse. On one of the last days with glimpses of the sun before the dark season begins, I am off to Tana. After a two-hour drive from the nearest airport in Vadsø, I approach my destination. In a desolate and sparsely populated landscape covered in snow, three kilometers from the center of the municipality, I see a sign with the words "Polmakmoen Guesthouse" and turn into the courtyard.

The spiritual entrepreneurship of Esther Utsi in Tana, Finnmark, illustrates many of the tendencies referred to earlier and is, in addition, perhaps the most elaborate example in my material. Today in her mid-sixties, Esther in 1997 resigned from her job as head of the local social department in Finnmark county to set up Polmakmoen Guesthouse—a venue designed to meet the needs of spiritual seekers, tourists, and companies in search of an inspirational break and facilities for team building. The hostess collaborates with various local tourist entrepreneurs, and her business is supported by Innovation Norway, the Norwegian government's most important instrument for innovation and development of Norwegian enterprises and industry (see Fonneland 2012a).

Polmakmoen Guesthouse is a tourist and conference center situated on the banks of the Tana River in Norway's northernmost county, Finnmark, often presented as the heartland of Sámi culture (see Figure 7.2). "Come to Tana and the fairy tale is yours" is the title of a promotional video on Polmakmoen Guesthouse's website. Polmakmoen is here presented as a place where guests can feel at home and in a different world at the same time. Words such as tranquillity, magic, and wild nature are central in the marketing and combine to create a picture of Polmakmoen as a resort far away from hectic everyday life; the website

FIGURE 7.2
Polmakmoen Guesthouse.

presents this place as a land of fairy tales, where your longings for peace and inner harmony will be fulfilled.

Polmakmoen used to be the home of Esther's grandparents. Here, in the early twentieth century, Esther's grandmother started a private overnight inn for clergy and other public officials visiting Polmak. The story has it that she refused to budge when the whole area of Neiden was burned to the ground during the Second World War; and by doing so, she prevented her house from being set on fire by the German soldiers. As the hostess at Polmakmoen Guesthouse, since 1985, Esther is in many ways continuing her grandmother's life project, albeit in different and expanded forms.

Standing in the yard at Polmakmoen, looking out over the large bare area she has been told to convert into an attractive tourist and conference venue, Esther feels anxiety about how to pay for all the necessary investment. Suddenly the calming voice of her grandmother fills the air. "Ale moraš" it says—the Sámi for "leave your anxiety behind—do not worry." From that day on, the slogan, "ale moraš" became Esther's trademark, and the central content in everything she wishes to convey to her guests.

The idea behind the whole concept at Polmakmoen is to provide guests with an integrated package—a package that incorporates both an outer and an inner level. In the interview, Esther emphasizes that the trip to Polmak is a starting point for an inner journey, with wilderness adventures, meditation, healing, Sámi shamanism, and self-development courses as boosters. The website proclaims that this is: "one of the most exciting journeys you will ever experience."[7] Constructing Polmak as a unique destination paves the way for a variety of experiences and inner development, in contact with nature and in association with a Sámi hostess, and a niche product thus takes shape that has value in today's market.

Polmakmoen represents a tourism site that in many ways is unique and innovative in the northern Norwegian and perhaps also in a larger Norwegian context. The philosophy of the New Age market is here mixed with tourism and conference enterprises, offered both to spiritual seekers and the general public. The guest resort presents a vision of crossovers between religion, local development, and tourism, combining local traditions with global trends.

The Guesthouse can be seen as a venue for self-development designed to meet the needs of spiritual seekers, tourists, and companies in search of an inspirational break, and facilities for team building. The premises consist of several modern equipped Sámi turf huts, a large star-shaped hut—used for meals, entertainment, and spiritual offers—an Indian style sweat lodge, and a house used as conference venue. Visitors are welcomed with narratives about Esther's own spiritual calling and development, including communication with Sámi ancestors and native Canadian Indians. During dinner, which she herself cooks and serves, she entertains guest with tales from Sámi traditions, along with meditation sessions accompanied by Sámi folk music, *joik*.

Outside of meals, guests can choose between various products typical of the New Age scene, but here presented as rooted in Sámi shamanism, including crystal therapies, individual healing sessions, and self-development courses, the latter offered to groups as well as to single persons. Among other activities offered are salmon fishing in the Tana River, snowmobile tours, mountain hiking, and social gatherings with stories about local Sámi culture and performances of the traditional Sámi *joik*.

The creation of a narrative about a product is a strong tool in the contemporary experience economy (Mossberg 2007:321). In the context of tourism, such narratives are ways of encoding customers' reading of a place and steering their perceptions of a culture as an attractive and unique "experience package." At Polmakmoen Guesthouse as well as in the pilgrimage, Esther's personal life story plays a central part in the product that is being marketed. The main themes in the story expressed are her Sámi background and her spiritual calling to build a tourist resort.

Esther talks of how she grew up in a Sámi family. Her father was a reindeer herder and her mother took care of their farm and nine children while her husband was away watching reindeer. She describes her parents as opposites, her mother representing a rational world concerned with the family's economy and well-being, and her father connected to the spirituality of nature and to Sámi traditions. He came home telling Esther and her siblings stories about *gufihtar*, "the invisible people," and all the strange and mysterious things that happened to him and the herd while away. Esther remembers the excitement she felt listening to him. She points out that he communicated with the spiritual world of his ancestors and received messages from his spiritual helpers concerning the farm, his family, and friends. According to Esther, she has inherited both her father's and her mother's qualities. In our conversation she says:

In the first thirty-five years of my life, I was guided by my mum's rational thinking, but after the age of thirty-five I came closer to the stories

and experiences my dad had contributed. Alternative books started fall-
ing into my lap. I began reading these books and learned that we have
spiritual helpers and that we can communicate and get information
from them just as my father had told me—though the books used dif-
ferent words for it. But when it came to the point that my helpers told
me that I should quit my job as chief of the social department in Tana
municipality and begin to heal, and that I was to start a centre here at
Polmakmoen, it felt like a rather dramatic and scary life change that
I was not certain I could follow.

Esther points out that she had for a time felt burned out in her work
as leader of the local social department. She felt exhausted and pow-
erless and started reading alternative literature to find new ideas and
answers. She describes this period as a crossroads and as an opening in
which adopting New Age perspectives allowed her to get in touch with
her Sámi ancestors and her spiritual helpers.

In our conversation, she describes how these helpers had contacted
her twice delivering the same message each time. The third time was
a turning point. According Sámi traditions, a third message is the last
one the spirits will bring, meaning if you relate to the spirits as a reality, there are no spirits coming the fourth time (see Alver 1999:156).
Being familiar with this tradition, Esther says she finally realized the
seriousness of the message and she promised to leave her job in Tana
municipality, a safe and well-paid job she had held for eighteen years,
and by the summer 1997 she slowly started developing what would be
known as Polmakmoen Guesthouse.

Esther started marketing Polmakmoen as a place where visitors can
let go of their anxiety, stress, and worries, and she finds that there is
a great need in society for this type of experience—the experience of
spirituality, silence, and tranquillity:

TRUDE: *But when you market Polmakmoen, what do you choose to*
present as the core values of this place?
ESTHER: *The main factor is that people feel very harmonic and peaceful*
when they arrive here. I used to say that troubled kids sleep here and

stubborn men turn into butter (laughter). Something happens to peo-
ple at Polmakmoen. It is the peace that does it first and foremost ...
that visitors get an opportunity to seek inwards. I have seen what
happens to people when they come here, and that is what happens.
That is what I say has happened and surely is going to happen next
time as well. Other factors that I promote are the good homemade
Arctic food and the homey atmosphere.

By setting up Polmak as a unique destination that paves the way for
a variety of experiences and inner development in contact with nature
and in association with a Sámi hostess, a niche product takes shape
that has value in today's economy market.

ENVISIONING A NEW BUSINESS COMMUNITY

In our conversation, Esther emphasizes that when Polmakmoen was
turned into a tourist, healing, and conference center, her spiritual helpers told her that her second task was to take part in the creation of a
new business community and to help change the ideas and perspectives
of people in key business positions. Esther's vision for Polmakmoen
Guesthouse thus goes beyond being a destination for vacationers
and conference participants. Her hope is that the personal, spiritual,
and cultural experience she offers her guests will have an impact at a
higher, political level and will contribute to the development of a new
economic era:

ESTHER: *I got a message relating to what kind of people would come*
to Polmakmoen. My helpers told me that I would be working with
the top rung in Norwegian politics, business, and industry. They were
to come here and get new ideas related to the new knowledge that is
reflected in the Age of Aquarius, which we entered about twenty years
ago. And it was the people at the top level who needed this knowl-
edge first, to be able to change their thinking. Above all things, I was
told that I should participate in building a new business community,
and I was forced to wonder; "Should I work with the new business

community, I who have zero bearing on economics?" But later I have found out that this is exactly why, because if I had been an economist I would have had too much ballast with me from all the things that should not be with us anymore. So I have since been commissioned to use what I have built up here to bring the new business community into reality.

As Stef Aupers and Dick Houtman emphasize, New Age spirituality has taken root within the public domain of business organizations, and courses focusing on spirituality are held for the purpose of promoting both well-being and efficiency—in happiness and profit (2006:211–214). Polmakmoen Guesthouse is used as a site for conferences and courses by firms such as Statoil and Volvo, by the Norwegian government as represented by some of its ministries, and by the Sámi Parliament. Even if they do not take part in organized New Age courses, these firms and politicians are all introduced to Esther's standard repertoire concerning her spiritual experiences in developing Polmakmoen Guesthouse. For these and other visitors, Esther says she wants to be a mediator—a bridge between the normal and the paranormal, between human beings and spiritual powers, in order to bring about a new business community based on the values of a Sámi indigenous spirituality. These are values relating to spirituality, to a premodern local Sámi society and to "slow money"—to the exchange of gifts and services rather than money exchange:

TRUDE: *But when you talk about the new business community, what is the core of it?*

ESTHER: *It is that we will work out a business that is driven by the joy of creating, not profit. It is creativity, not money that you should have as the core in everything you do when you build something up. For it is not that we shall be without money, for one or other means of exchange we need. And that's fine; money does have value. However, I think we will see a development toward exchanging goods and services.*

Esther's visions about changing the current business community are related to her experiences in developing Polmakmoen Guesthouse. The first years were marked by economic uncertainty and the bankruptcy of the guesthouse in 2004. Esther was subsequently able to buy the resort back, and these experiences created the seed for what Esther today proclaims as the core values in the new economy. On several occasions, Esther has lectured on this topic and relates it to the development of a creative rural economy and to a new sustainable northern Norwegian region.

To create a package that is both appealing and believable, in the interview and on the website, Esther walks a fine line between a rational and a spiritual worldview. To survive in the tourist market and to be able to take part in changing the business community, she argues, you cannot focus on spirituality alone. She stresses that, by inheriting both her mother's and her father's qualities, she has a foot in the rational as well as in the spiritual world. Though a well-known healer, Esther never takes part in the popular alternative markets mentioned earlier; and by keeping a distance from the most iconic New Age marketplaces, she can be said to maintain a seriousness that is required in the tourist industry. Her focus on the rational also serves to counter and to play with national myths describing people in the northern region as both "noble" and as "ignoble savages" (see Mathisen 2010). The balance between the spiritual and rational in the marketing of Polmakmoen creates credibility and strengthens Esther's role as an entrepreneur in the tourist market.

Through the Sámi slogan "ale moraš," Esther's goal is to reshape both her visitors and the business community. These words encapsulate the values that she perceives as fundamental for a new economic era and a new industrial life to develop for the best, both for the individual and for the environment. In the process of bringing the message of "ale moraš" to the world, Esther even recruited President Barack Obama as one of her helpers. When the President was awarded the Nobel Peace Prize in 2010, Esther knew she had to go to Oslo to give him the words her grandmother had been telling her. Dressed in her Sámi kofte, with a small handmade *lavvo* of reindeer skin with the slogan "Ale moraš" neatly embroidered in silver, she took off to the capital to greet the president. The *lavvo* was handed over to the Nobel Institute and later given to Obama himself. Local and national media took up the case, and Esther thus had the opportunity to convey her message through TV, radio, and the press.

Just how much people change, if at all, after their visit to Polmakmoen is uncertain and beyond my focus in this chapter. In the interview it thus remains unclear how the relaxation of key business people in the tranquil environment of Polmak, and the loosening of their ties to the modern world, can trigger a real change in the business community. What is significant is how Esther promotes this as a central value of the location, and that the media has become involved in this marketing.

"THE SEVEN COFFEE STOPS"

Guests who wish to explore further the local area or their own inner depths are invited to take part in the wandering "The Seven Coffee Stops" by foot, on skis, or by car, according to the seasons (see Figure 7.3). This tourist offer can be related to a concept within the global field of tourism that in recent years has steadily increased in popularity, namely the pilgrimage. In Norway, the interest in pilgrim walks has increased substantially from the late 1990s. Pilgrim routes have been marked and, according to the national pilgrimage center, the number of organized trips and number of walkers rises annually.[8] "The Seven Coffee Stops" is organized as a walking route with related stories and experiences from the first to the seventh coffee stop. According to the hostess, the goal is that the journey, in addition to implying a physical movement and an experience of new places, will also lead to increased self-awareness and inner well-being. Esther Utsi herself draws parallels to Santiago de Compostela, which is one of the oldest and most popular pilgrimages in Europe, and describes "The Seven Coffee Stops" as a northerly and modern variant.

According to Ian Reader, modern pilgrimages "provide a way of dealing with individual needs without commitment to organised

FIGURE 7.3
"The Seven Coffee Stops."

traditions and even with the rejection of religion as an organised entity" (2007:226). "The Seven Coffee stops" belongs under this category and more precisely, it can be described as a New Age pilgrimage. A primary concern related to these types of pilgrimages is that the wandering is highlighted as a discovery project in which the wandering is a goal in itself and the religious insight, the self-development, an individual process in which no religious answers are given in their final form (see Kraft 2007a:47; Selberg 2011:124–126).

New Age pilgrimages like "The Seven Coffee Stops" are marketed toward those who do not exclusively wish to travel to see a new place, take pictures, and travel on, but toward those who wish to take part and become one with a chosen destination, through meditation, healing, and other types of ceremonies and rituals (Attix 2002; Ivakhiv 2003). The New Age pilgrim nevertheless shares many characteristics with other middle-class tourists. In addition to the focus on self-actualization and religious self-development, more pro-saic motives like nature experiences, culinary adventures, and social-izing are included in the New Age pilgrimage (see Gilhus and Kraft 2007:15–17).

Rountree notes that the pilgrim urge among New Age pilgrims is motivated by a nostalgia for the values that they feel have been lost in modern Western society. To go to places that are being marketed as sacred is an attempt to satisfy this nostalgia. The New Age pil-grim seeks an inner development through a journey to places that are regarded as more primitive and natural, removed from an urban and Western everyday life (2002:491). This further indicates an understat-ing of remote places of the world, as places where age-old traditions have been preserved in unchanged forms and kept alive in the shadow of dominant ideologies (see Selberg 2015). The past here takes on a mythological dimension and is said to add a new dimension to the modern pilgrim's life and understandings. It is also these perspectives that Esther highlights as key marketing tools with regard to "The Seven Coffee Stops":

> We will take you on a journey that will reveal what the reindeer herders of the Utsi family experienced and still experiences accompanying the herd from inland to coast. We follow the way the reindeer move from winter to summer pastures in spring and autumn.... On this exciting journey, you can drive a car or bus, paddle, bike, walk or be transported by boat between the various coffee stops along the route—or you can choose to focus on only one or two of the coffee stops. Each coffee stop is connected to a theme that describes the area and through activities, food, and stories you will get to know more about Sámi culture.... We will do our best to make you leave not only with a full stomach but also with a filled HEART. (http://www.polmakmoen-gjestegard.no/kaf-fekok1.html, my translation)

The pilgrimage is organized according to the participants' needs and their available time. On Polmakmoen Guesthouse's homepage, eight optional tours are presented that vary in length and in forms of organization. A coffee stop is a local measurement related to three factors: distance, time, and relationships. Traditionally a coffee stop referred to selected sites of rest in the landscape where one stopped to take a break and to boil coffee on the fire. These sites were also seen as social gathering places where relationships were created.

This pilgrimage at one level refers to particular places in the landscape where a chosen narrative and tastes and smells connected to Sámi reindeer herding traditions are carried out. Esther has made a repertoire of stories from her own family's life and work on the Varanger plateau with topics that emphasize key tasks and challenges related to the work of the reindeer herders and their families.

At another level, it refers to the seven chakras of the human body. A chakra is in New Age literature presented as the connecting link between body and soul; for a person to be healthy, the seven charkas must be in balance, and if imbalance occurs, it will spread through the body and cause disease (see Sherwood 2009; White 2000). Each coffee stop is meant to represent one of the body's chakras and on an inner level the pilgrimage thus is a journey starting at the root chakra and ending at the crown chakra. Esther emphasizes:

> So every coffee stop then has a theme which describes the culture, the nature, food, and history so that the guests will learn more about the area. This is the first dimension. The second dimension is the human body's seven chakras that you are helping to open when you travel through the coffee stops.

"The Seven Coffee Stops" thus involve old wisdom and more recent mythology, along with wildlife experiences and the physical challenge and joy of walking. It also involves, last, but not least, a link between the Sámi herders of the past and late modern pilgrims. Here the Sámi past is unfolding through links to both New Age core values and to a Sámi heritage. The growth in the pilgrim's inner landscape therefore does not occur in a vacuum, but occurs through meeting and interacting with nature, with other pilgrims, the guide, and in this case also through the mediation of a selected Sámi cultural history expressed through stories about Esther family's life on the Varanger plateau. This presence involves an invocation of old wisdom and mythology, a connection between place and practice and a mythical connection between Sámi reindeer herders who worked in the area and late modern pilgrims (see Coats 2011:122).

SPIRITUALITY AS CULTURAL MARKER

Esther Utsi can be placed in the religious landscape of late modernity—being inspired both by New Age thinking and by her father's relation to the spirits of nature. This type of spirituality can be seen according to the frames of what I have referred to as indigenous spirituality. Indigenous spirituality is at the core of Esther's personal narratives, of her self-understanding and of the product she markets. At Polmakmoen Guesthouse and during the pilgrimage, a Sámi mythology is connected to a selected New Age mythology, which together create an understanding of the landscape as unique.

The opening scene in the advertisement video on Polmakmoen Guesthouse's website further highlights the role of this discourse as a marketing tool. Here we meet a Sámi man singing the *joik*. He looks out over the Finnmark plateau and takes us to an old Sámi sacrificial stone, where he ritually hands over a piece of reindeer meat to his ancestors, saying: "*Nature has given us this as a loan. With thanks we give nature back its share.*" Further along in the promotional video, we meet men and women dressed in traditional Sámi clothes, the *gákti*, gathered around the fire in a traditional Sámi tent, the *lavvo*. We see white snow-covered landscape, herds of reindeer, and people traveling in the countryside enjoying activities such as fishing, hunting, and berry picking. The special character of the destination is strongly linked to experiencing nature, an exotic culture, local food, and entertaining narratives. The video illustrates an inner and outer tranquillity, far from the bustle of the city, where the landscape and activities surrounded by nature invite one to experience inner peace. During the ten minutes that the video lasts, a picture is established, of the Sámi as a people living in harmony with their surroundings and in close contact with the traditions of the past, and underlines that visitors coming to Polmak will be able to experience and take part in the same values themselves.

The commercial relationship at Polmakmoen and in the pilgrimage is presented as characterized by intimacy. Visitors' meetings with their Sámi hostess are clearly meant to contribute beneficially to their inner, personal development. Here, tourists are not just tourists or anonymous customers; instead, they are able to become part of a homelike atmosphere that goes beyond a routine tourist scenario. Tourists coming to Polmakmoen and tourists taking part in "The Seven Coffee Stops" are being invited into an indigenous community and, by this means, to taste the magic and holism of nature.

The term "indigenous spirituality" is in many ways a cultural marker set in contrast to Western society, Western religions, and Western worldviews. Values related to nature and to the landscape mark a distinction between a place-oriented, peaceful, holistic, traditional, and eco-friendly indigenous culture and a modern Western capitalistic society (Kraft 2009:188). In this context, indigenous spirituality represents a unique product that adds value to a destination by telling a different story and representing a unique experience far removed from the daily Western life. The performance of an indigenous spirituality can be seen here as a powerful instrument for creating strong and persuasive experiences. As researchers have underlined, at the heart of the tourist industry and the new economy lies a quest for what is different, and one of the primary narratives in the tourism industry concerns precisely the relationship between the modern and the traditional (Kirshenblatt-Gimblett 1998:153; Gilmore and Pine 1999; Wang 2000; Olsen 2006).

Anthropologist Ronald Niezen has referred to notions of an indigenous *we* (2003, 2009, 2012) as one outcome of the processes of indigenous resistance and revival. As one of several scholars, he points to a religious dimension of indigenous people's identity making, consisting of elements such as shamanism and animism, sacred places, environmental awareness, and holism (see also Beyer 1998; Kraft 2009). He claims that in contemporary times, "the notion of 'indigenous religion' has been so thoroughly conventionalized that most Euro-American lay people presented with it would likely have some notion of what is meant by it, probably by drawing upon related ideas associated with such things as shamanism and forest spirituality" (2012:119). These notions have a widespread reach, but their main locations seems to be UN forums, academia, music, festivals, and tourism contexts (see Graham and Penny 2014).

The fact that Sámi culture has become part of an international indigenous community in which discourses about indigenous spirituality are part of the symbolic repertoire has considerable consequences for how the Sámi culture is staged in the tourist industry. Polmakmoen Guesthouse and "The Seven Coffee Stops" are clear examples of such new marketing and communication of Sámi as indigenous, in which words like *spirituality, holism, harmony, closeness to nature,* and *a mythological past* are central themes. As a spiritual entrepreneur, Esther's mission here is to showcase Finnmark as a country of resources, rich in delicate ingredients, great scenery, lighting, colors, and not least, spiritual energies.

MEDIA DISCOURSES

Perhaps the single most interesting ingredient of Esther's business is the more or less complete lack of criticism typically granted to spiritual entrepreneurs promoting New Age values. Much like elsewhere in the Western world, New Age is situated low on the Norwegian scale of good, decent, or even real religions. Considered as a fake more than a "real" religion, New Age is commonly represented as a money-making machine, whose professional agents are cynical and greedy, on the one hand, and naive and silly, on the other (Kraft 2011). Esther, in sharp contrast to the status of her New Age colleagues, has established herself as a media darling and a local hero. She has several times been nominated for the title "Finnmarking of the Year," based upon votes to local candidates on the basis of personal achievements, and both local and national media portray her as a courageous, enterprising, and creative entrepreneur whose novel projects and ideas have helped put Finnmark on the map.[9] In the words of her local newspaper:

> Utsi is a driven woman in the travel industry in eastern Finnmark. She runs both Kjølnes lighthouse and Polmakmoen Guesthouse. And the number of this year's visitors has been overwhelming. (*Finnmark Dagblad*, July 23, 2010)

This then, is the image of a creative woman, able to keep alive the traditions she has inherited and adjust them to the needs of modern society. In line with this image, the spiritual dimension of her endeavors is commonly referred to as Sámi spiritual traditions. Placed in the traditional surroundings of Polmakmoen Guesthouse and the pilgrimage "the Seven Coffee Stops," even well-known New Age markers like crystals, pendulums, and chakras are interpreted as a natural part of ancient Sámi traditions. My argument is that the positivity surrounding her is also connected to the distance she keeps from the New Age market, both through her remote geographical location (Finnmark being far away from the New Age core area) and through her deliberate linking of the marketing of spirituality to Sámi local traditions.

Esther's two sources of inspiration, New Age and Sámi indigenous spirituality, have come to symbolize two different sets of values. In a market and media context, Esther's latest inspiration, New Age, is often characterized as lacking roots in tradition—as fake. Indigenous spirituality, on the other hand, seems to enjoy a positive image, associated with values such as wisdom, the ancient, heritage, environmental protection, and knowledge about nature (Kraft 2009). When, on the website, healing with crystals and pendulums are transferred from their New Age context and presented as a natural part of a Sámi indigenous religion, here known as Sámi shamanism, this can be seen as a move to enhance the attractiveness of the product and to maintain a distance between the traditional and the modern. By keeping a distance from the typical New Age markets and by connecting the site's religious aspects to Sámi culture more than to New Age, Esther increases the significance of Polmakmoen Guesthouse and the pilgrimage in the tourist industry.

In contrast to the perceived shallowness of the New Age, the link to a Sámi past and Sámi indigenous spiritual traditions offers a strikingly distinctive brand, and it projects the assurance of a unique product, experience, or service.

The relatively frequent and solely positive media attention can also be said to make Esther and her spiritual entrepreneurship a central actor in regional development processes.

CONCLUSION

Through the selection of symbols and stories that Esther presents to her guests, Polmakmoen Guesthouse and "the Seven Coffee Stops" are cast as vacation destinations that are also portals to a magical world where untamed nature and spirituality are central values. The location in a rural environment and contact with Sámi culture are projected as generating internal growth and development. However, the story of Polmakmoen Guesthouse and the pilgrimage is also a story about politics and about a woman who, using her remote location as a starting point, wants to reform the world community. Tourism includes both politics and power. As Michael Hall argues:

> Despite its common consumer association with pleasure and leisure, perhaps as far away from politics as one can get in the popular mind, tourism does not occur in a political vacuum. In fact few subjects better illustrate the political dimensions of tourism than the issues associated with indigenous tourism. Whether it be decisions as to where tourism development occurs or more humanistic concerns associated with commodification and representation of heritage and identity, tourism is political. (2007:306)

Though Polmakmoen Guesthouse is a place of relaxation and well-being, it is also a place in which the local and global are intertwined. The story of power and politics that is illustrated through my conversation with Esther can be seen in the context of a whole raft of cultural events and projects in northern Norway in recent years. Both the Mandela concert, held in Tromsø in June 2005, and Tromsø's application for the Winter Olympics in 2014/2018, point toward a common aim which we can glimpse in Esther's story (see Kraft 2008; Guneriussen 2008). In different ways, they all involve replacing the traditional image of northern Norway.

In late modernity, the construction of local and specific identities positions people, products, and services as particularly valuable and authentic. This is a positioning that allows adaption to a global world and at the same time opens up responses and opposition (Robertson 1992; Featherstone 1995; Beyer 1998). Globalization and communications technology make it possible for local communities to relate to other places in the world and to create networks that cross national borders. This is also a process where new narratives about the local community's culture and history occur: narratives that challenge familiar notions of what is central and what is peripheral. Though not necessarily denying a position as peripheral, the juggling with symbolic representations can be said to counter hierarchical relations from within. At this point places that have so far been peripheral in a national context, such as Northern Norway, are made central in global stories (see Granås 2009).

It is precisely this transformation of the northern Norwegian landscape that Esther reveals in our interview. By assigning a local community values as spiritual, magical, and mythical, as well as rational, Esther's story challenges established representations in which northern Norway represents the peripheral, and is economically, ethnically, and culturally marginalized. The intellectual balance of her representation, and the distance she maintains from the iconic New Age markets, contradict the image of Finnmark as an uncivilized outpost of modernity. At the same time, they point to values of a spiritual character which the Western community is lacking—values that Esther argues are central in contemporary economic processes for setting a new business community in motion.

On February 24, 2011, Esther was a key guest on the TV show "Svendsen om Hansen og Jensen" on TV2, one of Norway's largest national TV channels, a show which sets out to investigate whether myths about people in the different regions of Norway match reality. This broadcast discussed myths related to the Sámi and the fact that most Norwegians have the impression that all Sámi are reindeer herders and that they are rough and superstitious. The TV host, Truls Svendsen, took a trip to the Finnmark plateau to check out the myths, and here he visited, among other places, Polmakmoen Guesthouse.

At Polmakmoen, Esther gave Truls a lecture about her visions for her guest resort. The TV host also participated in a healing session in Esther's healing room decorated with Native American dream catchers. After the meeting with Esther, the myth that Sámi are superstitious was examined and revised: no longer presenting Sámi people as superstitious, but rather, as spiritual, in a positive sense.

In the TV show Esther was presented as a representative for all Sámi, thus casting the Sápmi region or nation as exotic and spiritual. To a national audience of TV viewers, the Sámi people were in one turn "demythicized" as superstitious and "remythicized" as spiritual. The change in mythical content also implies a change in status and power. Spirituality was here seen as a resource, not as an emblematic stigma locating the Sámi population outside modern life and development (see Mathisen 2010). From being seen as an outside civilization, the landscape of the Sámi was presented as a center—with Esther and her spiritual businesses as the context.

With the Sámi slogan "Ale moraš," Esther wants to make Finnmark a site for innovative change in economics and business—a small handmade *lavvo* in the White House symbolizing the big step from periphery to center.

PRESENTATION
OF INTERVIEWEES

Ailo Gaup (1944–2014) was born in Guovdageaidnu (Kautokeino) in the county of Finnmark, Northern Norway. At the age of seven, he was adopted and moved south to grow up in a Norwegian family and lost access to Sámi language and culture. He studied to become a journalist, and he is also a known Sámi author. Ailo trained as a shaman at Michael Harner's institute at Esalen, California. He has written several books on shamanism and held extensive shamanic training courses across the country, known as *Saivo shaman school*.

Ronald Kvernmo who is in his forties works full time as a Sámi shaman and is the leader of the shamanic festival Isogaisa. He was trained by Ailo, who encouraged him to embrace his Sámi roots and to further develop the field of Sámi shamanism. Ronald has held several courses in Sámi shamanism, explicitly focusing on Sámi gods and goddesses. He has also written the book *The Shaman's Secrets* (2010) and runs his own shaman blog http://isogaisablogg.blogspot.no/.

Kyrre Gram Franck is the founder and the leader of the denomination Shamanistic Association on a national level. He is in his forties and his shaman name is White Cougar. He emphasizes that Sámi as well as North and South American religious traditions inspire him. Kyrre is also the vision keeper and cofounder of *The World Drum Project*.[1] On his mother's side of the family, Kyrre is of Sámi descent.

Lone Ebeltoft is a Norwegian woman from Vadsø, Northern Norway, and the leader of the Shamanistic Association's local branch in the county of Troms. She is in her forties and runs her own design firm known as Alveskogen, where she designs new clothes and accessories inspired by the Middle Ages and Arctic indigenous clothing. These clothes are popular among shamanic practitioners and are often used at ceremonies and during rituals.

Eirik Myrhaug started practicing as a shaman in the late 1990s, and he claims to have had Sámi shamans in his family for centuries. Eirik who is in his seventies became known throughout the country due to his participation in a popular TV show "Jakten på den 6.sans" (The quest for the sixth sense) in Norway in 2008, a competition where he gained second place. Eirik also organizes courses in shamanism and is the leader of the denomination "Kosmologisk Livstro" (Cosmological Life Faith).

Arthur Sørrensen is a shaman in his seventies from Bergen, Western Norway. Like Gaup he received his training as a shaman at Michael Harner's institute and has written a book about his experiences at Esalen, *Sjamanen: en rituell invielse* (*The Shaman a Ritual Initiation*) (1988). Since the late 1980s Arthur has organized shamanic courses and gatherings and was for a time leader of the Shamanistic Association's local branch in Hordaland.[2]

Anita Biong is in her seventies and grew up in a small community on the Finnmark coast. She claims to come from a family that for generations has practiced clairvoyance and healing. In her youth, she moved to Oslo, the Norwegian capital. She has been educated as an NLP (Neuro-Linguistic Programming) practitioner and works full time as a shaman. Anita has also been a staple exhibitor on the Alternative fairs since the fairs' start-up in 1992.

Esther Utsi is a Sámi woman in her mid-sixties from Tana in Finnmark, northern Norway. She has been involved in the Sámi tourism industry for many years and ran until recently her own Guesthouse at Polmakmoen in the county of Finnmark. At the guesthouse, Esther organized conferences for firms seeking facilities for team building. Esther also offers guests and others healing inspired by Sámi shamanism and is the head organizer of the pilgrimage "the Seven Coffee Stops" that combines elements of shamanism and New Age with stories of Sámi cultural life.

Anna (fictional name) is in her forties, and for several years, she has run her own alternative therapist firm in a city in northern Norway. She has been studying Neuro-Linguistic Programming (NLP) and attended Ailo's Saivo Shaman School. Through her firm, she organizes yearly vision wakes in a national park in the region.

Lisa (fictional name) is in her forties, lives in northern Norway, and works as an alternative therapist focusing on healing and Neuro-Linguistic Programming (NLP). She is a member of The Norwegian Healer Association (Det Norske Healerforbundet) and has been apprentice to Ailo Gaup and Eirik Myrhaug.

NOTES

CHAPTER I

1. The quote is a statement by Lone Ebeltoft, leader of the Shamanistic Association in the county of Troms.

2. The Sámi people are the indigenous people inhabiting northern Fennoscandia, which today encompasses parts of Sweden, Norway, Finland, and the Kola Peninsula of Russia. In Norway the Sámi are recognized under the international conventions of Indigenous people and are the northernmost indigenous people of Europe. Their livelihood has traditionally been based on different types of hunting, fishing, gathering, husbandry, and agriculture, with considerable variation between different Sámi groups. The most commonly used Sámi languages in Norway today are South-, Lule-, and North Sámi. In this book, I use the North Sámi orthography.

3. *Helgeland Arbeiderblad*, October 17, 2014; *Klassekampen*, October 10, 2014; *Nordlys*, October 2, 2014.

4. The Western world's fascination with shamanism is by no means a recent phenomenon. The historical background has been meticulously documented among others by Ronald Hutton (2001), Kocku von Stuckrad (2003), and Andrei Znamenski (2007).

5. https://www.manataka.org/page1563.html, accessed February 1, 2017.

6. The Church of Norway's membership comprises per 2016 approximately 77 percent of the country's 5 million inhabitants.

7. Several artists experienced the conflict as a "cultural awakening," and the Alta affair had a strong impact on Sámi art.

8. Sweden, Finland, and Russia have not yet ratified the ILO Convention.

9. ILO Convention 169, ratified by Norway in 1990, claims that governments must "respect the special importance for the cultures and spiritual values of the people concerning their relationship with the lands or territories" (Article 13, 1). Further, Article 12 and 25 of the 2007 United Nations Declaration on the Rights of Indigenous Peoples (UNDRIP) asserts that indigenous people have "the right to manifest, practice, develop and teach their spiritual and

religious traditions" (Article 12) and "the right to maintain and strengthen their distinctive spiritual relationship with their traditionally owned or otherwise occupied and used lands, territories, waters and coastal seas and other resources" (Article 25).

10. Salomonsen has also later published books with great relevance to the field of neopaganism, among them *Enchanted Feminism: Ritual, Gender and Divinity among the Reclaiming Witches of San Francisco* (2002).

CHAPTER 2

1. Jørgen I. Erikson—interview with Ailo Gaup (2009:236, my translation). The picture was printed in the newspaper *Klassekampen* March 11–12, 2006.

2. Although an increasing number of Sámi took part in the demonstrations, large parts also regarded the demonstrations as improper behavior toward governmental authorities and feared they would disrupt future interethnic relationship (Thuen 1995:45).

3. During the struggle, the first Sámi flag was designed and used as a symbol in the demonstrations. The flag's official design, differing slightly, was adopted in 1986.

4. As noted by Thomas A. Dubois, Joseph Campbell's romantic neo-Jungian approach to mythology has also exerted a major influence on many contemporary shamans (2009:266–267).

5. The Scandinavian Center for Shamanic Studies was founded in 1986. The center leads a purely virtual existence, and it is administered as an Internet website. Høst is regarded as a pioneer in bringing the ancient Norse tradition to light. In 2005, her book *Jorden synger Naturens kraft og nordiske rødder* (The Earth Sings, Nature's Power and Nordic Roots) was published. It presents an exploration of the roots of shamanism in Nordic spiritual traditions, myth, and nature.

6. Globally, Lynn Andrews (*Medicine Woman* 1983; *Jaguar Woman* and *The Wisdom of the Butterfly Tree* 1990) and Marlo Morgan (*Mutant Message from Down Under* 1995) became bestsellers on the subject.

7. Seid is a ritual practice known from Norse religion, mainly performed by women called *volver*.

8. "Wise man" is in Norwegian synonymous with a healer of folk traditions.

9. On the "reader" and the reader's characteristics, see Myrvoll 2010:148–153.

10. The development of the Isogaisa festival and the Shamanistic Association (SA) will be further discussed in Chapters 5 and 6.

11. In the highly accurate description of preserved drums presented by Ernst Manker in his two-volume book *Die lappische Zaubertrommel* (1938–1950),

eighty-one drums are described. These are found in European museums, mostly in Scandinavia (Christoffersson 2010).

12. One obtains a clear sense of these types of descriptions when looking at the titles of some of the missionaries' books: *The Muting of Idolatry* (Afguderiets dempelse) (Kildal 1727) and *On the Delusion and Superstition of the Laps* (Om lappernes vildfarelser og overtro) (Olsen 1716).

13. The term *noaidevuohta* is a literal translation of the word *shamanism*.

14. *Joik* and drums have, for instance, been forbidden in the local churches in Guovdageaidnu (Kautokeino). *Joik* was until the 1990s also banned in the local schools in the same area (see Graff 2016).

15. See Isaksen Kjellaug and Dikka Storm (2014).

16. The symbol for Internet Explorer and E6 are found to the right on the lower part of the drum skin.

17. The quote is taken from http//www.sjaman.com. This site was closed when Gaup died in September 2014.

18. http://www.shamanism.org/workshops/coreshamanism.html, accessed November 14, 2016.

19. On June 10, 1993, at the Lakota Summit V, an international gathering of US and Canadian Lakota, Dakota, and Nakota Nations, about five hundred representatives from forty different tribes and bands of the Lakota unanimously, passed a "Declaration of War Against Exploiters of Lakota Spirituality." For the text of the declaration see http://www.aics.org/war.html.

20. Asprem 2013, available at: http://arkiv.humanist.no/sjamanisme.html, accessed January 15, 2015, my translation.

CHAPTER 3

1. In Norway, the romanticism did not have real progress until the 1830s related to the works of Henrik Wergeland (1808–1845) and Johan Sebastian Welhaven (1807–1873).

2. The book *The One Dimensional Man* (1964), by philosopher Herbert Marcuse, is regarded as one of the greatest written inspirational sources of the radical youth of the 1960s and 1970s. Marcuse was inspired by the Frankfurt School, where Max Horkheimer and Theodor Adorno spearheaded criticism of the effects of the modernization process.

3. Whether the New Age movement still represents a counterculture is debatable. Some of the ideas that are expressed, particularly ideas that have to do with environmental protection, are currently so widespread that they can be said to be a part of the cultural majority. According to Hammer, the contemporary New Age should be depicted as a collective consciousness rather than

as a heterogeneous and clearly defined socioreligious movement (Hammer 2001:74).

4. Beyer gets the term "counter structure" from the religious historian Victor Turner, who analyzed the antistructural dimensions of religious rituals (Turner 1969).

5. https://www.nrk.no/sapmi/viser-stotte-til-standing-rock-sioux-folket-med-vannseremoni-i-tromso-1.13137507, accessed October 20, 2016, my translation.

6. A focus of several of the demonstrations has also been to demand that DNB, Norway's largest bank, withdraw their investment in the Dakota Access pipeline (DAPL).

7. http://www.shamanism.dk/moderneshamanisme.htm, accessed October 18, 2015, my translation.

8. The oldest dating from offering material including bones and metal objects indicate that the tradition began in ca. 500–1300 AD (compare with Salmi et al. 2015).

9. VG (February 15, 2009), my translation.

10. In summer 2016, the number of participants was reduced to 12,000. According to the organizers, the low attendance was due to the event falling on a weekday and that the event coincided with international football games involving England and Wales.

11. The action is based upon the way one defines the situation, and it corresponds to one's own ideas independently of whether the premises for the action are "true" or "false." If one defines the situation as real, it will have real consequences (see Alver 1993:8).

12. Nora has been criticized for presenting memories as something solely in the past, whereas history is localized in the modern world. This constructed division in a past and a present, where the science of history is being presented as being in contrast to a premodern culture of memory, which places Nora in the same trap as several other modernity theorists—describing premodern society as a golden age brimming with innocence and nature (see Eriksen 1999:88).

13. Seid is a divination technique described in the sagas, which involves religious possession. In the Norse society, seid was mainly exercised by women called volver. Seid magic concerns actions and techniques that by themselves are believed to be so powerful that they work without the help of Gods. It is said that the person who practiced seid could see everything that was hidden in the past and the future. She could still the sea and storm and find lost objects. This kind of knowledge made the seid-woman both feared and respected.

14. http://da2.uib.no/cgi-win/WebBok.exe?slag=lesside&bokid=ngl1&sideid=383&innhaldid=6&storleik=, accessed May 19, 2016.

15. http://www.sommersel.no/naturnar_selvutvikling.html, accessed January 9, 2013, my translation.
16. http://sjaman.com/content/view/142/2/, accessed January 28, 2013.
17. http://pagesperso-orange.fr/ville-en-mouvement/interventions/John_Urry. pdf, accessed May 28, 2009. This article was also published in *Sociology* 46 (2) in 2002.

CHAPTER 4

1. Both Salomonsen (2002) and Greenwood (2000) argue that menstrual blood is the most central symbol for womanhood in the pagan milieus they are studying.
2. At the festival, the *volve* is referred to as a female shaman in Norse traditions.
3. "Vision quests" are in most New Age literature described as being one of the most intensive shamanic rituals (see Sørenssen 1988: 84). Even if the content of the ritual varies, a well-known characteristic is that participants will spend one or more nights alone in nature, see Chapter 3.
4. Thomas von Westen (1682–1727) was a Norwegian priest and missionary among the Sámi. From 1709 he was a parish priest in Veøy in Romsdal, where he led the priest's deed "Syvstjernen" (the Pleiades), which developed a strategy for the conversion of the Sámi.
5. This is a perspective one can trace in Rose 1984, Grenn 1988, Sørbø 1988, Torgovnick 1990, Vindsetmo 1995, Myrhaug 1997, Klesse 2000, York 2001, Churchill 2003, and Wernitznig 2003. See further discussion of the subject in Chapter 2.
6. Critique against what is perceived as reactionary and wishful essentialism has also been leveled by feminist evaluations of the politics within pagan movements (see among others Eller 2000). Jone Salomonsen has a slightly different approach. According to Salomonsen, the association of women with nature, and reproductive cycles, may at first seem disturbing and even reactionary to a person committed to sexual equality (Salomonsen 2002:223). Still, Salomonsen argues, strategic essentialism contributes to a stronger sense of self among the women in these movements (245).

CHAPTER 5

1. http://www.isogaisa.org/, accessed November 1, 2013.
2. This chapter builds on a previously published chapter "The Festival Isogaisa; Neoshamanism in New Arenas" (Fonneland 2015a) in *Nordic*

Neoshamanisms (2015), Siv Ellen Kraft, Trude Fonneland, and James Lewis (eds.), New York: Palgrave Macmillan.

3. In the long term, the arrangers of the festival want to have Isogaisa Siida evolve into a spiritual center focusing on indigenous culture.

4. The Association Isogaisa consists of forty-five members and has its own board where Lars Henrik Cock is chairman, Frid Eva Karlsen and Ronald Kvernmo are board members, and Beate Sandjord is an alternate member. Isogaisa also hosts several co-arrangers; among them are Spansdalen Sameforening (Spandsdalen Sámi Association) and Foreningen Kystsamene (Costal Sámi Association).

5. http://www.isogaisa.org/, accessed February 2, 2015.

6. http://www.isogaisa.org/, accessed February 27, 2015.

7. On their webpage, one can find information on this year's and last year's programs, exhibitors, central themes, practical information, and registration forms for voluntary workers. On their home page, one can also find a YouTube link, where those who are interested may see, listen, and take part in a special Isogaisa dance, which is accompanied by a special festival *joik*.

8. See http://www.isogaisa.org/, accessed June 28, 2011.

9. http.www.isogaisa.org, accessed June 17, 2011.

10. http://www.isogaisa.org/tur-til-en-samis-offerplass.php, my translation, accessed August 12, 2016.

11. http://www.isogaisa.org/spennende-personligheter-2015.php, accessed October 20, 2016.

12. http://www.salangen-nyheter.com/boer-vernes-mot-isogaisa.5899558-28288.html, my translation, accessed August 31, 2016.

13. See, for instance, *Vårt Land*, August 25, 2016 (Kirken i klinsj med sjamanfestival), *Nordlys*, August 23, 2016, and *Fremover*, August 25, 2016 (Sogneprest meiner samer bør vernes mot innholet i bygdefestival).

14. In 2011, Kvernmo published his first book on Sámi shamanism entitled *Sjamanens hemmeligheter* (The Secrets of the Shaman).

CHAPTER 6

1. http://sjamanforbundet.no/, accessed November 25, 2016 (my translation). Shamanistic Association's logo is made by Cecilie Strøm.

2. This chapter builds on two previously published articles, "The Rise of Neoshamanism in Norway: Local Structures-Global Currents" (Fonneland 2015b) and "Approval of the Shamanistic Association: A Local Norwegian Construct with Trans-Local Dynamics (Fonneland 2015c).

3. This was not the first time a pagan group gained official recognition as a religious community in Norway. Ásatrú groups have preciously achieved the

same status. The first group, *Odins Ætlinger* (Kindred of Odin), was registered in 1994 and in 1996 the government officially recognized the Ásatrú
umbrella organization *Bifrost*. After a schism in the milieu, the *Foreningen
Forn Sed* emerged as an officially recognized religious movement in 1998
(see Asprem 2008).

4. The core of this project is a shamanic drum, made by the Sámi shaman
Birger Mikkelsen. This drum has traveled and still travels to various destinations all over the world and is intended to be a "wakeup call to humanity."
According the project's homepage on the Internet, the intention behind the
world drum is to bind people together across race, religion, borders, culture,
ethnicity, color, and political conviction in a common struggle for humanity and Mother Earth. http://www.theworlddrum.com/index.html, accessed
November 28, 2016. At present (December 2016) the World Drum is located
at Standing Rock, North Dakota.

5. According to Kyrre, this notion is rooted in Mayan mythology.

6. http://sjamanforbundet.no/blog/archives/1240, accessed September 9, 2016,
my translation.

7. With members and other devotees spread throughout the country, the
Internet has become a key component in the organization of the Shamanistic
Association in large part because it allows widely separated individuals to
communicate with each other and information to be disseminated more
easily.

8. In Norwegian the two terms are *livsynsorganisasjon* and *trossamfunn*.

9. See "Lov om trudomssamfunn og ymist anna," §§ 13–14.

10. In 1996, an application from a group named *Det Norske Åsatrusamfunn*
(The Norwegian Åsatru Society) was turned down by the Ministry of
Justice due to claims that the group was against "public morals" (see
Asprem 2008).

11. The text is taken from the letter to the County Governor; http://www.face-
book.com/groups/291273094250547/files/#!/groups/291273094250547/
doc/302374349807088/, accessed January 29, 2013 (my translation).

12. According to Roy Wallis, shamanistic practitioners highlight archeological
sites as places where ritual practices "work best" (2003:141).

13. According to Kyrre, northern peoples for millennia, also in ceremonial contexts, have used *chaga* (a mushroom found on birch trees). He points out
that there are few sources for how such a ceremony took place, but also that
some guidelines still exist. Kyrre says he has used these sources, combined
with channeled information from ancestors, to construct their own *chaga*
ceremony for shamanic practitioners in the present.

14. The first shamanic wedding ritual was held at the Ireland Tysnes, outside of
Bergen on July 27, 2012 with the shaman Arthur Sørenssen as ceremonial
leader.

15. I have also been invited to take part in this group as a researcher, and all members have been informed and have accepted my participation.
16. https://www.facebook.com/groups/223599101100554/, accessed October 20, 2016, my translation.
17. http://sjamanforbundet.no/filosofi/2016/10/06/om-a-holde-seremoni/, accessed November 28, 2016, my translation.
18. https://www.facebook.com/groups/223599101100554/files closed group at Facebook—discussion September 10, 2012, my translation.
19. A search for the Shamanistic Association in the *A-tekst* database, which contains editorial articles from more than fifty Norwegian newspapers, resulted in fifty-three hits as of February 5, 2013.

CHAPTER 7

1. http://www.polmakmoen-gjestegard.no/tilbud.html, accessed November 6, 2015.
2. See http://www.sarahkkas.com/
3. See http://www.elinkaaven.com/
4. At what level "The Seven Coffee Stops" can be referred to as a pilgrimage will be discussed later.
5. Polmakmoen Guesthouse is now called "Gaiatun," but all of the tourist programs, included healing sessions, are still offered. The new owner, Anne Gard, according to the newspaper *Finnmarken* (July 2, 2015) has worked with healing and coaching for fifteen years. She is a trained hypnotherapist, Reiki master teacher, certified theta healer, and has basic training in kinesiology.
6. My analysis builds on my visit to Polmakmoen Guesthouse and my interview with Esther in November 2010 and on participation in the pilgrimage "The Seven Coffee Stops" in August 2011. The journey from Polmakmoen to Berlevåg lasted for three days with two overnights in a *lavvo* (a traditional Sámi tent). The pilgrimage is based upon the tracks of Esther's reindeer herding ancestors, from inland to coast, from winter to summer pasture, and is led by Esther herself and a local guide.
7. http://www.polmakmoen-gjestegard.no/index.html, accessed February 2, 2011.
8. http://www.pilgrim.info/index.aspx, accessed April 12, 2014.
9. A search for Esther Utsi in the database A-tekst that contains editorial articles from more than fifty Norwegian newspapers resulted in 161 hits.

NOTES

PRESENTATION OF INTERVIEWEES

1. The core of this project is a shamanic drum, made by the Sámi shaman Birger Mikkelsen. This drum has traveled and still travels to various destinations all over the world and is intended to be a "wakeup call for humanity." According to the project's website the intention behind the world drum is to bind people together across race, religion, borders, culture, ethnicity, color, and political conviction in a common struggle for humanity and Mother Earth. See http://www.theworlddrum.com/index.html, accessed February 6, 2015.

2. This interview is not referred to through direct quotes, but it still part of my analysis.

REFERENCES

Ahlin, L. 2007. *Krop, sind—eller ånd? Alternativve behandlere og spiritualitet i Danmark*. Højbjerg: Forlaget univers.

Äikäs, T. 2011. "What Makes a Stone a Sieidi or How to Recognize a Holy place?" *Culture Kultūras krustpunkti* 5, 14–24.

Äikäs, T. 2015. "From Boulders to Fells—Sacred Places in the Sámi Ritual Landscape." *Monographs of the Archaeological Society of Finland 5*. Available from http://www.sarks.fi/masf/masf_5/masf_5.html

Äikäs, T., and A. K. Salmi. 2013. "'The Sieidi Is a Better Altar/the Noaidi Drum's a Purer Church Bell'—Long Term Changes and Syncretism at Sámi Offering Sites." *World Archaeology* 45 (1) (Archaeology of Religious Change), 20–38.

Äikäs, T., Fonneland T., S. E. Kraft, Perttola W, and Thomas S. 2017. "'Traces of Our Ancient Religion'": Meaning-making and Shamanism at Sami Offering Sites and the Isogaisa Festival, Northern Norway". In *Archaeological Sites as Space for Modern Spiritual Practice*

Albanese, C. 1990. *Nature Religion in America: From the Algonkin Indians to the New Age*. Chicago: University of Chicago Press.

Alver, B. G. 1993. Er Fanden bedre end sit rygte? Fakta og fiktion i folkelig fortælling. *Tradition* 23, 1–17.

Alver, B. G. 1999. "Det magiske menneske. Magi som perspektiv for Identitetsarbejde." In Alver B. G. et al. (eds.), *Myte, Magi og Mirakel. I møte med det moderne*, Oslo: Pax Forlag AS, 147–164.

Alver, B. G. 2006. "'Ikke det bare vand'. Et kulturanalytisk perspektiv på vandets magiske dimension." *Tidsskrift for kulturforskning* 2, 21–42.

Alver, B. G. 2008. *Mellem mennesker og magter. Magi i hekseforfølgelsernes tid*. Oslo: Scandinavian Academic Press.

Alver, B. G. 2015. "More or Less Genuine Shamans! The Believer in an Exchange between Antiquity and Modernity, between the Local and the Global." In T. Fonneland, S. E. Kraft, and J. Lewis (eds.), *Nordic NeoShamanisms*. New York: Palgrave MacMillan, 141–174.

Alver, B. G., I. S. Gilhus, L. Mikaelsson, and T. Selberg. 1999. *Myte, Magi og Mirakel. I møte med det moderne*. Oslo: Pax Forlag AS.

Alver, B. G., and T. Selberg. 1992. *Det er mer mellom himmel og jord. Folks forståelse av virkeligheten ut fra forestillinger om sykdom og behandling*. Sandvika: Vett & Viten AS.

Andreassen, B. O., and T. Fonneland. 2002/2003. "Mellom healing og blå energi. Nyreligiøsitet i Tromsø." *Din. Tidsskrift for religion og kultur* 4/ 2002 + 1/2003, 30–36.

Andrews, L. 1983. *Medicine Woman*. San Francisco: Harper Collins.

Andrews, L. 1990. *Jaguar Woman and The Wisdom of the Butterfly Tree*. San Francisco: Harper Collins.

Askeland, H. 2011. *Hovedmodeller for relasjonen mellom stat og trossamfunn: Finansiering av majoritetskirker i Europa*. KA-note 27.4.2011. [unpublished].

Asprem, E. 2008. "Heathens Up North: Politics, Polemics, and Contemporary Norse Paganism in Norway." *The Pomegranate* 10 (1), 41–69.

Asprem, E. 2013. "Trommereiser og guddommelige sopper: Sjamanismen og myten om urvisdommen." *Humanist tidsskrift for livssynsdebatt*, published online at http://arkiv.humanist.no/sjamanisme.html.

Aupers, S., and D. Houtman. 2006. "Beyond the Spiritual Supermarket: The Social and Public Significance of New Age Spirituality." *Journal of Contemporary Religion* 21 (2), 201–222.

Attix, S. A. 2002. "New Age Oriented Special Interest Travel: An Exploratory Study." *Tourism Recreation Research* 27 (2), 51–58.

Bachelard, G. 2000. *Rummets poetikk*. Lund: Skarabé.

Bäckman, L. 1975. *Sájva: föreställingar om hjälp och skyddsväsen i heliga fjäll bland samerna*. Stockholm: Almqvist & Wiksell.

Baglo, C. 2011. *På ville veger? Levende utstillinger av samer i Europa og Amerika*. PhD dissertation, Department of Archaeology and Anthropology, University of Tromsø.

Beckford, J. A. 2003. *Social Theory and Religion*. Cambridge: Cambridge University Press.

Bell, C. 1997. *Ritual: Perspectives and Dimensions*. New York: Oxford University Press.

Bendix, R. 1997. *In Search of Authenticity. The Formation of Folklore Studies*. London: University of Wisconsin Press.

Berger, H. 1994. *A Community of Witches: Contemporary Neo-Paganism and Witchcraft in the United States*. Columbia, SC: University of South Carolina Press.

Beyer, P. 1998. "Globalisation and the Religion of Nature." In J. Pearson and G. Samuel (eds.), *Nature Religion Today. Paganism in the Modern World*. Edinburgh: Edinburgh University Press, 11–21.

Birch, M. 1996. "The Goddess/God Within: The Construction of Self-Identity Through Alternative Health Practices." In K. Flanagan and P. C. Jupp (eds.), *Postmodernity, Sociology, and Religion*. London: Macmillan, 83–100.

Bjørklund, I. 2000. *Sápmi—Becoming a Nation*. Exhibition catalog. Tromsø University Museum.

Bjørnson, B. 1907. "En ny feriefart." In B. Bjørnsons, *Fortællinger. Jubilæumsudgave. Fortællingerne og Digteren af Moltke Moe*. Kristiania, Centraltrykkeriet, Gyldendalske Boghandel. (First published in *Fortællinger* 1872).

Blain, J. 2005. "Heathenry, the Past, and Sacred Sites in Today's Britain." In M. F. Strmiska (ed.)., *Modern Paganism in World Cultures: Comparative Perspectives*. Santa Barbara, CA: ABC Clio, 181–208.

Bowman, M. 1995a. "The Noble Savage and the Global Village. Cultural Evolution in New Age and Neo-Pagan Thought." *Journal of Contemporary Religion* 10 (2), 139–149.

Bowman, M. 1995b. "Cardiac Celts. Images of the Celts in Paganism." In G. Harvey and C. Hardman (eds.), *Paganism Today. Wiccans, Druids, the Goddess and Ancient Earth Traditions for the Twenty-First Century*. London: Thorsons, 242–251.

Brattland, C., and M. Myrvoll. 2014. *Etiske problemstillinger ved støtte til Sámisk nyreligiøsitet*. Rapport NIKU, Barents Secretariat. Tromsø.

Briggs, C. L. 1986. *Learning How to Ask. A Sociolinguistic Appraisal of the Role of the Interview in Social Science Research*. Cambridge: Cambridge University Press.

Brown, M. F. 2003. *Who Owns Native Culture?* Cambridge, MA: Harvard University Press.

Brynn, G., and B. Brunvoll. 2011. *Eirik Myrhaug. Sjaman for livet.* Oslo: Nova Forlag.

Capra, F. 1982. *The Turning Point.* New York: Simon & Schuster.

Casey, E. 2001. "Body, Self and Landscape. A Geophilosophical Inquiry into the Place-World." In P. C. Adams, S. Hoelscher, and K. E. Till (eds.), *Textures of Place. Exploring Humanist Geographies.* Minneapolis: University of Minnesota Press, 403–425.

Castaneda, C. 1968. *The Teachings of Don Juan. A Yaqui Way of Knowledge.* Los Angeles: University of California Press.

Christensen, C. 2005. "Urfolk på det nyreligiøse markedet—en analyse av Alternativt Nettverk." Master thesis in religious studies, University of Tromsø.

Christensen, C. 2007. "Urfolksspiritualitet på det nyreligiøse markedet. En analyse av tidsskriftet Visjon/Alternativt Nettverk." In *Din. Tidsskrift for religion og kultur* 1, 63–78.

Christensen, C. 2013. *Religion som samisk identitetsmarkør: Fire studier av film.* PhD dissertation, Department of History and Religious Studies, University of Tromsø.

Christensen, C., and S. E. Kraft. 2010. "Religion i Kautokeino-opprøret. En analyse av Sámisk urfolksspiritualitet." *Nytt norsk tidsskrift* 1, 19–27.

Christensen, O., and A. Eriksen. 1993. "Landskapsromantikk og folketradisjon." *Norveg* 2, 27–40.

Christoffersson, R. 2010. *Med tre röster och tusende bilder: Om den samiska trumman.* PhD dissertation, Uppsala University.

Churchill, W. 2003. "Spiritual Hucksterism. The Rise of the Plastic Medicine Men." In Harvey, G. (ed.), *Shamanism: A Reader.* London: Routledge, 324–333. (First published in *Fantasies of the Master Race.* Monroe: Common Courage Press 1992).

Clifford, J. 2013. *Returns. Becoming Indigenous in the Twenty-First Century.* London: Harvard University Press.

Coats, C. 2011. "Spiritual Tourism—Promise and Problems: The Case of Sedona Arizona." In E. M. Hoover and M. Emerich (eds.), *Media, Spiritualties and Social Change.* New York: Continuum, 117–126.

Cogswell, D. 1996. "Niche for the New Age". *Travel Agent*, October 21, 1996.

Conrad, J. 2004. "Mapping Space, Claiming Place. The (Ethno-) Politics of Everyday Geography in Northern Norway." In B. Klein, S. R. Mathisen, and A. L. Siikala (eds.), *Creating Diversities. Folklore, Religion, and the Politics of Heritage*. Helsinki: Studia Fennica, 165–189.

Cowan, T. 1993. *Fire in the Head: Shamanism and the Celtic Spirit.* New York: HarperCollins.

DuBois, T. A. 2009. *An Introduction to Shamanism.* Cambridge: Cambridge University Press.

DuBois, T. A. 2000. "Folklore, Boundaries and Audience in the Pathfinder." In L. Pentikäinen (ed.), *Sami Folkloristics.* Turku: NIF, 255–274.

Ehn, B., and O. Löfgren. 1982. *Kulturanalys. Et etnologiskt perspektiv.* Lund: LiberFörlag.

Eisler, R. 1988. *The Chalice and the Blade: Our History, Our Future.* Cambridge, MA: Harper & Row.

Eliade, M. 1964. *Shamanism: Archaic Techniques of Ecstasy.* Princeton, NJ: Princeton University Press.

Eller, C. 2000. *The Myth of Matriarchal Prehistory: Why an Invented Past Will Not Give Women a Future.* Boston: Beacon Press.

Eriksen, A. 1999. *Historie, Minne og Myte.* Oslo: Pax Forlag AS.

Eriksson, J. I. 1988. "Att använda kraft i goda syften." In J. I. Eriksson, M. Eriksson, M. W. Gejel, and M. Hedlund (eds.), *Sejd—en vägledning i nordlig shamanism.* Stockholm: Vattumannen Forlag.

Eriksson, J. I. 2005. *Att bita av ôdets trådar. Ett Shamanskt manifest.* Upplands Väsby: Norrshaman.

Eriksson, J. I. 2012. *Rune Magic & Shamanism: Original Nordic Knowledge from Mother Earth.* Upplands Väsby: Norrshaman.

Eriksson, J. I., and L. Bäckman. 1987. *Sámisk Shamanism.* Hägersten: Gimle.

Eriksson, J. I., and A. Grimsson. 2006. *Runmagi och shamanism 2.0.* Upplands Väsby: Norrshaman.

Featherstone, M. 1995. *Undoing Culture. Globalisation, Postmodernism and Identity.* London: Sage.

Fitzgerald, T. 2000. *The Ideology of Religious Studies.* New York and Oxford: Oxford University Press.

Fjell, T. I. 1998. *Fødselens gjenfødelse. Fra teknologi til natur på fødearenaen.* Kristiansand: Høyskoleforlaget.

Fonneland, T. 2007. "Med fokus på det nære og lokale. Tromsø—ein Sámisk urfolksby?" *Din, tidsskrift for religion og kultur* 1, 79–88.

Fonneland, T. 2010. *Samisk nysjamanisme: i dialog med (for)tid og stad.* Doctoral dissertation, University of Bergen.

Fonneland, T. 2011. "Sami Tour: urfolksspiritualitet i ei samisk turist-næring." *Chaos. Dansk-norsk tidsskrift for religionhistoriske studier* 55, 153–172.

Fonneland, T, 2012a. "Spiritual Entrepreneurship in a Northern Landscape, Tourism, Spirituality and Economics." In *Temenos. Nordic Journal of Comparative Religion* 48 (2), 155–178.

Fonneland, T. 2012b. ""De syv kaffekok": spirituelt entreprenørskap i et samisk landskap." *Tidsskrift for kulturforskning* 2, 27–44.

Fonneland, T. 2015a. "The Festival Isogaisa: Neoshamanism in New Arenas." In T. Fonneland, S. E. Kraft, and J. Lewis (eds.), *Nordic NeoShamanisms*. New York: Palgrave MacMillan, 215–234.

Fonneland, T. 2015b. "The Rise of Neoshamanism in Norway: Local Structures—Global Currents." In T. Fonneland, S. E. Kraft, and J. Lewis (eds.), *Nordic NeoShamanisms*. New York: Palgrave MacMillan, 33–54.

Fonneland, T. 2015c. Approval of the Shamanistic Association: A Local Norwegian Construct with Trans-Local Dynamics. In James R. Lewis and Inga Bårsen Tøllefsen (eds)., *Handbook of Nordic New Religions*. Leiden: Brill, 291–309.

Fonneland, T. 2017a. "Ein sieidi si rolle i religionsutøving i samtida: Skiftande tolkingar og tilnærmingar." *Tidsskrift for kulturforskning* 1, 71–84.

Fonneland, T. 2017b. "Indigenous Spirituality and the Staging of Sami Culture in Northern Scandinavia." In A. Viken, and D. K. Müller (eds.), *Tourism and Indigeneity in the Arctic*. Bristol: Channel View Publications, 262–286.

Fonneland, T., and S. E. Kraft. 2013. "Sami Shamanism & Indigenous Spirituality." In I. Gilhus and S. Sutcliffe (eds.), *New Age Spirituality: Rethinking Religion*. London: Equinox, 132–145.

Fonneland, T., S. E. Kraft, and J. Lewis. 2015. "Introduction: Nordic Neoshamanisms." In T. Fonneland, S. E. Kraft, and J. Lewis (eds.), *Nordic NeoShamanisms*. New York: Palgrave MacMillan, 1–12.

Freidman, J. 1999. "Indigenous Struggle and the Discreet Charm of the Bourgeoisie." *Journal of World-Systems Research* 2, 391–411.

Frykman, J. 2002. "Place for Something Else. Analyzing a Cultural Imaginary," *Ethnologia Europea* 32 (2), 47–68.

Frykman, J., and O. Löfgren. 1994. *Den kultiverade människan*. Stockholm: Liberförlag.

Frykman, J., and N. Gilje. 2003. *Being There. New Perspectives on Phenomenology and the Analysis of Culture.* Lund: Nordic Academic Press.

Gaski, L. 2008. "Sámi Identity as a Discursive Formation. Essentialism and Ambivalence." In H. Minde (ed.), *Indigenous Peoples. Self-Determination, Knowledge, Indigeneity.* Delft: Eburon Academic Publishers, 219–236.

Gaup, A. 2005. *The Shamanic Zone.* Oslo: Three Bear Company.

Gaup, A. 2007. *Inn i naturen: Utsyn fra Sjamansonen.* Oslo: Tre bjørner forlag.

Geertz, A. 1991. "Indianere i New Age." In J. Aagaard (ed.), *Religiøsitet og religioner.* København: Anis, 236–255.

Gilhus, I. 2012. "Post-Secular Religion and the Therapeutic Turn. Three Norwegian Examples." In T. Ahlbäck and B. Dahla (eds.), *Postsecular Religious Practices.* Scripta Instituti Donneriani Aboensis 24. Åbo: Donner Institute for research on Religious and Cultural History, 62–75.

Gilhus, I., and L. Mikaelsson. 2015. "A Study of New Religiosity in Norway." In J. Lewis and I. B. Tøllefsen (eds.), *Handbook of Nordic New Religions.* Brill Academic Publishers, 175–189.

Gilhus, I. S., and S. E. Kraft. 2007. "Innledning." In I. S. Gilhus and S. E. Kraft (eds.), *Religiøse reiser. Mellom gamle spor og nye mål.* Oslo: Universitetsforlaget, 11–21.

Gilhus, I. S., and L. Mikaelson. 2001. *Nytt blikk på religion. Studiet av religion i dag.* Oslo: Pax Forlag AS.

Gilmore, J. H., and J. B. Pine. 2007. *Authenticity: What Consumers Really Want.* Boston: Harvard Business School Press.

Gilmore, J. H., and J. B. Pine. 1999. *The Experience Economy.* Boston: Harvard Business Scholl Press.

Gjessing, G. 1973. *Norge i Sameland.* Oslo: Gyldendal Norsk Forlag.

Graburn, N. H. H. 1989. "Tourism the Sacred Journey." In V. L. Smith (ed.), *Hosts and Guests. The Anthropology of Tourism.* Philadelphia: University of Pennsylvania Press, 21–36.

Graff, O. 2016. *Joikeforbudet i Kautokeino. Musikketnologisk, historisk analyse av kulturutvikling i etterkrigstida i Kautokeino.* Monografi, Davvi Girji.

Graham, L. R., and H. G. Penny. 2014. "Performing Indigeneity: Emergent Identity, Self-Determination, and Sovereignty." In L. R. Graham and H. G. Penny (eds.), *Performing Indigeneity: Global Histories and Contemporary Experiences*. Lincoln and London: University of Nebraska Press, 1–31.

Granås, B. 2009. "Constructing the Unique—Communicating the Extreme Dynamics of Place Marketing." In T. Nyseth and A. Viken (eds.), *Place Reinvention. Northern Perspectives*. Farnham: Ashgate, 111–125.

Green, R. 1988. "The Tribe Called Wannabee: Playing Indian in America and Europe." *Folklore (Journal of the American Folklore Society)* 99 (1), 30–55.

Greenwood, S. 2000. *Magic, Witchcraft and the Otherworld: An Anthropology*. Oxford: Berg.

Gregorius, F. 2008. *Modern Asatro: Att konstruera etnisk och kulturell identitet*. Doctoral dissertation, Centrum for Theology and Religious Studies, Lund University.

Guneriussen, W. 2008. "Modernity Re-enchanted: Making a 'Magic' Region." In J. Ole Bærenholdt and B. Granås (eds.), *Mobility and Place. Enacting Northern European Peripheries*. Aldershot: Ashgate, 233–244.

Guneriussen, W. 2012. "Nord-Norge—et opplevelsesamfunn" In S. Jentoft, J. I. Nergård, and K. A. Røvik (eds.), *Hvor går Nord-Norge? Et institusjonelt og perspektiv på folk og landsdel*. Stamsund: Orkana forlag, 343–354.

Hætta, O. M. 2002. *Samene: Nordkalottens Urfolk*. Oslo: Cappelen Damm.

Hall, M. 2007. "Politics, Power and Indigenous Tourism." In R. Butler and T. Hinch (eds.), *Tourism and Indigenous Peoples*. Oxford: Elsevier, 305–318.

Hansen, K. 2002. "Festivals, spatiality and the New Europe." *Ethnologia Europea* 32 (2), 19–36.

Harner, M. 1980. *The Way of the Shaman a Guide to Power and Healing*. San Francisco: Harper & Row.

Harner, M. 2013. *Cave and Cosmos. Shamanic Encounters with Another Reality*. Berkeley, CA: North Atlantic Books.

Harvey, D. 2000. *Spaces of Hope*. Edinburgh: Edinburgh University Press.

Harvey, G. 2003. "General Introduction." In G. Harvey (ed.), *Shamanism: A Reader*. London: Routledge, 1–24.

Harvey, G. 2005. *Animism: Respecting the Living World*. London: Hurst & Co.

Harvey, G. 2009. *Religions in Focus: New Approaches to Tradition and Comtemporary Practices*. London: Equinox.

Hammer, O. 1997. *På spaning efter helheten. New Age en ny folketro?* Stockholm: Wahlström & Widstrand.

Hammer, O. 2001. *Claiming Knowledge. Strategies of Epistemology from Theosophy to the New Age*. Leiden: Brill.

Hammer, O. 2004. *På spaning efter helheten. New Age en ny folketro?* (Omarb. Utg. 1997). Stockholm: Wahlström & Widstrand.

Hammer, O. 2015. "Late Modern Shamanism: Central Texts and Issues." In T. Fonneland, S. E. Kraft, and J. Lewis (eds.), *Nordic NeoShamanisms*. New York: Palgrave Macmillan, 13–29.

Hanegraaff, W. J. 1996. *New Age Religion and Western Culture. Esotericism in the Mirror of Secular Thought*. Leiden: E. J. Brill.

Hauan, M. A. 2003. "Riddu Riđđu—et sted å lære." In M. A. Hauan, E. Niemi, H. A. Wold, and K. Zachariassen (eds.), *Karlsøy og verden utenfor. Kulturhistoriske perspektiver på nordnorske steder. Festskrift til professor Håvard Dahl Bratrein på 70-årsdagen 13.02.2003*. Tromsø Museums Skrifter XXX. Tromsø Museum, Universitetsmuseet, 186–207.

Heelas, P. 1996. *The New Age Movement*. Malden, MA: Blackwell.

Helander, E. 2004. "Myths, Shamans and Epistemologies From an Indigenous Vantage Point." In E. Helander et al. (eds.), *Dreamscape Snowscape*. Vassa: Fram Oy. Tampere Polytechnic Publications, 552–562.

Hess, D. J. 1993. *Science in the New Age: The Paranormal, Its Defenders and Debunkers, and American Culture*. Madison: University of Wisconsin Press.

Hetherington, K. 1998. *Expressions of Identity*. London: Sage.

Hodgson, D. L. 2014. "Culture Claims: Being Maasai at the United Nations." In L. R. Graham and H. G. Penny (eds.), *Performing Indigeneity: Global Histories and Contemporary Experiences*. Lincoln: University of Nebraska Press, 55–82.

Høst, A. 2001: "Moderne shamanistisk praksis. Om 'neo-shamanisme', 'kerne-shamanisme', 'by-shamanisme' og andre betegnelser." In *Spirit Talk Nyheitsbrev for Scandinavian Center for Shamanic Studies*. (http://www.shamanism.dk/moderneshamanisme.htmhttp://www.shamanism.dk/moderneshamanisme.htm).

Høst, A. 2005. *Jorden synger: Naturens kraft og nordiske rødder*. København: Møntergården.

Hovland, A. 1996. *Moderne urfolk. Sámisk ungdom i 90-årene.* Oslo: Cappelen Akademisk Forlag.

Hutton, R. 2001. *Shamans: Siberian Spirituality and the Western Imagination.* London: Hambledon.

Isaksen, K., and D. Storm. 2014. "Duodjo-Dáidda." In M. A. Hauan (ed.), *Sami Stories: Art and Identity of an Artic People.* Stamsund: Orkana Forlag.

Ivakhiv, A. 2003. "Nature and Self in New Age Pilgrimage." *Culture and Religion* 4 (1), 93–118.

Jackson, M. 1996. "Introduction: Phenomenology, Radical Empiricism and Anthropological Critique." In M. Jackson (ed.), *Things as They Are. New Directions in Phenomenological Anthropology.* Bloomington: Indiana University Press.

Jakobsen, M. D. 1999: *Shamanism. Traditional and Contemporary Approaches to the Mastery of Spirits and Healing.* New York: Berghahn Books.

Järvinen, M. 2005. Interview i en interaktionistisk begrepsramme. In M. Järvinen and N. Mik-Meyer (eds.), *Kvalitative Metoder I Et Interaktionistisk Perspektiv. Interview, observationer og dokumenter.* København: Hans Reitzels Forlag, 27–48.

Jenkins, P. 2004. *Dream Catchers. How Mainstream America Discovered Native Spirituality.* Oxford: Oxford University Press.

Johnson, G., and S. E. Kraft. Forthcoming 2017. "Introduction." In G. Johnson and S. E. Kraft (eds.), *The Brill Handbook of Indigenous Religion(s): Pathways—Being, Becoming, Back.* Leiden: Brill.

Kalland, A. 2003. "Environmentalism and Images of the Other." In H. Selin (ed.), *Nature Across Cultures. Views of Nature and the Environment in Non-Western Cultures.* Amsterdam: Kluwer Academic Publishers, 1–17.

Kalvig, A. 2001. "Himmelske samtaler om sex—friske fråsegn og gammalt grums." *Din: Tidsskrift for religion og kultur* 2 and 3, 30–37.

Kalvig, A. 2015. "Shared Facilities: The Fabric of Shamanism, Spiritualism, and Therapy in a Nordic Setting." In T. Fonneland, S. E. Kraft, and J. Lewis (eds.), *Nordic NeoShamanisms.* New York: Palgrave MacMillan, 67–88.

Kildal, J. 1727. Afguderiets dempelse. In M. Krekling (ed.) 1945. *Nordlands og Troms finner i eldre håndskrifter.* Oslo: A.W Brøgger Boktrykkeri.

King, U. 1995. *Religion and Gender.* Oxford: Blackwell.

Kippenberg, H. G. 2002. *Discovering Religious History in the Modern Age*. Princeton: Princeton University Press.

Kirshenblatt-Gimblett, B. 1998. *Destination Culture. Tourism, Museums, and Heritage*. Berkeley, CA: University of California Press.

Klein, B. 1995. "Innledning." In B. Klein (ed.), *Gatan är vår! Ritualer på offentliga platser*. Stockholm: Carlssons, 10–11.

Klesse, C. 2000. "Modern Primitivism: Non-Mainstream Body Modification and Racialized Representation." In Featherstone, Mike (eds.), *Body Modification*. London: Sage, 15–39.

Kraft, S. E. 2000. "New Age og den nye kvinnen." *Historie. Populærvitenskapelig magasin* 1, 78–82.

Kraft, S. E. 2004. "Krokhenging. Nær-livet opplevelser og "primitiv" maskulinitet." *Din. Tidsskrift for religion og kultur* 2–3: 3–11.

Kraft, S. E. 2005. *Den ville kroppen. Tatovering, piercing og smerteritualer i dag*. Oslo: Pax Forlag AS.

Kraft, S. E. 2007. "En senmoderne pilegrimsreise. Prinsesse Märtha Louise og Ari Behns fra hjerte til hjert." In I. S. Gilhus and S. E. Kraft (eds.), *Religiøse reiser. Mellom gamle spor og nye mål*. Oslo: Universitetsforlaget, 39–50.

Kraft, S. E. 2008. *Place-Making through Mega-Events*. In J. O. Bærenholdt and B. Granås (eds.), *Mobility and Place. Enacting Northern European Peripheries*. Aldershot: Ashgate, 219–231.

Kraft, S. E. 2009. "Sámi Indigenous Spirituality. Religion and Nation Building in Norwegian Sápmi." *Temenos. Nordic Journal of Comparative Religion* 45 (2), 179–206.

Kraft, S. E. 2010. "The Making of a Sacred Mountain. Meanings of Nature and Sacredness in Sapmi and Northern Norway." *Religion an International Journal* 40, 53–61.

Kraft, S. E. 2011. *Hva er nyreligiøsitet*. Oslo: Universitetsforlaget.

Kraft, S. E. 2015. "Shamanism and Indigenous Soundscapes: The Case of Mari Boine." In T. Fonneland, S. E. Kraft, and J. Lewis (eds.), *Nordic NeoShamanisms*. New York: Palgrave MacMillan, 235–262.

Kvernmo, R. 2011. *Sjamanens hemmeligheter*. Own imprint.

Lehtola, V. P. 2004. *The Sámi People. Traditions in Transition*. Inari: Kustannus Puntsi Publisher.

Lewis, J. 2015. "New Age Medicine Men versus New Age *Noaidi*: Same Neoshamanism, Different Sociopolitical Situation." In T. Fonneland,

S. E. Kraft, and J. Lewis (eds.), *Nordic NeoShamanisms*. New York: Palgrave MacMillan, 127–140.

Lindquist, G. 1997. *Shamanic Performances on the Urban Scene: Neo-Shamanism in Contemporary Sweden*. Doctoral dissertation, Studies in Social Anthropology, 39. Gotab, Stockholm.

Lorentzen, J. 2004. *Maskulinitet: blikk på mannen gjennom litteratur og film*. Oslo: Spartacus.

Lowenthal, D. 1985. *The Past Is a Foreign Country*. Cambridge: Cambridge University Press.

Lowenthal, D. 1998. *The Heritage Crusade and the Spoils of History*. Cambridge: Cambridge University Press.

MacCannell, D. 1976. *The Tourist. A New Theory of the Leisure Class*. New York: Schoken Books.

Macnaghten, P., and J. Urry. 1998. *Contested Natures*. London: Sage.

Magliocco, S. 2004. *Witching Culture: Folklore and Neo-Paganism in America*. Philadelphia: University of Pennsylvania Press.

Manker, E. 1938. *Die Lappische Zaubertrommel. Eine ethnologische Monographie*. 1. Die Trommel als Denkmal materieller Kultur. Acta Lapponica 1. Stockholm: Thule.

Manker, E. 1950. *Die Lappische Zaubertrommel. Eine ethnologische Monographie*. 2. Die Trommel als Urkunde geistigen Lebens. Acta Lapponica 6. Stockholm: Hugo Gebers förlag.

Manker, E. 1957. "Lapparnas heliga ställen. Kultplatser och offerkult i belysning av nordiska museets och landsantikvariernas fältunder-sökningar." *Acta Lapponica XIII*, Uppsala.

Marcuse, H. 1964. *The One Dimentional Man. Studies in the Ideology of Advanced Industrial Society*. London: Routledge & Kegan Paul.

Massey, D. 1997. "En global stedsfølelse." In J. Aspen and J. Pløger (eds.), *På sporet av byen. Lesninger av senmoderne byliv*. Oslo: Spartacus, 306–318.

Massey, D. 2005. *For Space. London*. Thousand Oaks, CA: Sage.

Mathisen, S. R. 2001. "'Den naturlige samen': Narrative konstruksjoner av 'de andre' i norsk tradisjon." In L. A. Ytrehus (ed.), *Fortellinger om "den andre"*. Kristiansand: Høyskoleforlaget, 84–98.

Mathisen, S. R. 2002. "Sted, etnisitet og fortelling. Lokaliseringer av det samiske i Skånland." *Tidsskrift for kulturforskning* nr. 3/4, 73–91.

Mathisen, S. R. 2010. "Indigenous Spirituality in the Touristic Borderzone. Virtual Performances of Sámi Shamanism in Sápmi Park." *Temenos. Nordic Journal of Comparative Religion* 46 (1), 53–72.

Mathisen, S. R. 2014. "Nordlys, magi og turisme." In *DIN: Religionsvitenskapelig tidsskrift* 1, 69–92.

Mayer, G. 2008. "The Figure of the Shaman as a Modern Myth. Some Reflections on the Attractiveness of Shamanism in Modern Societies." In *The Pomegranate. The International Journal of Pagan Studies* 10 (1), 70–103.

McCutcheon, R. T. 2000. "Myth." In W. Braun and R. T. McCutcheon (eds.), *Guide to the Study of Religion.* Cassell: London, New York, 190–208.

McGregor, G. 1988. *The Noble Savage in the New World Garden: Notes Toward a Syntactic of Place.* Toronto: University of Toronto Press.

Meadows, K. 1991. *Shamanic Experience: A Practical Guide to Extrasensory Perception.* London: Rider.

Mebius, H. 2000. "Historien om den samiska nåjden." In T. P. Larsson (ed.), *Schamaner. Essäer om religiösa mästare.* Nya Doxa, 41–75.

Melucci, A. 1992. *Nomader i nuet. Sosiala rörelser och individuella behov i dagens samhälle.* Uddevalla: MediaPrint.

Minde, H. 2008. "Constructing 'Laestadianism': A Case for Sami Survival?" *Acta Borealia: A Nordic Journal of Circumpolar Societies* 15 (1): 5–25.

Morgan, M. 1995. *Mutant Message from Down Under* Mossberg, L. 2007. "At skabe oplevelser ved hjælp af storytelling." In J. O. Bærenholdt and J. Sundbo (eds.), *Oplevelses Økonomi. Produktion, forbrug, kultur.* Fredriksberg: Forlaget Samfundslitteratur, 321–340.

Mossberg, L. 2007. "At skabe oplevelser ved hjælp af storytelling." In J. O. Bærenholdt and J. Sundbo (eds.), *Oplevelses Økonomi. Produktion, forbrug, kultur.* Fredriksberg: Forlaget Samfundslitteratur, 321–340.

Mulcock, J. 2001. "Creativity and Politics in the Cultural Supermarket." *Continuum* 15 (2), 169–186.

Myrhaug, M. L. 1997: *I Modergudinnens fotspor. Sámisk religion med vekt på kvinnelige kultutøvere og gudinnekult.* Oslo: Pax Forlag.

Myrvoll, M. 2010. *"Bare Gudsordet duger." Om kontinuitet og brudd I samisk virkelighetsforståelse.* Doctoral dissertation, University of Tromsø.

Niezen, R. 2003. *The Origins of Indigenism: Human Rights and the Politics of Identity*. Berkeley: University of California Press.

Niezen, R. 2009. *The Rediscovered Self: Indigenous Identity and Cultural Justice*. Montreal and Kingston: McGill-Queen's University Press.

Niezen, R. 2012. "Indigenous Religion and Human Rights." In J. Witte and M. Christian Green (eds.), *Religion and Human Rights. An Introduction*. Oxford: Oxford University Press, 119–134.

Nora, P. 1996: "From Lieux de Mémoire to Realms of Memory. Preface to the English- Language Edition." In P. Nora (ed.), *Realms of Memory. The Construction of the French Past*. New York: Colombia University Press, xiv–xxiv.

Norman, A. 2012. "The Varieties of the Spiritual Tourist Experience." *Literature & Aesthetics* 22 (1), 20–37.

NOU (2013:1)—*Det livssynsåpne samfunn. En helhetlig tros- og livssyns-politikk*. Available at https://www.regjeringen.no/no/aktuelt/nou-2013-1-det-livssynsapne-samfunn-en-h/id711620/

O'Dell, T. 2010. "Experiencescapes. Blurring Borders and Testing Connections." In T. O'Dell and P. Billing (eds.), *Experiencescapes. Tourism, Culture, and Economy*. Køge: Copenhagen Business School Press, 11–34.

Olsen, I. 1716. P, lappernes vildfarelser og overtro. Redigert av Just Qvigstad. Trondheim, 1910. (Skrifter utgitt av Det Kongelige norske videnskabers selskab; no 4; 1910).

Olsen, K. 2003. "The Touristic Construction of the 'Emblematic' Sami." *Acta Borealia* 20 (1), 3–20.

Olsen, K. O. K. 2006. "Making Differences in a Changing World: The Norwegian Sámi in the Tourist Industry. The Touristic Construction of the 'Emblematic' Sámi." *Scandinavian Journal of Hospitality and Tourism* 6 (1), 37–53.

Olsen, L. 1997: "Om runebommen (1885)," *Ottar—populærvitenskaplig tidsskrift fra Tromsø Museum* 217, 4–7.

Ortner, S. B. 1974. "Is Female to Male as Nature Is to Culture?" In M. Z. Rosaldo and L. Lamphere (eds.), *Woman, Culture, and Society*. Stanford, CA: Stanford University Press, 68–87.

Owen, S., and T. Teemu. 2015. "The Category of 'Religion' in Public Classification. Charity Registration of the Druid Networl in England

and Wales." In T. Stack, N. Goldenberg, and T. Fitzgerald (eds.), *Religion as a Category of Governance and Sovereignty*. Leiden: Brill, 90–114.

Paine, R. 1965. "Læstadianisme og samfunnet." *Tidsskrift for samfunnsforskning* 1, 60–73.

Partridge, C. 2004. *The Re-Enchantment of the West*. London: A Continuum Imprint.

Paulgaard, G. 2012. "Geography of Opportunity: Approaching Adulthood at the Margins of the Northern European Periphery." In U. D. Bæck and G. Paulgaard (eds.), *Rural Futures? Finding One's Place Within Changing Labour Markets*. Stamsund/Oslo: Orkana Akademisk Forlag, 189–215.

Pedersen, P., and A. Viken. 2009. "Globalised Reinvention of Indigenuity. The Riddu Riddu Festival as a Tool for Ethnic Negotiation of Place." In T. Nyseth and A. Viken (eds.), *Place Reinvention; Northern Perspectives*. Farnham: Ashgate, 183–202.

Penny, G. H., and J. Rickard. 2014. "Surrogate Indigeneity and the German Hobbyist Scene." In L. R. Graham and H. G. Penny (eds.), *Performing Indigeneity: Global Histories and Contemporary Experiences*. Lincoln: University of Nebraska Press, 169–205.

Phipps, P. 2009. "Globalisation, Indigeneity and Performing Culture." In *Local-Global: Identity, Security, Community* Vol. 6, 28–48.

Phipps, P. 2010. "Performances of Power: Indigenous Cultural Festivals as Globally Engaged Cultural Strategy" *Alternatives* 35, 217–240.

Pike, S. M. 2001. *Earthly Bodies, Magical Selves: Contemporary Pagans and the Search* for Community. Berkeley: University of California Press.

Pike, S. M. 2004. *New Age and Neopagan Religion*. New York: Columbia University Press.

Pollan, B. 2002. "En nålevende samisk sjaman. Møte med Eirik Myrhaug." In *Noaider, Verdens Hellige Skrifter*. De Norske Bokklubbene, 259–266.

Prins, H. 2002. "Visual Media and the Primitivist Perplex: Colonial Fantasies, Indigenous Imagination, and Advocacy in North America." In F. D Ginsburg and L. Abulughod, and B. Larkin (eds.), *Media Worlds: Anthropology on New Terrain*. Erwing, NJ: University of California Press.

Prothero, S. 1996. *The White Buddhist. The Asian Odyssey of Henry Steel Olcott*. Bloomington: Indiana University Press.

Reader, I. 2007. "Pilgrimage Growth in the Modern World: Meanings and Implications" *Religion* 37, 210–229.

Richard, J. 1998. "Alterity, Mimicry, and German Indians." In M. Becher and A. Robbins (eds.), *Bavarian by Law German/Indians*. Syracuse NY: Light Word, 30–31.

Robertson, R. 1992: *Globalization. Social Theory and Global Culture*. London: Sage.

Robertson, R. 1995: "Glocalization: Time-Space and Homogeneity-Heterogeneity." In M. Featherstone (ed.), *Global Modernities*. London: Sage, 25–44.

Rønnow, T. 1998. *Den nye pietismen. Miljøvernet i religionsvitskapelig perspektiv*. Hovudoppgåve i religionshistorie, Universitetet i Oslo.

Rønnow, T. 2000. "Den nye pietismen. Miljøvern og religiøs revitalisering." *Sosiologi i dag* 2, 23–52.

Rønnow, T. 2003. "Moder Jord: et moderne nøkkelsymbol." *Din tidsskrift for religion og kultur* 2, 34–43.

Rose, W. 1984. "Just What's All This Fuss about Whiteshamanism Anyway?" In B. Schöler (ed.), *Coyote Was Here*. Aarhus: Department of English, 13–24.

Roszak, T. 1969. *The Making of a Counter Culture. Reflections on theTechnocratic Society and Its Youthful Opposition*. Garden City, NY: Doubleday.

Rothstein, M. 1993. *Er Messias en Vandmand?* København: G.E.C. Gad.

Rountree, K. 2002. "Goddess Pilgrims as Tourists: Inscribing the Body Through Sacred Travel." *Sociology of Religion* 63 (4), 475–496.

Rountree, K. 2012. "Neo-Paganism, Animism, and Kinship with Nature." *Journal of Contemporary Religion* 27, 305–320.

Rountree, K. 2013. "Introduction: Context Is Everything: Plurality and Paradox in Contemporary European Paganisms." In K. Rountree (ed.), *Modern Pagen and Native Faith Movements in Europe*. New York: Berghahn, 1–23.

Rydving, H. 1993. *The End of Drum-Time. Religious Change among the Lule Saami, 1670s–1740s*. Acta Universitatis Upsaliensis. Historia Religionum 12, Uppsala.

Rydving, H. 2003. "Innledning" In A. Sveen (ed.), *Mytisk landskap. Ved dansende skog og susende fjell*. Stamsund: Orkana Forlag, 9–23.

Rydving, H. 2011. "Le chamanisme aujourd'hui: constructions et décon-structions d'une illusion scientifique." In *Études mongoles et sibériennes, centrasiatiques et tibétaines* 42 (DOI: 10.4000/emscat.1815).

Salmi, A-K, Äikäs, T., Fjellström, M., Spangen, M. 2015. "Animal Offerings at Sámi Offering Site Unna Saiva—Changing Religious Practices and Human-Animal Relationships." *Journal of Anthropological Archaeology* 40, 10–22.

Salomonsen, J. 1991. *Når Gud blir kvinne. Blant hekser, villmenn og sja-maner i USA.* Oslo: Pax Forlag AS.

Salomonsen, J. 1996. *"I am a Witch—A Healer and a Bender": An Expression of Women's Religiosity in Contemporary USA.* PhD disser-tation, University of Oslo.

Salomonsen, J. 1999. *Riter. Religiøse overgansritualer i vår tid.* Oslo: Pax Forlag AS.

Salomonsen, J. 2002. *Enchanted Feminism: The Reclaiming Witches of San Francisco.* London: Routledge.

Schanche, A. 2004. Horizontal and Vertical Perceptions of Saami Landscapes." In M. Jones and A. Scanche (eds.), *Landscape, Law and Customery Rights.* Report from a symposium in Guovdageaidnu-Kautokeino, 26–28 March 2003. Dieđut 3: 1–10.

Selberg, T. 1998. "Fortidslengsel i moderne folkelig religiøsitet." *Tradisjon* 2, 83–89.

Selberg, T. 1999. "Magi og fortryllelse i populærkulturen." In T. Selberg et al., *Myte, Magi og Mirakel. I møte med det moderne.* Oslo: Pax Forlag AS, 122–133.

Selberg, T. 2001. "Ideas about the Past and Tradition in the Discourse about Neoshamanism in a Norwegian Context." *Acta Ethnographica Hungaria* 46 (1–2), 65–74.

Selberg, T. 2005. "The Actualization of the Sacred Place of Selja and the Legend of Saint Sunniva." *Arv. Scandinavian Yearbook of Folklore* 61, 129–164.

Selberg, T. 2007a. "Magiske reiser og magiske steder." In I. S. Gilhus and S. E. Kraft (eds.), *Religiøse reiser. Mellom gamle spor og nye mål.* Oslo: Universitetsforlaget, 66–73.

Selberg, T. 2007b. "Mennesker og steder. Innledning." In T. Selberg and N. Gilje (eds.), *Kulturelle landskap. Sted, forteljing og materiell kultur.* Bergen: Fagbokforlaget, 9–20.

Selberg, T. 2011. "Pilegrimsveien som kulturarv: Den norske pilegrimsre-nessansen." *Din, tidsskrift for religion og kultur*, 120–131.

Selberg, T. 2015. "Shamanism—A Spiritual Heritage?" In T. Fonneland, S. E. Kraft, and J. Lewis (eds.), *Nordic NeoShamanisms*. New York: Palgrave MacMillan, 89–102.

Sherwood, K. 2009. *Chakra Therapy for Personal Growth and Healing*. Woodbury, MN: Llewellyn.

Sky, J. 2007. *Kjønn og religion*. Oslo: Pax Forlag A/S.

Smith, J. Z. 1998. *Å finne sted. Rommets dimensjon i religiøse ritualer*. Oslo: Pax Forlag AS.

Solbakkk, A. 2008. *Hva vi tror på: Noaidevuohta—en innføring i nor-dsamenes religion*. Karasjok: CálliidLágádus.

Solheim, S. 1952. *Norsk Sætertradisjon*. Skrifter serie B XLVII. Oslo: Institutt for samanliknande kulturforsking.

Solli, B. 2002. *Seid. Myter, sjamanisme og kjønn i vikingenes tid*. Oslo: Pax Forlag AS.

Sørbø, J. I. 1988. *Svar til ein sjaman. New Age, overmennesket - og ei kyrkje på flukt*. Oslo: Samlaget.

Sørenssen, A. 1988. *Shaman. En rituell innvielse*. Oslo: Ex Libris.

Spangen, M. 2016. *Circling Concepts: A Critical Archaeological Analysis of the Notion of Stone Circles as Sami Offering Sites*. Dissertation, Stockholm University.

Stausberg, M. 2011. *Religion and Tourism: Crossroads, Destinations and Encounters*. London & New York: Routledge.

Stordahl, V. 1996. *Same i den moderne verden. Endring og kontinuitet i et Sámisk lokalsamfunn*. Karasjok: Davvi Girji O.S.

Strmiska, M. F. 2003. "The Evils of Christianization: A Pagan Perspective on European History." In T. Wadell (ed.), *Cultural Expressions of Evil and Wickedness: Wrath, Sex, Crime*. New York: Rodopi, 59–73.

Strmiska, M. F. 2005. "Introduction: Modern Paganism in World Cultures—Comparative Perspectives." In M. F. Strmiska (ed.), *Modern Paganism in World Cultures: Comparative Perspectives*. Santa Barbara, CA: ABC-CLIO, 1–53.

Stuckrad, K. V. 2002. "Reenchanting Nature: Modern Western Shamanism and Nineteenth-Century Thought." *Journal of the American Academy of Religion* 70 (4), 771–799.

Stuckrad, K. V. 2003. "Discursive Study of Religion: From States of the Mind to Communication and Action." *Method and Theory in the Study of Religion* 15, 255–271.

Stuckrad, K.V. 2005. *Western Esoterisicm. A Brief History of Secret Knowledge.* London: Equinox.

Svanberg, J. 1994. *Den skandinaviska nyschamanismen. En revitaliserande rörelse.* Unpublished M.A. thesis in Comparative Religion. Åbo: Akademi University.

Svanberg, J. 2003. *Schamanantropologi i gränslandet mellan forskning och praktik: En studie av förhållandet mellan schamanismforskning och neoschamanism.* Åbo: Åbo Akademis Förlag.

Szerszynski, B. 2005. *Nature, Technology and the Sacred.* Oxford: Blackwell.

Tedlock, B. 2005. *The Woman in the Shaman's Body: Reclaiming the Feminine in Religion and Medicine.* New York: Bantam Books.

Thompson, W. I. 1986: *Pacific Shift.* San Francisco & California, Sierra Club Books.

Thuen, T. 1995. *Quest for Equity: Norway and the Saami Challenge.* St. John's Newfoundland: Institute of Social and Economic Research.

Thuen, T. 2003. "Stedets identitet." In T. Thuen (ed.), *Sted og tilhørighet.* Oslo: Høyskoleforlaget, 11–38.

Tøllefsen, I. B. 2016. "Gender and New Religions." In R. Lewis and I. B. Tøllefsen (eds.), *The Oxford Handbook of New Religious Movements.* New York: Oxford University Press, 239–253.

Torgovnick, M. 1990: *Gone Primitive: Savage Intellects, Modern Lives.* Chicago: University of Chicago Press.

Tørum, G.-H. (in co-operation with T. Skagestad). 2012. *Sjaman på høye hæler: Min reise i ukjent landskap.* Oslo: Cappelen Damm.

Trulsson, Å. 2010. *Cultivating the Sacred. Ritual Creativity and Practice among Women in Contemporary Europe*, doctoral dissertation, Department of History and Anthropology of Religions, Lund University.

Turner, V. W. 1969. *The Ritual Process. Structure and Anti-Structure.* Ithaca, NY: Cornell University Press.

Turner V., and E. Turner. 1978. *Image and Pilgrimage in Christian Culture.* New York: Columbia University Press.

Urry, J. 2002. "Mobility and Proximity. *Sociology* 46 (2), 255–274. http://pagesperso-orange.fr/ville-en-mouvement/interventions/John_Urry.pdf, accessed May 28, 2016.

Valkeapää, N.-A. 1997: *The Sun, My Father*. Translated by H. Gaski, L. Nordström, and R. Salisbury. Guovdageaidnu: DAT.

Vasenkari, M. 1999. "A Dialogical Notion of Fieldwork." *Arv. Nordic Yearbook of folklore*, 51–72.

Viken, A. 2002. Turismens Sameland: tradisjoner i transformasjon, 1–7. Available at http://utmark.nina.no/portals/utmark/utmark_old/utgivelser/pub/2002-1/art/viken-utmark-1-2002.html, accessed August 21, 2016.

Vindsetmo, B. 1995. *Sjelen som turist. Om religion, terapi og magi*. Oslo: Gyldendal Forlag.

Wallis, R. J. 2003. *Shamans/Neo-Shamans: Ecstasy, Alternative Archaeologies and Contemporary Pagans*. London: Routledge.

Wang, N. 2000. *Tourism and Modernity: A Sociological Analysis*. Amsterdam: Pergamon.

Wernitznig, D. 2003. *Going Native or Going Naive? White Shamanism and the Neo-Noble Savage*. Oxford: University Press of America.

White, L. 1967. "The Historical Roots of our Ecological Crisis." *Science* 155 (3767), 1203–1207.

White, R. 2000. *Using your Chakras: A New Approach to Healing your Life*. York Beach: Samuel Weise Inc.

Wilson, G. 2014. *Redefining Shamanisms. Spiritualist Mediums and Other Traditional Shamans as Apprenticeship Outcomes*. London: Bloomsbury Academic.

Winkler, G. 2003. *Jewish Magic of the Ordinary: Recovering the Shamanic in Judaism*. Berkeley, CA: North Atlantic Books.

York, M. 2001. "New Age Commodification and Appropriation of Spirituality." *Journal of Contemporary Religion* 17 (1), 361–372.

Ziehe, T. 1986. "Inför avmystifieringen av världen. Ungdom och kulturell modernisering." In M. Löfgren and A. Molander (eds.), *Postmoderna tider*. Stockholm: Norstedt, 345–361.

Znamenski, A., A. 2007. *The Beauty of the Primitive. Shamanism and the Western Imagniation*. Oxford: Oxford University Press.

REFERENCES

NEWSPAPER ARTICLES

Vårt Land: "Kirken i klinsj med sjamanfestival" (August 25, 2016)

Fremover: "Sogneprest meiner samer bør vernes mot innholet i bygdefestival" (August 25, 2016)

Nordlys: "Sogneprest meiner samer bør vernes mot innholet i bygdefestival" (August 23, 2016)

Helgeland Arbeiderblad: "Ailo Gaup til minne" (October 17, 2014)

Klassekampen: " Sjamanen Ailo Gaup er død" (October 10, 2014)

Nordlys: "Minneord" (October 02, 2014)

Nordlys: "Sjamanisme offentlig godkjent som religion i Norge" (March 14, 2012)

Dagen: "sjamanisme finner grobunn i norge" (March 15, 2012)

ABC Nyheter: "Derfor bør du reise til tromsø" (April 01, 2012)

Bergens Tidende: "Sjamaner inn fra kulden" (October 30, 2012)

Finnmark Dagblad: "Turister ønsker reiser i sitt indre" (July 23, 2010)

Troms Folkeblad: "Norge første sjamanfestival" (September 01, 2010)

VG: "Andeverden Kultur Esthers" (February 15, 2009)

Klassekampen: "Sjamanen" (March 11–12, 2006)

WEBSITES

http://sjamanforbundet.no/
http://www.theworlddrum.com/index.html
http://www.facebook.com/groups/291273094250547/files/#!/groups/
    291273094250547/doc/302374349807088/
http://www.trooglivssyn.no/doc//stl_livsfaseriter.pdf
http://www.aics.org/war.html
http://www.shamanism.dk/Artikel--moderne-shamanistisk-praksis.htm
http://magic.no/magic-magasin/reportasjer/sjamadamer-pa-reise
http://isogaisa.org
http://www.polmakmoen-gjestegard.no/
http://www.fbb.nu/artikkel/sjamanisme-og-kristen-tro/
https://tv.nrk.no/serie/ardna-tv/SAPP67006215/02-11-2015#t=30s
http://www.sarahkkas.com/
http://www.elinkaaven.com/

INDEX